MEMORY AND GENDER IN MEDIEVAL EUROPE, 900–1200

Elisabeth van Houts

*Lecturer in Medieval History at Emmanuel College,
University of Cambridge*

First published 1999 by
MACMILLAN PRESS LTD
Houndmills, Basingstoke, Hampshire RG21 6XS
and London
Companies and representatives throughout the world

ISBN 0-333-56858-3 hardcover
ISBN 0-333-56859-1 paperback

A catalogue record for this book is available from the British
Library.

This book is printed on paper suitable for recycling and made
from fully managed and sustained forest sources.

10   9   8   7   6   5   4   3   2   1
08   07 06 05 04 03 02 01 00 99

Copy edited and typeset by Password, Norwich, UK.
Printed in Hong Kong.

In memory of two sisters

Audrey Richards FBA, 1899–1984

and

Enid Faber (née Richards), 1902–1995

CONTENTS

General Editor's Preface

Few aspects of human life can be so fundamental and enriching as the memories conveyed within families. It is in the telling of the past by kin, by neighbours and friends, and by community that identity is forged, expectations and hopes are nurtured, and enmities and intimacies have their roots. This book sets out ambitiously to capture the ways in which medieval people in the north-western corner of Europe, between the years 900–1200, captured memories of the past – useful memory which was to serve them in their endeavours to marry well, to forge fitting alliances, and to do justice to the actions of ancestors and the achievements of successors alike.

In societies within which literacy was contained in distinct social and vocational niches, communication of family lore often took the form of instructive tale, of stories attached to objects, and was elicited from grey old heads, often older women who were closely consulted before important family decisions such as marriage. Memory of a family's past conflicts, extended kin and abiding grudges were fostered by the older folk and conveyed at crucial moments; they could be contained in object and image for future interpretation and use. Like the blood-kin son, the religious family nurtured the memories of its founders in support of its claim for holiness and in enhancement of its attraction to future donors. All these modes of memory interacted and coexisted with writing. They were closely tested in the societies related to the Norman conquest and settlement of England as peoples, traditions and languages met and clashed.

Elisabeth van Houts has brought to the delicate traces of memory a wide range of sources – historical, hagiographical, visual – in her expert discerning of wholly new ways of approaching the medieval past, and the modes it had for preserving its own past. She is particularly attuned to the operations of power and gender within families and communities, and is constantly aware of the question: who decides what is to be remembered, and how? Norman society in which northern memory is still alive, Norman England in which Anglo-Saxon is the language of common speech, or monasteries facing a new wave of reform inspired by Rome? The eleventh and twelfth centuries saw a reforging of states, peoples and kinship structures; as people moved from the new to account for the old, they wove narratives which could encompass, if not explain, change. Elisabeth van Houts has expertly teased out these processes – so central and yet hitherto so little understood. Here is a book which will strike poetical historians, historians of religion, of family and of gender, as timely and all too necessary.

Miri Rubin

Acknowledgements

I am grateful to the following for allowing me to use previously published material written by me. Chapter 2 contains material first published by Günter Narr as 'Genre aspects of the use of oral information in medieval historiography', in *Gattungen mittelalterlicher Schriftlichkeit*, ed. B. Frank, T. Haye and D. Tophinke, *Scriptoralia*, 99 (Tübingen, 1998), 297–312. Chapter 6 in an earlier version was published by the Boydell Press as 'The Memory of 1066 in written and oral traditions', in *Anglo-Norman Studies*, vol. 19 (1996), ed. C. Harper Bill (Woodbridge, 1997), 167–180.

I am also grateful to Oxford University Press for their kind permission to reproduce the following copyright material: the translation of Aethelweard's prologue to his chronicle from *The Chronicle of Aethelweard*, ed. and trans. A. Campbell (London, 1962); and my own translation of Robert of Torigni's genealogical material from *The Gesta Normannorum Ducum of William of Jumièges, Orderic Vitalis and Robert of Torigni*, vol. 2 (Oxford, 1995).

FOREWORD

I first conceived the idea of writing a book on the use of oral information by medieval historians while I was a Research Fellow at Girton College in the 1980s. During my short involvement in the Girton Oral History project, I interviewed several remarkable women who retained vivid and interesting memories of the college in the first decades of the twentieth century. This practical experience brought home to me that problems of acquiring and digesting oral information are the same regardless of the period of history we study. That the scope of the book ultimately changed from a relatively narrow focus on orality to a wider study of the collaboration between men and women regarding memories of the past is due to another influence originating from Girton. For that college is also the place where I met Miri Rubin, then my predecessor as Eugenie Strong Research Fellow and now one of the editors of this series. Little did we know then that one day ten years later, with young children at our feet, we would discuss the final present shape of this book. Miri's constant enthusiasm, encouragement and inspiration are primarily responsible for the fact that it finally saw light.

I owe deep gratitude to my other, now also former, college Newnham. I am grateful to the Principal and Fellows for the sabbatical term granted to me in 1995, which enabled me to start writing the book and for several research grants which financed visits to Continental libraries.

Several friends and colleagues have been helpful in answering queries, discussing particular points or solving mysteries for me. Their advice has been invaluable. Susan Kelly kindly explained the intricacies of the Anglo-Saxon land lease, while Richard Smith threw much needed light on patterns of aristocratic marriages in central medieval Europe. Neil Wright collaborated on the translation of Beatrix's Latin letter printed as Appendix 3. Patrick Geary, Renée Nip, Jean Dunbabin and Miri Rubin read the whole of the text. Their comments, criticisms and corrections saved me from many errors, any remaining are entirely my responsibility. I should also like to express my gratitude to Penny Simmons for her meticulous copy editing and to Laura Napran who prepared the index.

Last, but not least, I must thank my family. First of all members of my own family in the Netherlands who patiently answered queries about our past. In particular my uncle Frans van Houts who, as the sole surviving member of my father's generation, confirmed the story my grandmother told me when I was six. This exclusively oral story concerns her father, Simon Hooij, who as an 18-year-old boy from a Roman-Catholic enclave in protestant Holland, took up arms and went as a Zouave to Italy 'to support the defence of the Pope'. Today he is remembered less for this heroic behaviour than for his foundation of one of the first Roman Catholic bakers' unions in the Netherlands.

In England my husband's family made me more than welcome. In particular I owe great homage to my mother-in-law, Enid Faber (née Richards), whose love of stories about her extended family I exploited for the purposes of this book. As one of four sisters, she opened my eyes to the forces of sisterhood and, indeed, spinsterhood. It was she who preserved her sister Audrey's charming written portrait of their mother, Isabel Richards (née Butler). Regretfully, her death prevented her from seeing my book finished. My husband Tom, and my children Sophie and Benjamin have borne the brunt of this book with fortitude. I owe them more than gratitude.

Elisabeth van Houts
Cambridge, January 1998

1

Introduction

Remembering the past in the Middle Ages is a subject that is usually perceived as a study of chronicles and annals written by monks in monasteries. Following in the footsteps of early Christian historians like Eusebius (d. 339) and St Augustine (d. 430), the medieval chroniclers are thought of as men isolated in their monastic institutions writing in Latin about the world around them. As the sole members of their society versed in literacy, they had a monopoly on the knowledge of the past as preserved in learned histories, which they themselves updated and continued. A self-perpetuating cycle of monks writing chronicles, which were read, updated and continued by the next generation, began in the sixth and seventh centuries and, so the argument goes, remained the vehicle for a narrative tradition of historical writing for the rest of the Middle Ages. This view of medieval historical writing emphasizes the isolation of monks in monasteries separated from the rest of the world, an almost exclusively male view of society and its past, and a literary tradition of historiography rooted in Christian religion. This book will present a different view.

In the first place, there is scope to challenge the assumption that only men were responsible for the shaping of historical thought. Even if we argue that monasteries were exclusive centres of literacy, we have to accept the possibility that nuns may have contributed something to this process. And once the issue of gender is introduced, the scope of the study is greatly broadened. For if religious women are taken into account, should one look at the role of secular women as well? And if we admit the likelihood of members of the secular world influencing the way memories of the past are kept, then it is surely correct to speculate about the role of the laity (including men) as a whole. Interaction between the genders, then, is one of the central points of this study. The introduction of women, and the laity in general, into a study of the historical process and the shaping ideas of the past has another consequence. Instead of concentrating exclusively on literary traditions and written sources, we have to take into account the predominantly oral culture in which medieval men and women lived. Can we isolate the stories lying behind written sources, which are now the only testimonies left? As will become clear in the course of the book, for various reasons the contribution of women, in particular, is explicitly recorded very infrequently and can only be reconstructed by reading between the lines or by using other methods of probing the texts. It is this 'hidden' contribution of women which has led to the perception of their non-participation in the historical process and the exploration of oral testimonies is one way of exposing the concealed nature of the female contribution. Hence the importance of orality as a strand of this study.

Finally, remembrance of the past took shape in the form of memorial traditions in a wider sense than written and oral testimonies about the past. The material expression of memories of persons, often rooted in particular places, is crucial evidence for the participation of men and women in the memorial process. Besides texts there is the evidence enshrined in objects ranging from liturgical vessels to personal jewellery, clothing, memorial stones and tombs. The third main focus of the present study therefore will be the study of memory. Taking these strands together will enable us to recognize that knowledge and remembrance of the past was seen as a task to be shared by men and women. Specific gender roles can be distinguished for specific tasks in some periods and geographical areas more clearly than in others. Human life was frail, death omnipresent and neither men nor women could do without the other in preserving knowledge about the past for posterity. That the male gender seemingly had a louder voice and mightier pen is a foregone conclusion. That women informed men, stimulated men and actively collaborated with men to make sure that the past was not forgotten is a new concept.

The chronological and geographical scope of the study is limited. The focus will be on the central Middle Ages from c. 900 to c. 1200. This period saw varied types of historical writing with many local, regional and national chronicles being written. Yet, as we shall see, relatively few modern studies have tapped these sources for the kind of questions that will be raised in the present study. Recent monographs on orality, literacy and memorial tradition have left something of a gap between the Carolingian period of the late eighth and ninth centuries and the later Middle Ages from the thirteenth century onwards, although the gap is gradually diminishing. Geographically the book covers most of the western European countries from Scandinavia in the north to Italy and the Iberian peninsula in the south. The north and the south experienced different stages of development with Scandinavia, in particular, adhering much longer to the non-Christian culture at the roots of European history. The marked emphasis on England, France and Germany is due to the author's particular interest in their sources. These self-imposed limits in terms of time and space have been interpreted flexibly in order to mark certain contrasts more sharply or to draw on differences more poignantly. Any discussion of interchanges between oral and written memories must take into account the eighth-century hagiographies from the English men and women who worked as missionaries in Germany, while some evidence from thirteenth-century sources illuminate the increasing reliance on written modes of historical memory in post-Conquest England. Before we can begin to survey the evidence on the remembrance of things past in the central Middle Ages, it is essential to look at the present state of research in the three areas singled out for special attention: oral tradition, memory and gender.

Oral Tradition

Few of the veterans of the First World War, now aged over 90, are still alive to tell us their experiences in the trenches of Flanders and Northern France 80 years ago. Because the numbers of survivors are rapidly decreasing the efforts to salvage their collective memory are being stepped up. Their stories are being collected and recorded, not only in writing but also on tape, so that the oral history of those who fought in 1914–18 shall not be lost. There are, of course, many other reminders of this war in the form of books, articles and war memorials, but the direct testimony of those who were present is vital for our understanding of the past. In fact, the collecting of eyewitness accounts was once thought to be the main task of the historian, so in that respect our attempt today to catch the last vivid reminders of the Great War belongs to a long tradition of preserving oral stories of the past.[1]

From classical antiquity through the Middle Ages and Modern period up to our own times, historians have tapped the human memory for knowledge about the past.[2] Their techniques in collecting this information barely changed until, in our own day, technical inventions provided photography, radio and film for the recording of live sound and living images. As exact replicas of reality the recording of the past in these ways has steadily become more sophisticated, even though the historical 'documents' resulting from the use of such testimonies, as Raphael Samuel has shown, are not always taken seriously by historians.[3] Paradoxically, the availability of modern technology has influenced the way historians look back to a past when people relied entirely on orally transmitted information, perhaps supported with the occasional written record. For the abundance which faces us now makes us even more aware of the means people developed to record their memories in other times.

Historians have been helped in this respect by anthropologists who travelled the world studying 'primitive' people in underdeveloped countries. They opened the eyes of historians by suggesting parallels between the medieval world of western Europe and modern traditional countries, particularly by pinpointing illiteracy and orality as common characteristics. This is precisely the way Hannah Vollrath has argued in her influential study of 1981. She points out how medieval society before the middle of the thirteenth century resembles a modern less-developed country. As a predominantly oral society, medieval people relied above all on oral communication, while the literate clergy was engaged with written forms of philosophy and religion of greater sophistication than the elite of a 'primitive' society.[4] Instead of arguing that one set of norms – literacy – replaced another set of norms – orality – she suggests that we study the interaction of the two systems.

Vollrath's work reflects the ideas of the older generation of anthropologists, like Jan Vansina, who did so much for the establishment of oral history as a discipline in itself.[5] Both see a clear hierarchical difference between the oral traditions (medieval and present) and their written counterpart, where the latter is clearly higher placed than the former on the basis of some implicit notion of reliability. The recent critique of their work, as expressed by Elisabeth Tonkin, as well as James Fentress and Chris Wickham, rightly points out that they applied criteria for the study of documents to that of oral tradition thus arguing that oral traditions are unsafe, unreliable and distorting, whereas documents are trustworthy, safe and true.[6] It is much more fruitful to see oral traditions as informal and unstable, liable to change, but also bearing in mind that written narratives can be equally unsound. After all, as these scholars point out, literary modes of narration ultimately go back to oral narratives and result in a continuous dialectic between the oral and the written word. It is this dialectic tension, so their argument goes, which turns oral history into a social construction embedded in every society. Hence narrating the past, whether in oral or written mode, is a social occasion familiar to every society including the medieval one.[7]

Bearing this in mind helps to see how limited the arguments are of those historians of the Middle Ages who concentrate either on literacy or on orality as the main force in medieval society. Emphasizing the increase in literacy to the point where the argument is almost beginning to defeat itself, scholars of the early medieval period neglect over-whelming evidence for the oral component in policies implemented by Charlemagne.[8] Even Janet Nelson's admission that pragmatic literacy is, perhaps, a better way of describing the use of the written word in Carolingian society falls short of considering the significance of oral com-munication.[9] There are signs, however, that this lack of attention to the importance of orality is being remedied, particularly in the work of Matthew Innes who, taking up Tonkin's thesis, shows how crucial the oral modes of communication, especially in historiography, were.[10] He continues from Brian Stock's insight,[11] which emphasized the overwhelming local significance of interplay between orality and literacy in the 'textual communities' of monasteries and churches.[12]

Any study of orality in the past has to take literacy into account if only because all our knowledge of orality is, ultimately, based on written testimonies. That there was an increasing tendency to record events of the past and present into writing from the Carolingian period onwards is uncontested, and has been proven for central medieval England by Michael Clanchy in his *From Memory to Written Record*. But this increase in literacy did by no means *replace* the oral culture of daily com-munication, whether in government, law, popular culture or, last but not least, memories of the past. In all these areas, spoken words were recorded in writing and therefore preserved for posterity. The dynamics of shaping these records took place as much in the language of speech as in the language of writing. It will be the argument of this book to show that particularly in the recording of stories about the past, oral and written exchange produced the information on which we now rely.

Memory

It is common knowledge that for most people, in the past and the present, memories of previous generations usually stretch back no further than three to four generations. Thus a family's history can usually be traced back to the grandparents and great-grandparents. If we accept that in the Middle Ages each generation lasted for about thirty years, we may accept a period of between 90 and 120 years as a period of 'active memory'.[13] This constituted the period for which people could remember the names of the ancestors concerned, their place of origin and their occupations. People may also have been able to keep up with their relatives horizontally: cousins once, twice or three times removed. For most of the period, the information would be freely available, swapped and exchanged with other members of the family, and this mutual support would ensure that the names of grandparents or great-grandparents would still be known. The means of passing on the information from one generation to another would be by word of mouth and not normally in writing. The family context is by far the most outstanding characteristic of the study of memory in the central Middle Ages. Recently James Fentress and Chris Wickam have stressed how indispensable the family network is for the production of memories and recollections.[14] The facility to produce memories and the human instinct to wish to recall events make sense only if there are people to whom one can relate one's memories and who, in turn, can interpret them within the same referential system. In fact, they go even further and argue that the characteristic medieval remembrance tradition as expressed, for example, in genealogies, reflects the same kin-centred interest as do those of peasant memories in rural societies, whether present or past. Most of them are orally transmitted memories; they are only 'frozen' and become stable once they are written down. Until then they are fluent, unstable, changeable and adaptable to new circumstances.

From the early part of the time under consideration in this book, the late Carolingian period, to until the end of the twelfth century, there was a clear awareness that members of the third or fourth generation ought to put pen to paper, even though articulations of this awareness are rarer for the ninth than for the twelfth century. The relevance of this observation is that we cannot assume that there was no formation of memory before the memories were written down or cast into stone. The assumption has often been that the oral phase of memory is characterized by a constant shaping and reshaping of stories, customs and memories, depending on changing circumstances in the present.

Influenced by anthropological research amongst oral societies in the twentieth century, historians of the Middle Ages have come to realize the mutability of historical memory. Genealogies were adapted in the light of important contemporary situations. In the past leadership allegiances were transferred from a person belonging to one tribe to another person from another tribe if political expediency on the part of the genealogist required this. Customary oral law was continuously adapted and reshaped, and in the process precedents were being altered under the influence of what happened in one's own time. Clearly memory is not static but alive. Living memories result in the adaptability of the past to suit the present. Hence traditions transmitted in this 'live' way can help to reconstruct what the past was like up to a point, but they provide no reliability for a reconstruction of what the past was really like. I believe with many others that we cannot 'reconstruct' the past, but that this does not pose a problem. If, on the other hand, we are interested, as I am for the purposes of this book, in the process of remembering and the formation of memories, the criterion of historical reliability is of little or no importance in judging the significance of a memory.[15]

The study of memories of the past covering three to four generations and centred, usually, on a family, institution or an area dominated by one extended kin-group, is different from the study of memory in a more learned sense. The tradition of medieval memory as a rhetorical tool to assist scholars has received much attention over the last few decades, culminating in Mary Carruthers's important book.[16] She traced the development of mnemonic techniques inherited from classical antiquity which the monks used to help them memorize the many works they had to read. No monastery had enough books, Bibles, biblical commentaries or important classical texts for each monk to have his own bookshelf. Hence monks had to memorize a considerable amount of literature. To be able to understand and interpret the Bible, for example, one had to be sure that the text was firmly fixed in one's mind. All sorts of tricks were devised to make this job easier. Hugh of St Victor (d. 1141), who was a famous theologian and historian in the mid twelfth century, wrote a treatise on the use of memory for precisely these reasons. Having pointed out that knowledge is a treasury and the heart its strongbox, he sets out ways to imprint the knowledge so that it can be easily retrieved. One of the examples he uses is memorizing the Psalms by their first line, increasing the number of lines one learns each day, not only in the correct order but also back to front and randomly. As a historian he was very much aware of the infinity of historical information and of his pupils' struggle to retain details about the past. As a result he devised several schemes to help them memorize the essentials by suggesting that they select according to three principles:

> . . . there are three matters on which the knowledge of past actions especially depends, that is, the persons who performed the deeds, the places in which they were performed and the time at which they occurred. Whoever holds these three memorially in his heart will find that he has built a good foundation for himself, onto which he can assemble afterwards anything by reading and lecture without difficulty and rapidly take in and retain it for a long time. However, in so doing it is necessary to retain it in memory and by diligently retracing to have it customary and well known, so that his heart may be ready to put in place everything he has heard, and apply those classification techniques which he will have learned now to all things which he may hear afterwards by a suitable distribution according to their place and time and person.[17]

Hugh's scholarly advice was followed in the schools and universities of medieval Europe and his instructions for memorizing texts helped to keep the textual traditions of important authoritative works more or less intact. But his sophisticated programme, which after all was devised for literate people with access to books, had no following amongst those who either did not go to school or received only a rudimentary education. Hence his work and that of other medieval scholars who were preoccupied with memory and mnemonic techniques is only helpful for our present purpose in that it gives hints on how these scholars used information presented to them. It is totally unhelpful as a guide as to the ways non-scholastic memory worked.

There is another aspect with regard to learned memory that we have to discuss in this context, namely the institutional monastic urge that was aimed at obliterating individual monks' or nuns' personal memories. The clearest evidence comes from Cistercian writings, expounded in this light by Janet Coleman in her book *Ancient and Medieval Memories*. Again she is not concerned with the ordinary memories passed on from one person to another, but with a problem which monastic communities faced: how to concentrate the monk's or nun's mind on God and salvation and prevent him or her wallowing in memories of past life. In Benedictine monasteries most members entered as oblates and therefore had only limited memories of life in the outside world.[18] Later entrants usually took up monastic life out of free will or at least for a reason that made monastic life more attractive than a lay existence. The Cistercian movement did not accept oblates and preferred adult entrants, who had carefully weighed the pros and cons of life within a monastery. Therefore adults with experience of secular life were faced with considerable problems of adaptation, having to repress longings for their previous way of life. The most important advice Bernard of Clairvaux (d. 1153), who wrote extensively on the problem, could give was to repress one's memories. In a sense he proposed the opposite of what Hugh of St Victor suggested: non-memorizing. He encouraged adult newcomers to obliterate their memories of secular life and to purge their minds as much as possible. With hindsight it is extremely difficult for us to know exactly what Bernard meant by that. Perhaps the closest we can come to his attitude is by assuming that he encouraged them 'to come to terms with' their previous existence and accept their new environment.

In fact, the gap between monastic life and lay life was perhaps not as great as we once thought. Recent research into the economic and financial affairs of monasteries illustrates the profound interdependence of the lay and religious worlds, and the close association between monastery and its lay patrons and servants.[19] Such linkage was clearly a pre-condition for the collaboration between men and women, lay and ecclesiastical, to preserve the collective memories of their society. Neither monks nor nuns forgot their past or their family's connections. Indeed, most of our information points in the opposite direction and shows how very much of the knowledge of the past was kept alive by the very people who were supposed to forget about this past. These two facets of monastic life and memory contain a paradox: one was aimed at enhancing the memorial capacity, while the other attempted to suppress memorial faculties.

Family networks surrounding monasteries followed from the conscious monastic policies of the Carolingian period when commemoration of the dead was given place in the church liturgy: masses, funerals and commemorative services were performed for those who wished to be remembered and thus paid for posthumous prayers. In order to keep track of the dead, monks and nuns kept lists of the names of the friends, alive and dead, of the institution and recorded them in necrologies and memorial books. These are important repositories of institutional and family remembrance studied by the Munster school of German medievalists.[20] This book, however, will concentrate on a parallel phenomenon of the more ordinary memories and thus, for our purpose, liturgical commemoration is significant as a bridge between local and family-centred remembrance, as sketched above, and the learned memorial tradition of Hugh of St Victor and his followers who sought ways of retaining memory and displaying vast amounts of information in easily accessible ways. All three sorts of memory collections collapsed under the strain of too much information, which inevitably resulted in oblivion.

Medieval people were acutely aware of the fallibility of human memory. Many a charter has in its preamble one or two sentences expressing the purpose of the record as the prevention of knowledge of the transaction being lost to oblivion. Michael Clanchy showed how, for England in the eleventh and twelfth century, people developed tools to prevent knowledge of the past from disappearing. He conclusively argued that administrators, whether lay or ecclesiastical, were aware of the pitfalls of relying exclusively on oral memory. Tenure of land, heritability of offices and execution of laws all depended on legal enforcement against the background of a constant yardstick. Only written documentation could act as such a yardstick in order to withstand the change and permutations in a society that had only oral tools (based on the limited human faculty to remember everything consistently) to regulate itself. The knowledge of law and the knowledge of a country's past were gradually enshrined in writing that thence forward functioned as yardstick. However much the written traditions helped to stabilize memories, they never completely eradicated the inherent fluidity of memory.

The adaptability and fluidity of memory gave rise to another medieval phenomenon, characterized recently by Amy Remensnyder as 'imaginative memory'. Instead of discussing memory as the reflection of past events shaped by one person's or one group's memory and fixed in time and place, she draws attention to the fact that frequently a story or object preserved for a specific memorial tradition was transferred from one person or time to another. For example, relics were particularly vulnerable to this process. Over time, a relic of a particular saint could be reused or renamed to enshrine the remains of another saint, whose story then became attached to it. Due to the increased fame of Charlemagne as a heroic figure, the twelfth century saw the growth of many legends centred on his alleged actions, the defeat of the Muslims in Spain or his pilgrimage to Jerusalem are good examples. In the context of these legends, objects which were originally totally unrelated to Charlemagne became attached to him, and were subsequently known as part of the supposed Carolingian inheritance of a particular monastery. Remensnyder records such traditions from Conques which, from the late eleventh century onwards, claimed to be in possession of a reliquary given by Pepin and another from his son Charlemagne.[21] The reliquaries attached to the memory of a person, and preferably a famous person, turned them into something personal, a touch of past humanity, for the monastic community. According to Remensnyder, this results from the human urge to personalize memories of institutions, communities and families. No work comparable in depth and scope with Clanchy's study for England exists for Continental history. Occasionally studies have appeared looking at memorial traditions in Italy, such as Chris Wickam's stimulating article on the perception of history amongst Italian lawyers.[22] He sees the relative lack of local chronicles and histories in pre-eleventh-century Italy as a result of the legacy of public authority, in that legal documents embodied the knowledge of the past which made the production of local histories and chronicles superfluous. As a consequence, the Italian survival of private and personal memories are scarce in comparison with the northern historiographical tradition.

Gender

Thus modern historians accept that oral tradition and memory are inalienable parts of society and, indeed, that they precondition the functioning of a society. Narrating the past of any society can only happen by the application of oral techniques for exchange of information and for delving into past events. Since any society consists of men and women, it follows that both groups had a role in this process. And in particular, given the central role of women in families, the female contribution to knowledge about the past must, potentially at least, have been a significant one. Yet surprisingly, relatively little attention has thus far been paid to the study of gender, and in particular the study of women's role in the remembrance of things past. Two studies, though not concerned with the Middle Ages but with nineteenth-century Africa, deserve special attention because their methods of research are helpful in assessing the medieval evidence.

The most important of the two is Isabel Hofmeyer's study of the South African chiefdom of Lebowa in the North Transvaal.[23] She traced third and fourth generation oral stories from men and women about the traumatic Boer siege of the Ndebele people at Makapansgat in 1854 and compared them with contemporary written accounts which represented the Boer version of events. The majority of the oral stories came through an exclusively male tradition which concentrated on the escape of the male heir to the chiefdom, his rescue from Boer captivity and his return to political power. All men told Hofmeyer that they had heard the story told by their father or grandfather during meetings of the *kgoro*, an exclusively male meeting place in each village from which women and boys under the age of eight were excluded. The men added that nowadays, in the 1980s, such traditions were lost due to the loss of the *kgoro*. The women, on the other hand, also passed on stories about Makapansgat, but they were less concerned with the fate of the chief's heir than with the general suffering of men, women and children during the three-week siege in the caves, where water ran out and illness caused many deaths. Among the women, grandmothers, who told their stories in the kitchen area of the village, emerged as the authoritative informants of the siege's history. Hofmeyer's anthropological research into oral histories of the past enabled her to distinguish clearly defined roles for male and female story-tellers, each operating in segregated spaces and with very little amalgamation of the two traditions.

The other African study, by Leroy Vail and Landeg White, is limited to a specifically female genre of praise poems in South Africa.[24] The genre concerns poems which praise the women of Tumbuka, who in the mid nineteenth century had to adapt to a new political system imposed on them by the patriarchal Ngoni people. Due to the Ngoni conquest the women, accustomed to a matriarchy, lost land, power and status. Their feelings about this take-over were never written down, but can be traced in the so-called *vimbusa* poetry that has survived in exclusively oral form. Thus oral tradition enables historians to access women's opinions about a political revolution which took place in the 1850s and which thus far had only been studied from written, male documentation recording the conquerors' (Ngoni) version of events. These two South African examples illustrate the ways in which male and female stories about the past are often gender specifically transmitted, either in segregated oral traditions or in a written male and an oral female form. In both cases the female voice can only be traced in the oral tradition representative of the politically non-powerful section of the population. As we shall see in the course of this book, such a situation bears close similarity to the remembrance of things past in medieval society.

That few medieval women wrote history books has been acknowledged for a long time. The two best known female historians are Hrotsvitha of Gandersheim, a tenth-century nun from Germany who wrote her nunnery's history as well as a biography of King Otto I (936–73), and

Anna Comnena (d. 1153), the Byzantine princess who wrote a biography of her father Emperor Alexius I (1081–1118).[25] Many more women must have written history, but many of them did so anonymously and are only now receiving recognition. Janet Nelson has convincingly argued that the *Annals of Metz* were probably written at the Carolingian nunnery of Chelles, perhaps at the behest of Charlemagne's sister Gisla, and that the *Book of Frankish History* came from the pen of nuns from Notre Dame at Soissons.[26] The *Annals of Quedlinburg*, too, were almost certainly written by the nuns of that monastery, and there may be many more historiographical texts lying in libraries, waiting to be identified as the work of women rather than, as so often argued in the past, of the male officers attached to nunneries. Saints' lives, miracle stories and *translationes* texts, which describe the transfer of a relic from one place to another, were also composed in nunneries and were almost certainly the product of female authorship.[27]

There is thus some evidence of women who wrote histories. Is it too far-fetched to argue that they were instrumental in preserving historical information in other ways? A small trickle of studies has referred in pass-ing to the role of women as commemorators, as repositories of knowledge about ancestors and to their task of passing on this information.[28] The most comprehensive and recent is Patrick Geary's *Phantoms of Remembrance. Memory and Oblivion at the End of the First Millennium* (1994).[29] Concentrating on the tenth and eleventh centuries, Geary argues that a shift occurred from a family-based memorial tradition organized by women of that family to an institutionalized memorial tradition in which monks took the lead. Hence he concludes that the care of the dead and the preservation of ancestral knowledge, once the preserve of women, was taken over by the clergy and, in particular, by Benedictine monks. The latter legitimized this 'take-over' by using writing (chronicles, monastic records, charters) and making archival space (monastic archives and strong rooms) available for the marginalization of women. There is much to be said for such a conclusion and Geary discusses an impressive variety of evidence. However, the rel-atively limited geographical area of northern Italy, Ottonian Germany and French Neustria and the limited period studied tend to distort reality. The present study will show that a wider spread of evidence taken from a longer time-span does not support the thesis of 'a monastic take-over of memory'. On the contrary, what we shall see is evidence of continuous collaboration between monastery and lay world, and particularly of the mutual interdependence of monks and nuns, on the one hand, and lay men and women, on the other. The preservation of knowledge of the past was seen as a duty for all with particular tasks set aside for men and women.

The Present Study

The book is divided into three parts. In Part I, I shall be looking at the way historians (Chapter 2) and hagiographers (Chapter 3) acknowledged their sources and, in particular, their oral informants. Historians tended to publicly acknowledge male informants, particularly men of high ecclesiastical rank. Occasionally we find a veiled reference to a female informant, but this is the exception rather than the rule. Chapter 2 also contains a first attempt to categorize the different ways in which historians use oral witnesses, ranging from the eyewitness to the reporter who passes on a story that had been passed on to him through a recognizable chain of informants. This raises the question of how careful and conscientious historians were in reproducing the chain of reporters of a particular story. It will also focus on practical problems that historians faced, such as verifying the veracity of the story, assessing its reliability by characterizing the standing of the reporter and by detailing the time and distance of the reports involved. Like historians, hagiographers faced similar problems. They too wrote about the past and the present, they too used eyewitness accounts, they too had to acknowledge reports of dubious veracity, and they too needed men and women as their informants. However, the problems faced by the hagiographer merit a separate chapter because the nature of their material, the miraculous working of God through his saints at all levels of society, inevitably meant contact with women. So many miracles took place in the family circle and concerned children or the health of members of the household, for whom women were primarily responsible, that no hagiographer, whether a man or a woman, could have written about a saint or his miracles without taking into account the substantial number of stories told by women.

While Part I deals mainly with the ways in which historians and hagiographers acquired information, weighed and explicitly acknowledged it, Part II focuses on the implicit use they made of information about the past. It is precisely amongst the mass of unacknowledged material that we find women to be an important force behind the written narratives of the past. Chapter 4 discusses women as commissioners of chronicles, as addressees and as readers of history books. We find that heiresses, for example, were often the only people available for knowledge about the descent of estates in particular families. And there are fictional references to the role of women, spelling out their responsibilities for the commemoration of ancestors. Despite the fact that the precise function of women in this process is rarely spelt out in detail, there is enough evidence to reconstruct their role as informants about the past. They worked in the background and produced the raw material, usually in oral form, from which male authors constructed their narratives.

In Chapter 5 I shall be discussing how objects helped to preserve memories of the past. To what extent did the material culture help in the process of commemoration? In Scandinavia commemorative stones preceded chronicles in a time when literacy was not widely spread. Tapestries and jewellery could act as pegs for people's memories about their ancestors' deeds, while relics and other objects related to the veneration of saints also acted as repositories for information about the past. Women and men collaborated in the production of works of art to safeguard the memory of saints, ancestors or a lost child. Art objects operated as visual reminders of dead members of the community or of kinsmen and helped to preserve stories that would otherwise have been lost to oblivion.

Thus only by exploring oral and written culture, and the collaboration of men and women, can we come to a balanced idea of how medieval people remembered the past and preserved that knowledge. The variety of sources explored over a wide geographical area and spanning three centuries, taken with the scattered nature of some of the evidence, poses some problems which are acknowledged throughout. Part III, consisting of Chapter 6, therefore focuses on a single event, the Norman Conquest of England in 1066. The resonance of this formidable military achievement and the subsequent 'tenurial' revolution was felt throughout Europe, where the Conqueror's supporters trumpeted their admiration and his opponents continued to vent their anger on him for a long time after 1066. In England and Normandy we can trace in extensive detail the ways in which men and women remembered this event and its consequences over a period of four generations. Monastic authors, secular historians, as well as lay men and women all contributed to the process of the remembrance of things past.

In Chapter 7, the concluding chapter, the roles of women, who collected and passed on the family information and of men, who were responsible for recording it in writing, is discussed. Two main reasons for this endeavour will be explored. On the one hand, there is the political circumstance of landholding developing along patrilinear lines which concentrated families into much more narrowly defined kin-groups, the social groups from which the memories emanate. On the other hand, there is the demand from the church to prevent incest and marriage between individuals related to each other within seven degrees. The ecclesiastical law on marriage demanded much more sophisticated information about the family's past than had hitherto been produced. Each of these reasons stipulated specific gender roles in which men and women had their own tasks.

Finally, to avoid any confusion it is important to set out that this is not a book on the historical reliability or unreliability of the information provided by men and women. This book is primarily concerned with the ways in which medieval people perceived their fairly recent past and the tools they developed to recall it to the best of their abilities. The title of my book therefore indicates the remembrance of things past by medieval people who, to all intents and purposes, did the same as we still do today by recalling significant events, remembering beloved grandparents and treasuring precious mementoes. Some medieval texts in this book recur regularly. In order to enable readers to follow my interpretation and to trace the source material in its entirety, I have added these texts in translation in six appendices.

Part I

Gender and the Authority of Oral Witnesses

2

CHRONICLES AND ANNALS

Most information in chronicles necessarily derives in the first instance from people who had first-hand knowledge of the persons and places referred to, or who had witnessed, perhaps as participants, the events described. However, this information may have passed from mouth to mouth before being recorded in writing, and the version we have today may not be the original record; it may well have been copied from an older written version and perhaps deliberately modified in the process. Some chroniclers wrote from personal experience and most relied to some extent on oral evidence from others, but almost all made use of written evidence as well. Sometimes this written evidence was in the form of charters or letters, but more frequently it lay in the works of their predecessors, which they copied to an extent that would be unthinkable today. There were, of course, no copyright laws to restrain them, and the fact that texts had to be copied by scribes if they were to be disseminated at all must have encouraged the 'creative' copying which so often occurred. The creativity of the copier lay sometimes in correction of the original narrative and at other times in the chronological extension of it to bring it up to date. In the process he often made use of his own personal experience or of evidence not available to the original author.

In the present chapter I discuss a set of categories, ranging from the direct experience of the chronicler to tales so indirect as to possess the status of myths, into which examples of non-written evidence may fruitfully be divided. Such a division will raise questions, which I shall begin to answer, about the attitude which medieval historians had to evidence of different types. I shall illustrate some of the problems that confront a modern historian who wishes to interpret their work today.

The references to personal experience can be put in Category 1; information supplied at first hand by a witness of unimpeachable reliability, for example an eyewitness to whom the chronicler has evidently talked in Category 2; such information relayed by one or more named intermediaries in Category 3; hearsay evidence which the chronicler records without qualification in Category 4; hearsay evidence qualified by speculation about its reliability in Category 5; information derived from ballads, songs and jongleurs in Category 6; and tales about events so distant from the chronicler in time or place that he himself gives them little positive credence in Category 7. These categories are listed in what a modern historian might take to be their order of reliability. Did medieval historians view them in the same light? Did they follow any discernible rules of selection between sources where more than one was available to them? In so far as they preferred to rely on known witnesses rather than on general hearsay, who were these witnesses? Is there a pronounced gender-related preference for the witnesses quoted? For how many generations did their memories survive, and for how many generations did they remain trustworthy – both in the eye of the medieval chronicler and in ours? Do chroniclers tell us explicitly to which category their information belongs? If not, how may we, as modern readers, attempt to classify it ourselves? These questions sufficiently illustrate the purpose for this chapter, and we can now embark on a one-by-one consideration of the categories.

Category 1: Author as witness

Historians from Herodotus onwards have valued the immediate witness above any other as source for historical knowledge. In the early Middle Ages Isidore of Seville (d. 636), the author of the standard encyclopedic work, *The Etymologies*, formulated this attitude in Book I, Chapter 41, as follows:

> Among the ancient authors no one wrote history unless he had been present and had witnessed the events he described. For it is much better to learn with our eyes what happened than to gather it from hearing.[1]

Thus, in theory, anything other than an eyewitness account was considered second-rate information and the further away the account moved from the original event the more its value decreased. It is usually in the prologues of their works that medieval historians mention their own involvement, if any, in the stories they describe. They say, for example, that they have seen with their own eyes or heard with their own ears some of the people of whom they wrote. In such cases they rarely gave more details as to whom precisely they had met. For example, William of Jumièges, a Norman monk who wrote the *Deeds of the Dukes of Normandy* in *c.* 1070, says in his introduction that from the time of Duke Richard III (1026–27) he was an eyewitness of some of the events he describes, without identifying which particular events. However, his text reveals his exceptional knowledge about the castle of Tillières which, on the border with France, was the site of many skirmishes between Norman dukes and the French kings. It seems logical to conclude therefore that William himself either came from that area or visited it several times. Because of the formulaic character of phrases like 'I have heard', 'I have seen' or 'I was present' used in the prologues it is sometimes doubted whether we can put our faith in them.

In other words, it is sometimes believed that medieval historians would write such stock phrases even though in reality they had not been present on the occasions for which they claimed to give eyewitness accounts. This is unnecessary caution as the author's contemporary public, usually his fellow monks and the local aristocracy, would have known whether or not the historian spoke the truth. There is no reason to assume duplicity, as was already recognized by medieval scholars themselves. The Scandinavian historian and poet Snorri Sturluson, who was active in the early thirteenth century, expressed this attitude with regard to the scaldic or oral poetry which he had incorporated in his work. In the preface to his *Heimskringla* he says:

> We regard as true what is said in those poems that were declaimed in front of princes themselves or their sons. We accept as true all that those poems tell about their travels and battles. For it is the practice of skalds to praise most the man whose presence they are in, and nobody would dare to tell the man himself about deeds which everybody who heard – even the man himself – knew to be lies and deceit. That would be scorn, not praise.[2]

The Nordic skalds were court poets who described the Viking deeds of their contemporary masters. They were often eyewitnesses themselves or, if not, they used the eyewitness accounts of others. The important point here is that Snorri recognized that no reporter would lie about the sources of information in front of a contemporary audience. In a society that depended on the primary reliability of its eyewitnesses, much care was taken to maintain the idea that one could trust such accounts. As we shall see, in the absence of film cameras, sound recorders and other modern devices which can replay scenes as they happened, people had to be able to put their trust in the social system of mutual control over witness accounts.

Other places where the author might reveal his own contribution to the actions he described might well be in the story itself. He might explicitly say that he was present, or he might tell a particular story in the first person, thus making it fairly obvious that he had been involved. In the mid twelfth century Abbot Suger of Saint-Denis (d. 1151), the biographer of King Louis VI (1108–37), nowhere explicitly says that he was an eyewitness, but the way in which he describes some of King Louis's negotiations with members of the French nobility, referring to those present as 'we', leaves little doubt about his own role as royal adviser and thus as eyewitness. The same can be said about his contemporary Bishop Otto of Freising (d. 1158), the author of a world chronicle and a biography of his nephew Emperor Frederic I (1152–90). In neither history does he specifically single out his status as a witness to the events he described, though other evidence, such as letters and charters, confirm his authority as a prime witness.

While Abbot Suger and Bishop Otto speak in the first person and so indicate their involvement in the narrative, other historians refrain even from that degree of self-revelation. Frutolf of Michelsberg (d. 1103) and Ekkehard of Aura (d. 1125), for example, were both Bavarian monks who wrote important chronicles about their own monasteries without once revealing either their identity or their place in these communities. Their names were only subsequently revealed by later generations. In some cases the name of the author remains a mystery, even though they set out their eyewitness accounts in the first person. The anonymous author of the *Battle Abbey Chronicle*, clearly a monk of Battle, tells that he was present at a public penance ceremony in the early 1120s, an event he wrote about 50 years later. From the same period dates an eyewitness account by the anonymous monk of Waltham Abbey who, as a boy of about ten years old, witnessed a miracle in the abbey church, an occasion he wrote about in his late seventies. Whether or not they thought it positively desirable to remain in the background, these authors clearly recognized no rule or custom which made it obligatory for historians to explicitly acknowledge their own place in history.

Category 2: Information from a first-hand witness

Where authors quote witnesses, they normally go to some lengths to explain their own relationship to the informant and his link with the event described. Where the informant is not actually named, his trustworthiness is usually underlined by a qualification such as 'a reliable witness', 'a trustworthy man', 'true reports', ' faithful men' or similar phrases. Eyewitnesses, as we have already seen, are treated almost automatically as reliable persons. Otherwise, reliability seems to be attached to positions of authority and a high status in society, for in cases where 'trustworthy' informants can be identified they turn out to be monks or abbots, priests or bishops or other members of the clergy, or else members of the aristocracy. The Burgundian historian Ralph Glaber (d. *c*. 1050) acknowledged in *c*. 1040 Bishop Odolric of Orléans as the eyewitness of a miracle he relates. In the twelfth century the English canon Walter Map (d. *c*. 1200) quoted Archbishop William of Reims, whom he identifies as the brother of the queen of France (Adela of Champagne), as well as bishop Hugh of Le Mans and Bishop Philip of Naples, while Bishop Otto of Freising related affairs from India on the authority of Bishop Hugh of Djebele.[3]

Since many historians were monks they often quoted fellow monks or abbots as witnesses. Peregrin, the late-twelfth-century author of a monastic chronicle of the Aquitanian house Fontaine-les-Blanches, cites several old monks from his monastery, whom he mentions by name, who gave him information about the early history of his house. The English historian William of Malmesbury (d. *c*. 1143) related events in Germany on the authority of Walkelin, prior of Malvern, who had been an overseas visitor there. Another, younger, English historian, William Newburgh (d. *c*. 1201) told the story of King Henry II's penance after the murder of Thomas Becket on the basis of the eyewitness account of Abbot Roger of Beaulieu.[4] The anonymous author of the *Waltham Chronicle* reported the burial of King Harold of England, slain at Hastings in 1066, at Waltham on the authority of the sacristan Turketil, who had overseen the funeral. Priests and other members of the clergy frequently acted as trustworthy reporters. A story about the generosity of Duke Robert the Magnificent of Normandy (1027–35) was related by his former chaplain Isembert to the anonymous author of one of the many versions of the *Deeds of the Dukes of Normandy*. Ekkehard of Aura, the Bavarian chronicler, reported on the first crusade on the basis of reports given to him by one 'Herman the priest'.[5] In all these cases historians used the authority attached to the clerical or monastic status of the witnesses as an aid to convince readers of the reliability and trustworthiness of the story. Priests of whatever rank were learned and skilled in interpreting the *Scripture* and thus they were considered the most authoritative reporters of the events they witnessed.

This stance taken by the historians explains the relatively few reporters from the lay community who are mentioned as informants on specific events. The impression is that historians used those informants only by default and in the absence of ecclesiastical witnesses, even if the lay person belonged to the highest social strata. Walter Map refers to the nobleman William of Briouze for some specifically Welsh customs in the border area between England and Wales, while Dudo of Saint-Quentin (d. after 1015), the Norman historian, records his gratitude to Count Rodulf of Ivry who helped him with information on the early history of the duchy.[6] Against this background it becomes understandable why references to lay people further down the social hierarchy are extremely rare. Those that we find are mostly concerned with areas of life for which the clergy or the high nobility would be useless. For example, the historian Alpert of Metz (d. after 1005) relates the story of a brawl in a tavern on the authority of one of the servants at that establishment. Soldiers form a special group amongst the laity as informants on battles, but often we cannot be sure about their social standing. Were they common footsoldiers or members of the lower nobility? The author of the *Annals of Nieder-Alteich*, who wrote in 1075, mentions eyewitnesses of the Battle of Hastings as his source of information for the Norman Conquest of England. Presumably he had talked with Anglo-Saxon participants who had fled their native country and were on their way to take service with the Byzantine emperor. Another anonymous author, of the early-twelfth-century *Chronicle of Saint-Maixent*, was told of a local skirmish in Aquitaine in 1087 by some soldiers and Adémar of Chabannes, as we shall see below, conversed with Moorish soldiers captured near Limoges.[7]

If the highest authority of an eyewitness account could only be attributed to a member of the clergy or by default to a member of the high nobility, two almost exclusively male groups, it comes as no surprise that historians hardly ever claim to rely on the reports of women. In chronicles and annals such references are rarer than those to members of the laity below the rank of aristocracy. Only two testimonies can be found in the material used for this book; the first comes from the mid eleventh century in Novalesa (Italy) and the second from early-twelfth-century Iceland.

The anonymous monk from Novalesa acknowledges Petronilla of Susa as the best informed person on the history of his monastery's site:[8]

The men with the women of the city came to this woman [Petronilla] inquiring of her ancient traditions of the place, and she used to tell them many things, especially about the monastery of Novalesa. She told them many unheard of things she had seen or that she had heard from her parents (*progenitoribus*), especially about the number of abbots and the destruction that had been caused by the pagans. One day she was taken by some men to the place where she showed them the tomb of Walter, which previously had been unknown, just as she had heard from those who were born before her ancestors, since formerly no woman dared to go near that place. She also indicated how many wells there had formerly been in that place. For the neighbours claimed that this woman had lived almost 200 years.[9]

According to Patrick Geary, who discussed this passage, the old age of the woman was a necessary fiction of the author in order to link the past with the mid-eleventh-century discoveries in the church of Novalesa. It is, however, quite possible and indeed very likely that the ultimate source for the chronicler's details derived from this woman. She clearly was an elderly woman, but hardly 200 years old. Such exaggerations, as Shulamith Shahar has shown, are often found in chronicles and have to be taken with a large pinch of salt.[10] The importance of the passage for our purpose is surely that the only available witness for the early history of the monastery was a woman and that the author mentioned her by name and used her story. This is exceptional and as such deserves our attention. This very unusual fact in itself pleads for the author's veracity, for surely if he had invented the account, would it not have been more obvious for him to have invented a male witness?

The other example, equally exceptional, comes from a Scandinavian text which is a hybrid form of a lawbook and chronicle. It concerns the history of the Norse settlement of Iceland, the *Islendingabók*, written in the 1120s by Ari (d. 1148) about events which took place in *c.* 970, that is about 150 years previously. Ari quotes the information on the authority of three people whom he mentions by name, the last of whom is a woman:

> [A]ccording to the opinion of my foster-father Teit, the most informed man I ever knew, son of Bishop Isleif; and of Thorkel Gellison, my uncle, whose memory stretched far back; and of Thorid, daughter of Snorri the *godi* [a sort of priest], who was very well informed and reliable.[11]

He may have said more about his informants, including the woman Thorid and how she related to him, in the now lost first version of his book. This is suggested by the Icelandic author Snorri Sturluson (d. 1241), who quotes from this text in the *Heimskringla*. Unfortunately for us, Snorri elaborates on Ari's relationship with the male witnesses, Teit and Thorkel Gellison, but not on Ari's acquaintance with the woman Thorid:

> [Ari] was very learned and so old that he was born the winter after the death of King Harald Sigurdarson [1066–67]. As he himself says he wrote the lives of the kings of Norway according to the account of Odd, son of Kol, son of Hall of Sida, and Odd learned from Thorgeir Afradskoll, a man who was learned and so old that he was killed [995] . . . Priest Ari came to Hall Thorarinsson in Haukadal when he was seven years old and stayed there for 14 years. Hall was a very learned man with a good memory. He remembered being christened by priest Thangbrand when he was three – that was the year before Christianity became law in Iceland. Ari was 12 when Bishop Isleif died. Hall travelled from land to land and was in partnership with Olaf the Saint and benefited greatly from that. So he was well-informed about his reign. And Bishop Isleif died nearly 80 years after the fall of King Olaf Tryggvason [1000]. Hall died nine years after Bishop Isleif. He was then 94 years old. He had settled at Haukadal at the age of 30 and lived there 64 years. So Ari wrote. Teit, son of Bishop Isleif, was Hall's foster-son in Haukadal and lived there afterwards. He taught Priest Ari and told him many things worth knowing.[12]

Thus not only Ari himself was careful in noting the names of persons who told him about the early colonization of Iceland and the Norse settlers, but also his successor Snorri, who wrote about a century later and repeated his written account, thereby preserving the chain of reporters which linked Snorri and Ari to the earliest traceable informer of this particular history. On the assumption that Ari included details on the woman Thorid as well as on his male informants, it is particularly regrettable that these details were not copied by Snorri so that we do not now know how closely Ari was acquainted with her. Significantly, she was identified as the daughter of a priest, and the assumption must be that her father's ecclesiastical authority boosted the value of some, if not all, of her assertions. What remains important, however, is that women living as far apart as Italy and Iceland in the eleventh and twelfth centuries were occasionally regarded as sufficiently reliable and trustworthy informants to be singled out by male historians for specific acknowledgement.

Category 3: Information from a second-hand witness

There are fewer examples in this category, presumably because historians did not very often possess enough information on the individuals linking the original event with themselves. These chains were often, as we shall see, complicated. But on the whole the same remarks as the ones on Category 2 apply. Bishops, monks and priests predominate with some high-ranking laymen forming links in these chains. From eleventh-century Italy comes the story recorded by Leo of Ostia (d. 1115), the chronicler of Monte Cassino, on an early experience of Emperor Henry II (d. 1024). While still duke of Bavaria he once visited a monastery dedicated to St Benedict where his grooms, through a lack of stabling, were forced to shelter the royal horses in the monks' chapter house. That night the duke was warned and punished in a dream by the saint himself. According to Leo, the emperor told the story to Prince Pandulf IV of Benevento, who at the end of his life became a monk at Monte Cassino. There he passed on the tale to Abbot Desiderius (d. 1087), who in turn informed a certain Roffred, who told Leo. All links in this chain can be accounted for and there is no reason to doubt that the story originated with the emperor himself almost 90 years previously.[13] King Henry II of England (1154–89) as a layman is singled out by Walter Map as the source for his story on Count Theobald IV of Blois (d. 1152). Theobald's deeds were told by King Louis VII to the English king who himself passed them on to Walter.[14]

Another example can be found in Hugh of Flavigny's chronicle written in Burgundy in the early twelfth century. While discussing the deeds of the church reformer, Abbot Richard of Saint Vannes (d. c. 1042), Hugh colourfully describes the abbot's attitude to a miracle that he witnessed at Verdun sometime before 1004. Hugh of Flavigny had heard about it less than a century later during a visit in 1096 to Rouen, where he met people who in turn had heard the story from Archdeacon Hugh of Rouen (d. 1057). Before his move to Normandy this Hugh had been a monk at Verdun, where he had known Abbot Richard and had witnessed the particular occasion.[15] Hugh was well-informed about Norman affairs, partly because of his own involvement as secretary to a papal delegation visiting Normandy in 1096 and partly because of his fellow monk Gozelin, who originated from Bayeux. He told Hugh an interesting story in connection with Richard of Saint Vannes, for his father Gauzfrid and his grandfather Hubert had joined Richard's pilgrimage to the Holy Land in 1027. On their return they passed on stories about their adventures and told their family including Gozelin, who claimed to have heard the text of a prayer taught by Richard for those of simple and ignorant mind from his father and grandfather. The chain of information covering 70 years and recorded by Hugh of Flavigny prompted a reflection on how such oral information passed through three generations: 'And the fathers who saw it told it to their sons and the sons of the sons told it to their sons so that the next generation would know [about it].'[16]

Hugh of Flavigny's point was picked up and expanded by Walter Map and the anonymous author of the *Waltham Chronicle*. Both chroniclers explicitly state that stories told by the sons of those who witnessed events are valid sources of historical information, implying that such evidence constitutes a valid alternative to eyewitness accounts. The canon of Waltham, writing in *c.* 1177, refers back to the time of the Norman Conquest of England and thus covers a period of about a hundred years, while his exact contemporary Walter Map explicitly uses the same number of years, which he qualifies as the 'modern period' as opposed to the 'past' which starts beyond a hundred years:[17]

> It is in our own times that these things have arisen, and by our own times I mean this modern period, in the course of these last 100 years, at the end of which we now are, and of all of whose notable events the memory is fresh and clear enough; for there are still some centenarians alive and there are very many sons who possess, by the narration of their fathers and grandfathers, the certainty of things which they did not see. The century which has passed I call modern times – not that which is to come, though in respect of nearness to us the two are of like account.

With this particular passage Walter Map also unwittingly illustrates the medieval convention that it is often the members of the third generation who initiate the recording of the memories of the first and second generations. The assumption that the chain of informers consisted exclusively of men does not come as a surprise. That in practice women also played a large role is something we will discuss in later chapters.

Category 4:   General hearsay

This category contains all references to rumours, gossip or reports given by people and acknowledged by the chroniclers in the following terms: 'a man says', 'it is said', 'the rumour goes' and variations of these phrases. There is no way to distinguish between these expressions, which all indicate that the historian heard rather than read about the stories. Nor is there any indication as to the identity of the people responsible for the stories. Only very careful analysis of each author can clarify whether an author consistently used such a phrase for events he did not find described in any book or whether he used such expression arbitrarily. Among these general statements, however, there are some which are more specific. In a substantial number of cases reports are said to have been given by many people. There seems to be no doubt that the historians implied that the larger the number of people reporting a particular story, the greater the chance that the report might be true. These references are commonly phrased like: 'many people say/tell/relate', 'we have heard from our ancestors', 'we have heard from old people', 'many who then lived told us' and variations of this theme. They also illustrate the historians' reverence for the age of the informants. Old age is often equated with wisdom based on memory and knowledge. Memory and knowledge supply authority and authority is what the historians needed to 'authenticate' their information.[18] The Waltham chronicler, for example, speaks of hearsay reports in his monastery about Tovi, the founder who lived in the mid eleventh century and thus about 150 years before his own time.[19] William of Malmesbury reports on the inhabitants of the New Forest as still talking about the disasters befallen on the sons of William the Conqueror who created the forest.[20]

We can also include here the authors' explicit acknowledgements of members of his family, frequently uncles, who helped them with genealogical details about earlier generations. Fulk IV le Réchin of Anjou (d. 1109) relied on his maternal uncle Count Geoffrey Martel (d. 1060) for the brief history of his county which he wrote. Lambert of Wattrelos (d. c. 1170), who inserted an elaborate family history into the chronicle of his church, relied on his maternal uncle Abbot Richard for some stories of his ancestry, while Lambert of Ardres, writing c. 1200, says that his patron Arnold of Ardres heard stories about his ancestors from his uncle Walter of Clusa.[21] Though most references are to maternal uncles as the family authorities, the information conveyed is similar to that of unattributed hearsay. General hearsay is given credence by citing family authorities who have handed the information down to the author. The absence of women amongst these explicit acknowledgements is as interesting as the predominance of maternal uncles. Belonging to the kin group one generation removed from the author, these male relatives acted as authoritative channels through which the collective memory of a family passed. In Chapter 4 we shall come back to this observation to see that the maternal uncles must have heard the information from women in particular.

Some hearsay reports are specifically linked to objects, whether movable or immovable, and they illustrate the extent to which oral tradition was linked to specific articles, like swords, spears, jewellery, tapestries and paintings, which functioned as pegs for the survival of the collective memory. Although this theme is the subject of Chapter 5, it is important to give a few examples here in order to show the importance of objects as pegs for oral transmission of collective memory. Walter Map reports on a quarrel about the water basins used for the king, Henry II of England (1154–89), to wash his hands. William of Tancarville, hereditary chamberlain of Normandy, contested the right of an unnamed (in Map's story) official to carry the water basins, by pointing out that since the time of his father, who served Henry I (d. 1135), water basins for this purpose were kept as evidence of the right of the hereditary chamberlain in the church of Saint-Georges-de-Boscherville, a monastery founded by the Tancarvilles. A precious vase clinched the matter in another dispute about ownership related by William Newburgh, who reported it being returned by the Scottish king William I (1165–1214) to Henry II.[22]

Relics take a particularly important place amongst movable objects. Frutolf recalls that the Holy Lance in the possession of the German kings had once been acquired by King Henry I (d. 936) from King Rodulf II of Burgundy (d. 937).[23] We could not have realized that William the Conqueror gave the amulets he had worn during the Battle of Hastings to Battle Abbey had its chronicler 75 years later not recorded the sale of the relics in order to pay for William Rufus's gift of a precious cope to the monks of Saint-Germer at Fly in France.[24]

Category 5:   General hearsay evaluated

In this category the language of oral reports is similar to that of the previous one, but the authors either express doubt about the reports or compare them explicitly with information from other oral sources or with a written tradition. On several occasions the tenth-century authors of the *Annals of Fulda* refrain from giving details because they are not sure about the authenticity of apparently oral information.[25] William of Malmesbury often balances two different oral reports without necessarily expressing a preference for either.[26] Both Walter Map and William Newburgh are sceptical about some of the marvels which they say were reported orally. That they wrote the stories down illustrates their fascination with events such as the man who found his dead wife alive and dancing or the report of the existence of green children. At the same time, however, they refuse to silence their disbelief and struggle to find rational explanations for events which are neither miracles nor fantasy.[27] Such fantastic stories by their very nature were extremely difficult to verify, let alone establish as having taken place at all. Searching for witnesses or other evidence supporting the truth of the matter was one of the tasks of a good reporter. William Newburgh showed great enterprise and critical skill when he followed up the rumour that the archbishop of York had died of poison in 1154. He set out on a fact finding mission to Rievaulx where he knew that one of the archbishop's former servants had become a monk. This man emphatically refuted the poisoning reports and William clearly believed him.[28]

Most historians compared oral information with written material whenever possible. Ralph Glaber reported the sighting of a whale off the coast of Normandy and underlined the veracity of the story in two ways. First of all, he points to the fact that the whale was seen by many people, and secondly, he underpins their report by comparing it with the story of the *Journey of Saint Brendan*, which describes a similar large sea monster.[29] The occurrence of Siamese twins in the Breton border area is believed by William of Malmesbury on the same grounds of both oral and written reports.[30] The Norman historian Robert of Torigni (d. 1186) was puzzled to hear that King Alfonso of Portugal had transferred the body of Saint Vincent to Lisbon because, so he says, according to a much earlier written account of the monk Antony, Charlemagne had already done so.[31] Richard of Ely, author of the *Gesta Herewardi* written in the early twelfth century, said that he supplemented the Old English *Life of Hereward* written by Leofric the Deacon with oral reports from two of Hereward's companions as related to the abbot to whom he dedicated the *Gesta*.[32] We have already encountered the story of the sale of William the Conqueror's amulets at Battle Abbey, but in this context it is significant to emphasize that the Battle chronicler rejected a (now lost) written version of the event in favour of the oral one as told to him by Abbot Odo and the monk Richard, the delegates from Saint-Germer at Fly who had come to Battle Abbey to perform a public penance.[33] Despite the fact that the written account of what had happened at Fly represented the earliest testimony, what counted as more reliable and trustworthy at Battle was the oral story even though it was later.

Category 6:   Stories about ballads, songs and jongleurs

Ballads, songs and stories told by jongleurs warrant a separate category because medieval historians were worried about their lack of means to assess the veracity of these tales of the past. Their problems were twofold. On the one hand, there was the problem of orality, though, as we have just seen, oral information was regularly preferred above written texts. Much more serious was the problem of the vernacular language as the vehicle for the transmission of stories. When Orderic Vitalis (d. *c.* 1142), writing about the obscure ninth-century St William of Gellone, had the choice of two traditions, he spurned the ballad sung by jongleurs for the truthful account on the grounds that the former was in the vernacular and the latter in Latin:

> And since I have happened to mention St William, I will now insert a brief account of his life in this book. I have found it very hard to come by in this region, and a true account of the life of such a man will delight many. Anthony, a monk of Winchester, recently passed this way with a copy, and showed it to our eager eyes. Jongleurs sing a popular song about him, but a reliable account, carefully written by pious scholars and reverently read aloud by learned readers for the monks to hear, is certainly to be preferred to that.[34]

William of Malmesbury refers several times to songs without always specifying the language or expressing any opinion about their contents.[35] Walter Map deplores the fact that nobody celebrates the deeds of recent kings as opposed to the jongleurs who sung vernacular songs about the Charleses and Pippins of the past. Despite the ambiguity of the statement – is he regretting the lack of heroic kings like Charlemagne in his own time as well as that of stories about them? – he seems to betray no great concern about the jongleurs' artistic production *per se* nor, indeed, about their language.[36] Lambert of Ardres (d. *c.* 1200) juxtaposes the adventures of the past as told in fables and histories, presumably in Latin, and those of the deeds and fables of the Bretons (the *chansons de geste*) in the vernacular, with the deeds of the counts of Ardres. The implication is that both Latin and vernacular should be used as vehicles in the respective written and oral traditions. By adding that William of Clusa, the (great) uncle of his patron Count Arnold, was one of his informants, he stresses the oral and vernacular component even though he himself wrote in Latin. For him too, the vernacular and Latin traditions were complementary, whether transmitted orally or in writing.[37] Ekkehard of Aura, the Bavarian chronicler, also mentions vernacular songs which celebrate the deeds of Boto and Aribo, members, through their mother, of the *Immidingi* family. He adds the precise genealogy of the family and does not betray any anxiety as to the reliability of this information collected, it seems, in the vernacular.[38]

Canon Lambert of Wattrelos (d. *c.* 1170) also refers to family memories passed on by jongleurs. In his case the story concerned ten of his mother's (maternal) uncles who had all died on the same day in the same (unidentified) battle some 90 years earlier. He does not explicitly mention the language of the song, but that it was performed in French seems likely. Again there is no hint of disbelief in Lambert's story or of suggesting that the details may be wrong on account of the vernacular.[39] Thus the reaction of historians to texts in the vernacular and delivered by jongleurs is very mixed and on the whole not overly sceptical with regard to vernacular information. Assessment of the contents of the information reported on seems to have depended at least as much on the individual historian's opinion of the material involved as on some theoretical notion of what was and was not supposed to be acceptable as a reliable source.

Category 7:   Stories about people remote from the author in time and place

Most historians experienced problems in bridging remoteness of time and place, but relatively few explicitly expressed their concern with regard to oral information. For example Count Fulk IV le Réchin of Anjou (d. 1109), the author of his family chronicle, knew the names of four ancestors beyond his grandfather, but he could not give details about their actions because they had happened too long ago. Interestingly, he records the names of seven generations of ancestors, but knows only the life stories of the first three.[40] William of Malmesbury could not list the names of the sons of the Irish king because, he said, he had not heard them. He very briefly alluded to Empress Matilda's flight from the siege of Oxford, but he promised to give a more elaborate account once he had spoken to eyewitnesses.[41] Robert of Torigni had similar problems of lack of information, but they did not prevent him from saying of King Alfonso of Portugal, the father-in-law of his goddaughter Eleanor: 'and he did many more good things of which we, however, do not know', or of King Henry II while in war against King Louis VII of France (1137–80): 'and in this battle the king did many more things of which we have not heard, or if we have heard of them we have forgotten them'.[42]

The evidence for historians' explicit references to oral information raises several methodological problems. The first relates to the fact that some of the vocabulary applied by medieval chroniclers to oral tradition is also applied by some of them to stories which turn out to have been copied verbatim from written texts. Of the following examples, all belong to the fourth category of hearsay evidence. Ralph Glaber tells us about fourth-century St Evurtius, introduces the story with 'it is said' and then proceeds to copy part of the *Life of St Evurtius*.[43] William of Malmesbury in his *History of the Kings of the English* introduces stories taken from Asser's *Life of Alfred* and the *Life of St Dunstan* with phrases like 'they say', 'people recollect' or 'rumour has it'.[44] Such instances act as a warning to be careful in assigning stories to oral tradition on the evidence of phraseology alone. That modern scholars have made erroneous deductions in this way can be illustrated by the case of William Newburgh. Historians often quote his chapter on the burial of William the Conqueror at Caen as an example showing how an author writing at the end of the twelfth century still relied on oral tradition for an event which took place more than 100 years previously.[45] William says that something memorable happened at the burial in 1087, which he knew from a 'trustworthy account'. Then follows the tale of a poor man's claim that the ground in which the Conqueror was about to be buried belonged to his father and had been seized by the monks of Saint-Etienne at Caen. Since the story is told in numerous written chronicles of earlier date, like those of Orderic Vitalis, Eadmer of Canterbury, William of Malmesbury and Wace, there is no need to accept this particular case as an oral testimony.

Secondly, because historians often copied the work of a predecessor before they updated or interpolated it, they silently included their predecessors' references to oral sources. We have already seen how Snorri Sturluson quoted the now lost version of Ari's *Islendingabók* and so preserved precious information about the latter's oral sources. The practice of copying phrases describing the origin of stories, however, shows that for the medieval historian, careful copying of information about the past included copying the ways in which their predecessors had collected their information, that is whether this was in oral or written form. The relative faithfulness with which they did so is an important indication of how significant they thought it was to preserve every link in a chain of information. Modern scholars may be misled by this practice, which is particularly noticeable in cases of reference to general hearsay, and erroneously attribute such references to the wrong period. Robert of Torigni (d. 1186), abbot of Mont-Saint-Michel, interpolated and updated the *Worldchronicle* of Sigebert of Gembloux (d. after 1112). For Norman and English affairs he consulted the *History of the English* by Henry of Huntingdon. While reporting on the casualties of the Battle of the Standard in 1138 he says that rumour had it that 12 000 people were killed. The same passage occurs literally in Henry of Huntingdon's work, though the number of casualties there is only half as large.[46] Two centuries before Robert of Torigni compiled his *Chronicle*, the historian Regino of Prüm, writing about Hungary and Romania, digressed from his historical narrative by describing Scythia. His description is littered with phrases like 'they say' or 'rumour has it', which he copied word for word from Justin's description of Scythia dating from the third century.[47]

Thirdly, there is the fact that almost all oral information was received in the vernacular but written down in Latin, except in England and Scandinavia where the vernacular was written down well before Latin caught up with it. Therefore we have to allow for a considerable margin between the story as told and the final polished written product. As yet very little research has been done in order to trace the amount of literary and historical reshaping which took place in the process of transfer from the oral to the written mode in medieval historiography. Only glimpses of this process can be found and they pose more questions than answers. Take, for example, the wonderful story of the Moorish attack on the coast of Aquitaine in 1022, as reported by Adémar of Chabannes (d. 1034), monk at Limoges.[48] He tells us that the Moors themselves had afterwards told him what had happened. Twenty of them had been captured, two of whom were kept by the abbot of Limoges while the rest were sold. The implication is that the two Moors who remained as servants at Limoges were Adémar's informants. But did Adémar understand Arabic or did he use interpreters? He is scathing about their Arabic language and, in the same sentence, he shows off his own Latin vocabulary by using the rare verb *glattire* (to yelp) which Suetonius applies to the sound made by young dogs: 'the way they talk is not Arabic at all but it resembles more the squeaking of young dogs like yelping'.[49] The Latin gloss inserted by Adémar is a literary device which veils the essentially oral character of the original story.

Earlier on in this chapter it was pointed out that information relayed orally in the vernacular was not considered unworthy of inclusion in serious historical writing. Some residual scepticism about the vernacular language that lingered on gradually dissipated when the vernacular language became more widely used. From the middle of the twelfth century onwards historical narratives in the vernacular have survived from outside England and Scandinavia. Their survival begs the question whether vernacular historians approached the past in a similar way to their Latin contemporaries. Writing in the same language as the one in which the stories about the past were delivered to them removed the language barrier which existed between the learned Latin tradition and the 'vulgar' vernacular tradition. How could historians writing in the vernacular tell the truth if this could only be expressed in Latin? In fact, by the middle of the twelfth century, historians writing in the vernacular go to great lengths to establish their credentials not only as translators of Latin chronicles, but also as eyewitnesses of the contemporary parts of their stories.[49]

The Anglo-Norman poet/historian Jordan Fantosme claims that he was an eyewitness of the famous encounter between the kings of Scotland and England at Alnwick in 1173–74. This clearly establishes him as a prime reporter and ideal historian. He also, however, claims repeatedly that he cannot give the reader all the information because he was not present at other subsequent occasions. Rather than holding this statement against him as a sign of sloppiness, it should be accepted as the author's explanation that he was not an eyewitness of all that he wrote. The Norman canon Wace of Bayeux was also a poet who wrote in Anglo-Norman French. Between c. 1150 and 1175 he translated an impressive number of chronicles and saints' lives, inserted new information and expressed his opinion about the veracity of his sources. In fact, although he wrote in the vernacular, he was every bit as conscientious as his Latin contemporaries in selecting and reporting facts about the past. He even went so far as to explain that he had failed in establishing the truth of certain matters. His fruitless search for Breton magic and marvels in the Forest of Broceliande is the most famous of his statements about his research activities. As a practising canon of Bayeux cathedral he was used to dealing with Latin charters, juridical documents and he was well versed in canon law – the fact that he wrote in verse and in the vernacular does not mean that he was a less scholarly historian than his contemporaries who wrote exclusively in Latin.

In the light of these remarks we can now return to the questions proposed at the beginning of this chapter. The answer to the first question (did historians have preconceived ideas about the use of oral sources?) is *yes*. Most chroniclers at some stage in their work, usually in the prologue, say that they have used written sources and information which they themselves collected or received from others who were eyewitnesses or otherwise well informed.[50] But, except for the Waltham chronicler and Walter Map, none of the historians studied here explicitly explains for how long a period of time oral information is valid. In practice they seem to agree that the period is about one hundred years, or three to four generations. This was also the time it usually took chroniclers to pick up their pens in the first place to write a history of a church, a monastery or a family, or to continue a chronicle already in existence.[51]

The fact that it is to English chroniclers that we owe the clearest expressions of awareness that oral stories going back over more than 100 years may be unreliable is not surprising. They wrote in the 1170s, about a century after the Norman conquest of England, about the most dramatic event in the English past. By then conquerors and the conquered had become more or less one people, there being no distinction in law between them. In so far as disputes persisted concerning the ownership of land before and after 1066, they were being left unresolved because proofs which rested on oral testimony dating back to the period of the conquest were no longer acceptable.[52] Outside England there was perhaps less awareness of the limitations of oral evidence. The corollary of the idea that oral information is valid for about one hundred years, is the idea that any oral testimony going back beyond that period is untrustworthy unless it has been 'saved' in written form. If this argument is correct, it would follow that most medieval historians were aware of what constituted 100 years, and that the past beyond that point was more vague.

It is certainly true that chroniclers found it very difficult to place 'loose' information older than a century. The case of Frutolf of Michelsberg's query with regard to the Nibelungen story may serve as an example. He was puzzled by the fact that the 'vernacular fables' and the 'songs' from oral tradition represented the Germanic heroes Ermanaric, Attila and Theodoric who lived in the fifth and sixth centuries, as each other's contemporaries, whereas he found them in different periods in the *History of the Goths* by Jordanes.[53] In his discussion of this passage, Dennis Green suggests that the learned chronicler Frutolf, followed by Bishop Otto of Freising (d. 1158), represents the views of Latin historiographers and literate clerics who worked within a framework of the literary tradition of Christian chronology, knew Jordanes's standard history and took that as the truth. The vernacular oral tradition of the eleventh and twelfth centuries was still running autonomously alongside the stream of literacy and its representatives, presumably anonymous ballad singers or jongleurs, were unaware of the conflation of individuals and periods.[54] Thus medieval historians seem to have adopted the rule, though very often without commenting on it, that oral information remains reliable for about a century after which written sources should be preferred.

Then there is the question whether historians acknowledged the use of orality according to certain rules. The answer in this case is a clear *yes*. Chains of information derived from eyewitness accounts are presented in very similar ways. The agreement in presentation no doubt goes back to Bishop Isidore of Seville's claim that history is the story of true events, the truth of which can only be reported by eyewitnesses. The careful account of the individual links in such a chain is part of a conscientious attitude to reportage. The most striking aspect of the references to explicit eyewitness accounts is the status of the witnesses, who invariably belong to the higher echelons of society. Clearly, the greatest reliability was accorded by medieval historians to persons in positions of authority. General hearsay reports, which are far more numerous than the reports of eyewitnesses, are presented in a uniform way by medieval historians. I have already suggested that most of these are accounts of events which the authors did not derive from any specific source. Usually they concern stories which the author had not read, although we should be careful not to assume too quickly that all phrases like 'they say' or 'it is said' indicate exclusively oral sources. Medieval historians, writing in both Latin and the vernaculars, observed certain clear rules when making use of oral information. They were aware of these rules and by the twelfth century made some of them explicit. As society became more literate, para-doxically historians paid more attention to oral evidence rather than less.

The question about the gender of the informants can also be answered with some confidence. In those cases where the chroniclers acknowledged their sources, the overwhelming majority consisted of men. We have seen that in only two cases, Petronilla at Novalesa and Thorid in Iceland, were women singled out for explicit acknowledgement of their oral contributions about the past. The main reason for the lack of female informers is no doubt their perceived lack of status and authority. It was extremely rare for women in the Middle Ages to act as witnesses or sit on a jury in a court. Many secular law codes, in fact, forbid the participation of women altogether. Therefore, with no authority given to them in a legal context, how could they be perceived as a trustworthy witness for ordinary day-to-day events? With this knowledge in mind, it is not surprising that women feature so little as witnesses in medieval annals and chronicles.

Even the female historians, like Hrotsvitha of Gandersheim and Anna Comnena, conformed to this pattern. Hrotsvitha apologizes for her lack of knowledge about the court of Otto I (936–73) in her introduction to the verse biography she produced. And nowhere does she mention her abbess Gerberga (d. 1001), who as Otto's niece was the undoubted link between the court and Hrotsvitha herself. Neither does she mention explicitly the nuns of Gandersheim, or oral reports from them, as her main source of information for the history of Gandersheim which she wrote at the explicit request of Gerberga.[55] Anna Comnena's biography of Emperor Alexius (1081–1118) contains several references to oral reports, mostly relating to her father's military campaigns which she did not herself witness. She regularly acknowledges stories from soldiers and old veterans who had been present during his battles.[56] Her father himself features time and again as her oral informant, either directly as telling a story to her or indirectly as she overheard him talking to others.[57] An Italian envoy of the bishop of Bari was her main witness for the battle of Otranto and therefore represented an eyewitness in the enemy's camp.[58] Amongst members of her family apart from her father, she singled out maternal and paternal uncles, but without specifying their names.[59] But no woman is mentioned explicitly as a source for information or gossip. Ironically, however, Anna herself was the ultimate witness on which the story of her father is based. She does not apologize for acting as a female author. Her story is, in fact, the main exception to the rule that women could not act as explicit witnesses to historical events.

The seemingly meagre harvest of female participants in the historiographical process, as represented by a survey of oral testimonies in medieval historiography, cannot represent historical reality. Even if, for the sake of argument, we assume that men positively avoided information told by women, there remains too much evidence belying such an assumption, as we shall see in the following chapters. The hagiographical tradition, which itself was so closely linked to that of historiography, has an unexpected surprise in store in this respect.

3

SAINTS' LIVES AND MIRACLES

This chapter on hagiography and the problems faced by hagiographers in collecting and weighing information will revolve around two axes. The first concerns the close association between oral and written modes of gathering evidence on sainthood and miracles. The difficulty of collecting information many years after a saint's death, the first attempts at jotting down notes in the process of writing, the physical vulnerability of written records, as well as the reconstruction of the chain of informants, are similar to the problems faced by historians. Study of the saints' lives and of other hagiographical writings also suggests a development between the beginning and end of our period: from haphazard oral recordings of sainthood toward a much greater degree of scrutiny of witness accounts and other evidence in writing as demanded by the tightening of canon law regulations. The second axis concerns the differences in the degree of collaboration between men and women throughout Europe. Germany shows the greatest consistency in the positive attitude taken by men and women writing hagiography towards female oral witness accounts, whereas French and, more particularly, English sources display a far greater ambiguity in this respect.

As writers of saints' lives and miracle stories, hagiographers faced similar problems to those of the historians. It was their task to write the lives of saints, trace their relics and record the miracles performed through the intervention of the saints. Like historians they used written and oral information, justified the use of their sources and weighed the evidence used in the process of writing. The saint's life was normally a biography containing the bare-essential dates of birth and death, names of parents,

41

place of origin and the deeds which led to sainthood. Sometimes a saint's life was followed by an account of the saint's burial or the transfer (*translatio*) of the saint's body from one burial place to another. Especially during the period of the Viking invasions, many saints' bodies were taken away from the vulnerable coastal areas to safe sites further inland. Stories of such transfers became an integral part of hagiographical writing. The most numerous hagiographical accounts, however, concern miracles performed through the intervention of the saint at his place of burial or through his relics. Many of them contain stories about recovery from illness, miraculous healings, interpretations of dreams or finding of lost property. But whereas the historian was concerned with matters of chronology, accuracy of dates and in general making sure that the past was shaped according to the rules of a Christian order of time, the hagiographer had an easier task. The dating of events was only necessary to authenticate the miracles and there was no need to arrange them in a chronological order. Sanctity was timeless. All that mattered was an indication of the person and the place concerned. However, as we shall see, due to a variety of circumstances in the twelfth century in particular, people began to demand greater precision and more details on witnesses, whether for a saint's life or for a saint's miracles. A saint could no longer be created because a community declared someone a saint, but rather canon law laid down procedures which were scrutinized by the papal curia. This process resulted in a quite different way of recording memories, acknowledging witnesses and specifying oral and written traditions.

In the early and central Middle Ages it was relatively easy to proclaim someone as a saint. Usually a record of the saint's life was written at some stage and the hagiographer's task of collecting material very much resembled that of the historian. If the person was a contemporary or a near contemporary, the author could rely on eyewitnesses or receive oral information at first or second hand. It was common practice amongst hagiographers to follow the method of their historian colleagues of acknowledging the main informants and giving details of their status and their relationship with the saint concerned. They too preferred eyewitness accounts over second-hand information, even though sometimes they did not have the former and were forced to content themselves with the latter. An early example comes from the late eighth century and concerns a female hagiographer, Hugeburc. She was an Anglo-Saxon nun who in 761 had gone to Germany, where eventually she settled in Heidenheim. There, in 778, she wrote a life of St Willibald, an Anglo-Saxon missionary in Germany. Willibald had risen to become bishop of Eichstatt, while his brother and travelling companion Winnibald became abbot of the double monastery of Heidenheim. He died in 786/ 7. Hugeburc describes herself as his relative which clearly suggests a blood relationship, but not necessarily that of a sibling even though she refers to Willibald as her brother. On his deathbed Willibald told her the story of the pilgrimage he and his brother had undertaken to Jerusalem, while she, as she explains at the beginning of his *Life*, took down his own words:

> Of all these places Willibald has given us a faithful description. For this rea-
> son it did not seem right to allow these things to pass into oblivion, nor to be
> silent about the things God has shown to his servant in these our days. We
> heard them from his own lips in the presence of two deacons who will vouch
> for their truth: it was on the 20th of June, the day before the summer solstice
> [778] . . .. These facts were not learned from anyone else but heard from his
> own lips, we have taken them down and written them in the monastery of
> Heidenheim, as his deacons and other subordinates can testify. I say this so
> that no one may afterwards say that it was an idle tale.

Hugeburc stresses the fact that it was Willibald himself who gave her the details of his travels. Interestingly, she adds that her visits to him took place in the presence of two of Willibald's officials, presumably deacons of the cathedral of Eichstatt, who, if necessary, could act as witnesses to confirm what she had written down. Collaboration between men and women seems to have been normal and nothing out of the ordinary, despite Hugeburc's self-deprecating sentences in which she claims that 'many holy priests [would have been] capable of doing better' than her. But her protestations of humility and unworthiness turn out to be rather ironical if we take into account the clever way in which she hid the evidence of her authorship. Whether it was simply a joke or a way to hide her gender, we shall never know. Hugeburc cleverly disguised her name in a cryptogram and inserted it in the rubric at the end of Willibald's *Life*, where it was discovered this century by the distinguished German palaeographer, Bernard Bischoff.[1]

Hugeburc was of English origin and wrote about a compatriot who, like her, had settled in Germany. From the ninth century comes the example of Lupus of Ferrières (d. after 862), a German monk educated at Fulda who later became abbot of Ferrières, an abbey in northeast France. There he received an invitation from the abbot and monks of Hersfeld, a monastery just north of Fulda, to write a life of St Wigbert.

Born in England in 675, Wigbert had gone as a middle-aged man to Germany as one of the many English missionaries to convert the pagans. After a preaching career of 14 years he died in 747. The chronological gap of almost a century between Wigbert's death and his own time worried Lupus of Ferrières more than the geographical distance he had to cover. In his dedicatory letter to Abbot Brun, written in 836, he expresses his sense of frustration at having had to dig up information on a man who died 90 years previously:

> But let no one consider this little work inaccurate because I am writing it in the 836th year of our Lord's incarnation and the 14th indiction, and seem to be recalling things which took place 90 years ago, for certainly anyone with the slightest education knows that Sallustius Crispus and Titus Livius narrated not a few things which had occurred long before their time, and which they had learned, partly from hearsay, and partly from reading. And to come to our own writers, Jerome published his life of Paul, a man who certainly lived in a very remote past, and Bishop Ambrose has left us an account of the passion of the virgin Agnes who was surely not his contemporary. The negligence of our ancestors in leaving untold the deeds of so great a person is not strange, nor is it the only case which needs to be condemned, for we know of certain things of the highest importance which have been suppressed not only by writers who have lived shortly before our time, but also by those who have lived ever so long ago. Hence, I do not see why it should be to my discredit if indeed I clear ourselves of the blame resulting from our failure thus far to put into writing the deeds of this illustrious man.[2]

Abbot Lupus surely used informants belonging to the third or fourth generation, who provided him with details of Wigbert's career in Germany. While this example illustrates the author's consciousness of time stretching back for almost 100 years, it also shows the conscientiousness with which Lupus collected oral information and justified the results, which in his own eyes were very meagre due to the lapse of time. However, he had been lucky to catch the story of St Wigbert's life just in time before the collective memory of him had become detached from the last living person to possess information.

At about the same time his younger colleague, Ralph of Fulda (d. 863), composed a *Life of Saint Leoba*, another Anglo-Saxon nun who had emigrated from England to Germany as part of the missionary movement. He, born and bred in Germany, had not himself known her because she had died *c.* 779, that is half a century before he put his pen to paper.

Nevertheless, he had access, however indirectly, to the testimonies of
her female friends. His intermediary was a priest called Mago, who had
left notes of his conversations with four nuns who had known Leoba
while she was at the nunnery at Bishofsheim: Agatha, Thecla, Nana and
Eoloba. Ralph acknowledges their (indirect) help without any sense of
doubt about the validity of their statements or their status as witnesses:

> I have been unable to discover all the facts of her life, I shall therefore recount
> the few that I have learned from the writings of others, venerable men who
> heard them from four of her disciples, Agatha, Thecla, Nana and Eobola.
> Each one copied them down according to his [?] ability and left them as a
> memorial to posterity. One of these, a holy priest and monk named Mago,
> who died five years ago [831], was on friendly terms with these women and
> during his frequent visits to them used to speak with them about things prof-
> itable to the soul. In this way he was able to learn a great deal about her life.

Ralph, however, seems mostly concerned with the fact that the written
material which recorded Mago's interviews with the nuns who had known
Leoba was so scrappy:

> He was careful to make short notes of everything he heard, but, unfortu-
> nately, what he left was almost unintelligible, because, whilst he was trying
> to be brief and succinct, he expressed things in such a way as to leave the
> facts open to misunderstanding and provide no certainty. This happened in
> my opinion because in his eagerness to take down every detail before it
> escaped his memory, he wrote facts down in a kind of shorthand and hoped
> that during his leisure he could put them in order and make the book more
> easy for readers to understand. The reason why he left everything in such
> disorder, jotted down on odd pieces of parchment, was that he died quite
> suddenly and had no time to carry out his purpose . . .. The sequence of
> events, which I have attempted to reconstruct for those who are interested
> in knowing them, is based on the information found in their notes and on
> the evidence I have gathered from others by word of mouth. For there are
> several religious men still living who can vouch for the facts mentioned in
> the documents, since they heard them from their predecessors, and who can
> add some others worthy of remembrance. These latter appeared to me suit-
> able for inclusion in the book and therefore I have combined them with
> material from the written notes.[3]

The ultimate source for the information on St Leoba, then, was the testimonies of four nuns. Their words, however, were noted down by the priest Mago who died before he had time to put them in order. His slips of parchment were then copied by Ralph and amalgamated with extra oral information he received from other men who confirmed the contents of the stories on the basis of oral tradition. Here, male scrutiny supported female witness accounts, which in themselves seem to have been entirely acceptable.

Before we continue with more German hagiographical material from the tenth century, we will turn briefly to France to see what evidence we have of hagiographers' use of oral and written sources. Writing biographies or saints' lives of people who lived in one's own community made it slightly easier to collect information. The oral tradition was traceable within one church or one monastery and the author hardly needed to venture outside it. Normally, he would ask the monks or clerks of the church in question to tell him what they knew about the saint, or in the case of the transfer of the body to tell him about that event, or if miracles were performed, about the people who had benefited from the saint's intervention. It was in the interest of a church to record the rise of a cult of a particular saint as soon as possible. Thomas Head has made a study of this process for the cults of saints in the Loire valley between the ninth and the twelfth centuries. Tracing the methods followed by the hagiographers over several centuries, he concludes that oral and written traditions were used. Sometimes written texts had been produced shortly after the death of a saint, but because the manuscript containing the text had been lost, the story was in danger of disappearing. Head, however, points out several monasteries where monks managed to save the stories preserved in oral traditions which, in part, had been based on written work. Thus a clear interaction between oral and written traditions can be observed. The case of Letaldus of Micy's work on St Martin of Vertou illustrates the process well.

At the end of the tenth century the monk Letaldus was asked by the abbot of Saint-Jouin-de-Marnes, closely associated with his own monastery at Micy, to write the life of a local saint, Martin, not be confused with the better known St Martin of Tours (d. 397). Their interest derived from the fact that his body had been transferred to their monastery after the Viking raid of 843. Letaldus was told that a book of his life had been burned in a fire, was lost and needed to be replaced. This he did by adapting the contents of a poem about St Martin into prose, by using oral stories from the monks who remembered the text of the book and, finally, by using accounts which had not hitherto been committed to writing:

... and I expanded it [the new prose life] a bit upon the request of the brothers. But since a group of older men had lived up to our time, who had committed to memory many things from the book of the life of the blessed man,
and one of them, that is Rainald, is passing his venerable years right up to
today, we thought it right to put down separately whatever we discovered in
their account which had not been included in the above-mentioned book,
making, as it were, another collection of the volume, beginning with those
things which Martin did, while living in the body, and extending on to those
things which he accomplished, with Christ working through him, after death.[4]

Thus Letaldus used oral stories to supplement the oral information he
had received from the monks, who themselves depended for their
knowledge partly on the contents of a book that was lost. Since, however,
the book had been written shortly after the 'translatio' and many monks
were still alive who knew of the event through oral tradition, that is within
three or four generations, the story could be saved and kept for ever.
That the oral and written traditions were intertwined did not matter in
the least as far as the authority of the story was concerned.

Letaldus's contemporary, the learned Abbot Abbo of Saint-Benoît-sur-
Loire (Fleury) (d. 1004) wrote the *Life of Saint Edmund*, martyred at the
hands of the Vikings in England in 870, on the basis of evidence related
to him through an interesting chain of informants. Abbo wrote it more
than a century later in 987/8 at Ramsey Abbey at the request of the monks
there, who knew that Abbo had learned the story while at Canter-bury.
In the prologue to the *Life*, addressed to Archbishop Dunstan of
Canterbury (959–88), Abbo explains how he got to know the story of St
Edmund, which had never before been written down. At Canterbury he
was present on the occasion when Archbishop Dunstan told 'the memory
of antiquity put together in an historical manner' to the bishop of
Rochester, the abbot of Malmesbury and others. He continues:

You [Dunstan] said, your eyes full of tears, that in your youth you had learned
[the story] from an old man, who related it simply and in good faith to the
most glorious king of the English, Aethelstan, declaring by oath that he had
been armour-bearer to the blessed man, on the very day on which the martyr
laid down his life for Christ's sake.[5]

Thus Abbo put before Archbishop Dunstan the version he himself had
told on the basis of the eyewitness account of the murder of King Edmund
given by the latter's armour-bearer. The order of the successive reporters

in this chain is not as impossible as it may seem. King Edmund was murdered in 870 and his armour-bearer told the story as an old man at the court of King Aethelstan, that is between the years 925 and 939. Assuming the normal age of an armour-bearer, he was probably a teenager of, say, 15 at the time of the murder. That would make him approximately 65 at the start of King Aethelstan's reign and 79 at the time of the king's death. At that time, someone in his sixties or seventies was quite old, but that does not mean that he could not have told stories from his youth. In fact, Dunstan himself related this story at a similarly advanced age. Born in 909 he was in his early eighties when he related the account of King Edmund's murder which he in turn had heard in his youth. As a young man Dunstan had spent several years at King Aethelstan's court, where he met the aged armour-bearer. Clearly, the young Dunstan had an excellent opportunity to hear this particular story at the royal court, and to relate it when he himself was an old man just before his own death in 988. Abbo's careful report on the chain of informants, addressed to Archbishop Dunstan, closely resembles the examples of reportage going back three generations given in the previous chapter. It inspires great confidence and does not at all, as some historians argue, provide evidence of the mischievous concoction of a fictitious tale.

Like St Edmund, St Gerald of Aurillac (855–909) was both a layman and a member of the highest nobility in Aquitaine. His *Life* was written within a generation of his death, not because like Edmund he was a martyr, but because of his exemplary life-style and generosity. Abbot Odo of Cluny (d. 942), embarked on his biography having interviewed many of Gerald's contemporaries. Four of them were singled out by name and rank in the *Life*'s prologue: Hugh, a monk, Hildebert, a priest, and two laymen called Witard and another Hildebert. What distinguishes Odo's reference to his oral informants from the others we have read thus far, is his explanation of how he interrogated them about Gerald:

> I investigated his [Gerald's] behaviour and the quality of his life in detail. At times with the others and at times alone, I carefully investigated what each of them [the four witnesses] said and whether they agreed, silently pondering if his life was one in which miracles were fitting.[6]

Odo interviewed the ecclesiastical and lay witnesses both on their own and in groups to identify discrepancies and similarities, a surprisingly modern approach to establish the truth of Gerald's deeds. Unlike Letaldus or Abbo, Odo did not have problems with lost written evidence or a chain of informants covering many years. His problem, it seems, was the potential conflict in oral evidence from four witnesses whose testimonies he valued enough to single out and distinguish from 'the many others' whom he does not identify. The examples of the monks Letaldus, Abbo and Odo are most illuminating for our understanding of how and when saints' lives were written down on the basis of orally preserved material.

These examples were concerned only with men. Indeed very little material survives from France sketching the way in which nuns either wrote themselves or acted as witnesses. The evidence from Germany, on the other hand, is extremely revealing in this respect. The role of German abbesses in the process of the commemoration of ancestors and the commissioning of historical work will be discussed in the next chapter, but here it is appropriate to draw attention to their unquestioned position as oral witnesses in the hagiographical works that were written in their nunneries. This evidence will signal the continuity amongst German authors, male and female, in accepting oral testimonies from women from the late eighth and ninth centuries onwards.

Two abbesses in particular deserve a closer look, Richburga of Nordhausen (d. 1007) and Bertha of Vilich (d. after 1056). Abbess Richburga of Nordhausen began her long career as a royal servant of Queen Matilda I, wife of King Henry I of Germany (d. 936) and mother of Emperor Otto I (d. 973). When, in *c.* 962, the queen founded Nordhausen as a daughter house of Quedlinburg, she appointed her personal maid Richburga as abbess. Since the manuscript tradition of the two lives of this queen points towards Nordhausen as the place of origin, it is plausible to assume some involvement on Richburga's part. She was probably instrumental in asking her nuns to compose the two texts and in informing them about Matilda's personality. Secondly, she acquired royal authorization for its contents.

The first *Life* was written, according to the preface, at the request of King Otto II (973–83), Matilda's grandson, in 973 about five years after the queen's death. The contents provide a clue as to its origin because it records a dispute between Matilda and her son Otto I about land that she had given to Nordhausen which he had taken away from (but subsequently restored to) the nunnery. Richburga clearly wished that a record be made of the queen's life and her generosity if only so that her grandson, the new king, would fulfil his duty to protect the nunnery's estate. The second *Life* was dedicated to Matilda's great-grandson King Henry II (1002–24), in a new attempt to remind him of his obligations towards Nordhausen. It was written shortly after the king's accession and before Richburga herself died in 1007. Like the first *Life*, the text forms a record not only of Matilda's life but also of the history of the nunnery's patrimony. For more than half a century Richburga had been the living memory of the founder and the foundation of Nordhausen, a memory which she had also committed to writing.[7]

The other example of hagiography from Germany comes from the environment of Cologne and concerns the *Life of Saint Adelheid* about Abbess Adelheid of Vilich. She was the first abbess of Vilich, a nunnery founded by her parents Meningoz and Gerbirga in the 980s. After the death of her sister Bertrada, who had been abbess of St Mary's at Cologne, she also took over the abbacy of that house. The toll was high and shortly afterwards, in 1002, she died. Her *Life* was written in 1057 by a noble woman called Bertha who, although a nun at Vilich, had not herself known Adelheid personally. Like the male hagiographers we have discussed, she too relied on the eyewitness accounts of others who had known her very well. Moreover, besides the testimonies of younger contemporaries of Adelheid, Bertha also incorporated stories from Adelheid's maid, an old woman called Engilrada. Like Richburga who had been Queen Matilda's maid, Engilrada would have been in an excellent position of trust and intimacy with her employer and so to give evidence to her biographer. She seems to me to be the most likely source for the interesting genealogy of Adelheid's maternal ancestry incorporated into her *Life*. Presumably this oral information elucidated some of the origins of the property made over to the nunnery.[8] As in the case of Nordhausen, the narrative serves both as a record of sainthood and a history of the family and the nuns' estates. The very fact that a written narrative record was deemed necessary, alongside the charters which Bertha mentions, to protect the nunnery's endowments shows how similar the nuns' actions were compared with those of monks. Where historical and historiographical narratives were kept alongside documents, the use of female witness accounts and female authorship are tokens of comparatively great self-assurance and confidence, particularly if we compare the texts of Nordhausen and Vilich with those of Wilton and Barking written a little later in England.[8]

The survival of many accounts of saints' lives in England in the eleventh century is due to the prolific activity of the immigrant Goscelin of Saint-Bertin.[9] He is also the first male author who explicitly defended the use of female witnesses in hagiographical work against accusations of employing non-authoritative sources. Goscelin was a Flemish monk who came to England in *c.* 1058, probably as a clerk of Bishop Herman of

Sherborne (1058–78). During the next 50 years he travelled from monastery to monastery earning his living by writing down the lives and miracles stories of Anglo-Saxon saints. He worked at Wilton, Winchester, Peterborough, Barking Abbey, Ely, Ramsey, and St Augustine's at Canterbury where he died at the age of approximately 70 in *c*. 1107. His skills were particularly in demand after the Norman Conquest and he saved much of the Anglo-Saxon hagiographical tradition that thus far had survived exclusively in oral form. His most famous literary productions are those written for the nuns of Wilton, Romsey and Barking. They are also the most interesting for our investigation because he gives voice to the unease experienced by some people about the use of female sources for his hagiographical work.[10]

In the late 1070s Goscelin was asked to write the story of St Edith (Eadgyth) of Wilton by both Bishop Herman of Sherborne and the nuns of Wilton themselves.[11] At the beginning of this *Life* Goscelin sets out the sources for his information, amongst whom were nuns who had been told the story by older nuns who had known Edith herself. This statement in itself is quite traditional and perfectly acceptable historically. Edith was the daughter of King Edgar (957–75) and his concubine Wulftryth and lived from 961 to *c*. 984. Therefore Goscelin tapped the collective memory of the Wilton nuns, which covered a period of less than 100 years. This, as we have seen in the previous chapter, was the usual period of time that elapsed before oral testimony was committed to parchment. What is new, however, is that Goscelin goes on to justify his use of female testimony about the past by saying that he has no less faith in the nuns' words than he would have in books:

> Nor should the female sex be rejected as carriers of the truth, for [it was a woman] who carried the Word of God [that is Mary] and who with her faith argued against the incredulity of the Apostles and through an angel predicted the Lord's resurrection [that is Mary Magdalene]. Later God's maiden as well as his servants prophesied and spoke in different languages thanks to the intervention of the Holy Spirit.[12]

In this passage Goscelin combines several well-known texts from the New Testament, in which women tell the truth.[13] Since the Bible contains God's word and thus his truth, its stories about women's reporting are true and prove that women can speak truthfully. Goscelin's point is that there are precedents in writing, and not just any writing but in Scripture itself, testifying to women as valid witnesses. If these biblical women can speak truthfully, why not the Wilton nuns about their own history?

Goscelin repeats his argument for the validity of women's historical knowledge in his slightly later *Life* of Wulfhilda, the abbess of Barking Abbey who died in *c.* 1000.[14] Here too Goscelin begins with a statement on his sources which were almost exclusively female. His chief witness was the nun Vulfrunna, also named Judith, who apparently had two names or was renamed after becoming a nun. In her early youth she had been educated by Wulfhilda and knew her well. Vulfrunna's testimony thus stretched back until a time before her teacher's death in *c.* 1000 while she herself, according to Goscelin, 'is still alive in the reign of our King William [the Conqueror, d. 1087]'. As in the *Life of St Edith,* Goscelin addresses his readers:

> . . . that the faithful testimonies of this sex should not be rejected is shown by the first Mary [that is God's mother] and the angel's messenger of the Lord's resurrection [that is Mary Magdalene] and the many saintly female prophets . . .

He then continues by asking his patron, Bishop Maurice of London (1086–1107), to defend the nuns' stories 'against the gnawing teeth of the unbelievers', meaning those people who refused to accept a woman's word as valid testimony. These two passages are the clearest evidence we have for the male hagiographer's belief that he had to defend himself, and his female informers, against scepticism about the veracity of his, and their, narrative. It seems to me obvious that Goscelin is not defending the oral tradition which had kept the stories about the saintly women alive, but rather is clearly defending the fact that this tradition was transmitted by women. His defensive attitude must be seen as a confirmation that in his time it was thought unusual to quote female testimony as authority for the truthfulness of an account of the past.

Goscelin's younger contemporary and possible compatriot Herman, the author of the *Miracles of Saint Edmund,* ended up at Bury St Edmunds as an immigrant hagiographer from overseas. One of the miracles he relates in *c.* 1092 is presented as supporting evidence for the statement in the *Anglo-Saxon Chronicle* that the Danish occupation of England by King Svein of Denmark (1013–14) resulted in heavy taxes on the indigenous population of East Anglia. The miracle illustrates how, through the intervention of the saint, some local people received back the taxes collected by a certain Thurketil who considered them an unjust imposition. According to Herman this story was told to him by Thurketil's daughter, Aelfwen, then an aged recluse at St Benedikt of

Holm 'while reminiscing about the past'.[15] In the context of this chapter it is particularly noteworthy that in a later revision, Herman altered the slightly ambiguous word 'reminiscing' to the firmer 'she told [us]'. Was Herman here, like Goscelin, strengthening his claim that the evidence derived from a woman in the face of an audience that doubted female testimonies? In his text the juxtaposition of the written (male) authority of the *Anglo-Saxon Chronicle* and the oral (female) testimony of Aelfwen is particularly striking. What is not clear, however, is whether the apologetic attitudes of Goscelin and Herman were inspired by their English audience, or whether it was an opinion they brought with them from the Continent, and Flanders in particular.

The freedom with which the English nuns and missionaries in Germany had written saints' lives, letters and histories several centuries earlier, as we have seen above, suggests that Anglo-Saxon England was well acquainted with female witnesses. If, three centuries later their position had become less authoritative, we do not find any explicit evidence for such a change. As for a Continental Flemish source for the hagiographers' apologetic attitude – there is some, admittedly meagre, evidence to support such a suggestion. The *Life of Saint Arnulf of Soissons*, written by Bishop Lisiard of Soissons in the early twelfth century, is based on stories told by Arnulf's sister Adzela. Lisiard's unambiguous expression of thanks appears at the end of the *Life*. However, in a slightly later revision of the saint's life, the second author Hariulf of Saint-Riquier (d. 1143), who had become abbot of Oudenburg in Flanders, omitted Lisiard's acknowledgement of Adzela. Why he erased her name we do not know, but it is possible that his Flemish audience did not appreciate the use of a woman as source for some of the details quoted in the *Life*.[16]

Women as rememberers were frowned upon not only of past events but also of present ones in England and in France. This doubt on the part of male authors is clearly seen in the collections of miracles. There are numerous references to monks, abbots and bishops who witnessed miracles themselves or who reported them as having occurred to other people, whereas women are hardly mentioned explicitly as witnesses or reporters. The evidence from Normandy serves as an interesting example because much research has been done and some statistical information is available to back up our observations. Most miracle collections were written down by monks or members of the secular clergy attached to cathedrals. On the whole, they were the result of oral reportage, although occasionally we find traces of previous written traditions. The miracles of the Holy Virgin of Coutances illustrate the mixture of written and oral traditions lying behind the formation of the collection as we know it now.

The collection dates from the reign of King Henry I (1100–35) of England who from 1106 was also duke of Normandy. It was written by John of Coutances, canon of the cathedral and son of Peter, chamberlain of Bishop Geoffrey (1049–98). In his Prologue he explains that he used a previous collection written at the request of Geoffrey 'by a certain young man related by blood to the most important persons of the cathedral', presumably the son of a rival family whose members were cathedral officials.[17] Clearly, John disagreed with this work and replaced it with a new version based on information from his father Peter and his uncle Walter, also a priest and canon of Coutances. The miracles are very standard in that they relate recuperation from illness, recovery of lost property and other similar stories. At the end, however, occur three very unusual miracles. They concern three visions of the Holy Virgin that took place in the cathedral where Mary appeared to a lay woman called Daria.[18] According to John, who identified her, Daria was the grandmother of the wife of his father Peter's chamberlain Goscelin. Perhaps surprisingly, John does not cite his father or uncle as reporters of Daria's visions, but instead cites two anonymous priests (who may have been his relatives) who testified to the nature of the visions and authenticated Daria's experiences as genuine enough to be incorporated in the miracle collection. Of the 32 miracles 13 concern women, with Daria as the only one who experienced miracles. All other miracles concern men. Research on miracle collections in Normandy has shown that one-third of miracles devoted to women is a rather high rate. The average is closer to one-quarter.[19] Do these figures indicate that three times as many miracles happened to men than to women? Or do they show that more men than women reported miracles? Or should we conclude that men were believed more than women?

One way of answering these questions is to look at the place where the miracles were written and to assess the opportunity authors had for access to information from women. Most miracle collections were written in monasteries for monks, even though some, like the Coutances collection, survive from cathedrals. In Normandy, to stick to the same province for which we have statistics, no miracle collections have survived from nunneries. None the less, as we will see later on, miracles certainly happened there. Thus if monks and secular clerks were the authors and they relied on information from their own institutions, it seems hardly surprising that men were their most obvious reporters of miracles.

In Normandy, however, there are two clear exceptions to this rule and an examination of the circumstances under which they occurred provides the most satisfactory answers to the questions posed. The miracle collections from the monasteries of Le Bec and Saint-Wandrille give as many miracle stories on women as on men and explicitly quote many women as informants.[20] The two abbeys were monasteries for monks that housed sizeable communities for women in their grounds. They were not double monasteries, that is foundations for both men and women, but single-sex institutions where the monks offered a welcome to women. Most of them are referred to, either in charters or in the miracle stories themselves, as 'nuns' or 'veiled women' or 'widows'. As far as we can tell, many of them were widows who had retired to monasteries after the deaths of their husbands. The monks provided them with spiritual guidance and sheltered housing, whereas the women offered practical help with housekeeping and nursing and, most importantly, financial support. Very little is known about the precise housing arrangements. The women could not enter the cloistered area, so presumably they lived in separate communities in the grounds of the monasteries.

At Le Bec, in the second half of the eleventh century, at least three famous widows lived with some of their female relatives. Heloise, the well-to-do mother of Abbot Herluin, not only donated her estates to the abbey but also baked bread and washed laundry for the monks. Her younger contemporaries were Eva Crispin, Basilia of Gournay and Basilia's niece Ansfrida. Abbot Anselm was very fond of them and regularly mentioned them in his letters as 'the mothers of the monks of Le Bec'. All three of them died in January 1099: Ansfrida on 2, Basilia on 16 and Eve on 22 January. The last two died at the age of 90 years. At Saint-Wandrille the 'nun' Eulalia lived with her unnamed daughter. We know about the couple from the miracle collection entitled *The Finding and Miracles of Saint Vulfran*, written between 1053 and 1054 by an anonymous monk of Saint-Wandrille. He tells that one day the daughter handed a picture of Christ given to her by one of the monks to her mother for safe keeping. The mother hid it under the mattress of her bed, where unfortunately the family's pet fox found it and took it away. Three days later Eulalia recovered the picture unharmed somewhere outside the house. That it had survived the 'theft' without damage was a clear sign of St Vulfran's intervention. Eulalia told the miracle to the monk who wrote it down.

Such occasions of women living on monastic sites clearly brought the monks in touch with women. Their physical proximity might have persuaded the monks to accept the women as reporters of stories in the same way as they accepted them from their male colleagues. There is no evidence in any of these accounts that the authors despised the information of women or that they were in any way reluctant to use their reports. This is quite remarkable, for other Norman evidence illustrates vividly a nun's perspective that a great deal of persuasion was needed to convince monks of the reliability of her story.

Only one report of a miracle known to have happened in a nunnery and written down by a woman has survived from Normandy. In 1107 Abbess Marsilia of Saint-Amand at Rouen wrote a letter to Abbot Bovo II of Saint-Amand on the Flemish border with Hainault, reporting a recent miracle.[21] The case concerned a lay woman from the area of Lisieux, who had attempted suicide but was revived in order to repent her folly and to confess her sins. The woman had heard malicious gossip from a neighbour insinuating that her husband was in love with someone else. Despite the man's protestations that this was untrue, the woman went on believing the gossip. Concerned for her well-being, the husband and some of her relatives brought her to Saint-Amand to be looked after by the nuns. One night she escaped from the nuns' attention, went to the church and hung herself on one of the beams. The next morning she was found, lowered from the ceiling and laid out on the floor. She regained consciousness, confessed her sins to the archdeacon of Rouen who had been fetched, and fully recovered. The miracle was that through the intervention of St Amand she had been given the opportunity to confess so that she could live in peace.

What concerns us here are Marsilia's arguments in her attempt to persuade her Flemish colleague to accept her as a witness and the miracle as a genuine one. Her attempt to persuade Abbot Bovo reminds us of the possible scepticism in Flanders about female witnesses, which was discussed above. First of all Marsilia tells him that the miracle was not unique, but was one of many that had taken place at Rouen through the intercession of St Amand. In this way she makes it clear that St Amand did not only perform miracles in a male environment, but also in a female institution. She then goes on as follows:

[I]t is necessary to add to the virtues and miracles that have already taken place in our abbey through God and our holy father [St Amand], this famous miracle that took place in our presence in our church through the merit of our father. Therefore we consider it of sufficient importance to describe it briefly to your holiness. Despite the fact that we do not belong to the same sex, we are equal because in the castle of our eternal King we fight side by side under one leader; it is just that we rejoice unanimously in the virtue of his triumphant testimony in honour of God.[22]

Thus Marsilia underlines the fact that they share not only a common patron saint, but also a common purpose in life, namely a shared responsibility to lead a life of prayer and contemplation in their respective monasteries. However, she immediately qualifies this notion of equality by adding that they belong to a different sex, implying it seems, a paradoxical sense of inequality: monks were priests, while women were not. Drawing the abbot's attention to her gender after she had set out that she witnessed the miracle herself must signify that Marsilia was asking for her report to be taken seriously. She was clearly conscious of the fact that she was a woman reporting on another woman's life and pleaded for the case to be accepted as truth. Would she have written in the way she did had men normally believed a woman's testimony? I think not.

There is, however, another aspect to the matter. Presumably, Marsilia wrote to Abbot Bovo II in the hope that the miracle would be added to the canon of St Amand's writings, and that acceptance of her story by a male community would lend it an authority which it might not have had if it depended only on her and her nuns' testimonies. Thus incorporation into a male environment would authenticate the female miracle. Several abbots, including Bovo I (1077–85) and Hugh I (1085–1107), as well as the newly elected Bovo II (1107–21) were working hard to promote the cult of St Amand, judging by the saint's dossier now in the Municipal Library of Valenciennes. The oldest-known manuscript with all the works relating to this seventh-century saint is MS 502, commonly dated to the late eleventh century.[23] The last quire of this book on folios 137–43 is an addition of a slightly later date. In fact, it contains the full text of Abbess Marsilia's letter which, as we have seen, dates from 1107.[24] Two other twelfth-century copies of St Amand's dossier, both lavishly illustrated, were made at Saint-Amand and contain the letter. These three manuscripts provide the evidence that Abbot Bovo II and his community accepted Abbess Marsilia's story of the miracle as a truthful account that witnessed the continuous intervention of St Amand. This is one of the most exciting pieces of hagiography testifying to co-operation between men and women in the Middle Ages. For Marsilia depended on the monks' support for her story, while the monks, in the process of boosting St Amand's cult, were keen to incorporate her testimony.

The ambivalence felt by men in employing accounts given to them by women in the process of stimulating saints' cults persisted well into the twelfth century. During this period, our investigation into the perception of women as witnesses is hampered because of the influence of the Reform Movement. Ever since Pope Gregory VII (1073–85) claimed greater authority for the papal court in all matters pertaining to liturgy and the canonization of saints, written reports for the confirmation of sainthood proliferated. The procedure itself demanded the taking of statements in written or oral form which were then sent to Rome for scrutiny. The result was that the whole process of hagiographical writing became much more elaborate and detailed. It meant that statements by men as witnesses, as in the secular courts, were given greater authority. Whereas initially references to first name and occasionally social positions of the main witnesses were sufficient, in the course of the twelfth century the demand for more precise information was growing. One of the reasons was no doubt the increased demand by Church authorities that proper procedures for the pronouncement of sanctity should be followed. All claims to sainthood had to be supported by full references to witnesses' names. Just first names without patronyms or place of origin, or vague phrases like 'reliable people tell us' were insufficient. Without precise acknowledgements, doubt was expressed about the grounds on which someone could be claimed to be a saint. A good example from the second half of the twelfth century is that of Ailred of Rievaulx (1110–67).

Ailred was abbot of Rievaulx (1147–67), a Cistercian monastery in Yorkshire. He was a prolific author who wrote historiography, saints' lives and works of spiritual guidance. After his death one of his pupils, Walter Daniel, wrote his *Life* and detailed the many miracles that had happened around his burial place. But some people must have protested against the movement by the monks of Rievaulx to launch a campaign for Ailred's canonization, for Walter was forced to set out in a letter, which he later appended to Ailred's *Life*, the names of the witnesses to the miracles which he claimed to have happened through Ailred's intervention. The letter is addressed to a certain Maurice, who apparently had voiced the protestations of two prelates who had read the *Life* and disagreed with it. Walter apologizes for not having listed all the witnesses to all the miracles in the *Life* because, he claims, not very many hagiographers actually did so:

> Since only a few authors have made use of this kind of statement in their description of Lives of the fathers and given particular names of their sources, and in my view there should be no difficulty in believing that men of good life

are able to do what God wills, that little book of mine stands, by the counsel of my friends, as it was composed, the outcome of your command being transferred, as I have said, to the present page, so that may refer to it any unbeliever and especially those who have thought fit to suspect me of mendacity.

He then proceeds by listing some 30 witnesses by name, place and position, all of whom are male and are secular or regular ecclesiastical officers, and then goes on by saying:

> The powers of belief in the hearts of the faithful might have been satisfied by my assertion that I have written only the things which I had seen or what others had seen and told me; but those two prelates accept nothing that is not attested by formal and public proof, as though crime and virtue are established by one and the same easy canons of faith, and this and that admit of an equal appreciation.[25]

Clearly he accuses the unnamed bishops of wanting too much in the way of details, equating their wish for information with the demand of proof in the secular courts. The reference to the secular judicial system is interesting because it shows an awareness of two different procedures. Moreover, Walter is certainly right in claiming that an assessment of virtue is different from an assessment of crime. The former is a highly abstract attribute, while the latter can be settled through the application of reason.

Why are there no women amongst the witnesses Walter lists? Does their absence reflect the prejudices of the men in Ailred's milieu? That Ailred was deeply involved in spiritual guidance for women, and thus interested in their well-being, is proven by his advice written for recluses and his interferences in the case of the pregnant nun of Watton. But they were never asked for their opinion. Walter's comparison of the procedure of acknowledgements he had to follow with those of the secular courts, where women were not admitted as witnesses, may be an additional reason for their absence.

Women could not be avoided as witnesses in cases of female sainthood. Most of the evidence for the many female saints of the thirteenth century is contained in the records of their canonization processes. There we find a great many women testifying in favour of the saint's holiness from a young age onwards. Although the period from 1200 onwards falls, strictly speaking, outside the scope of this book, it important to take one example to put the dearth of material before this date into perspective. St Elisabeth of Hungary (1207–31) is one of the most famous female medieval saints. Born as the daughter of King Andrew II of

Hungary, she married Landgrave Louis IV of Thuringia in 1221. After his death six years later, she was evicted from her home by her brother-in-law and began a life of much greater austerity than the one she had led while married. She founded a hospital in Marburg where she helped the sick and poor and where she died of self-inflicted suffering in 1231. Within four years she was canonized by Pope Gregory IX on the basis of 600 witness accounts claiming her holiness and miracles.

One of the central documents submitted to the curia was the so-called *Book based on the testimonies of four servants of Saint Elisabeth*.[26] It consisted of a life composed of the testimonies of four women, charting the course of her brief career from childhood to death. The first two were Guda, her exact contemporary who had been educated with her since the age of five and later entered her service as a companion, and Isentrudis who, as a widow, became one of Elisabeth's maids after her marriage to Louis. Between them they covered Elisabeth's childhood, marriage and departure from her home. The other two were the nuns/servants (*ancillae*) Elisabeth and Irmengard, who shared her life in the hospital at Marburg. Besides their testimonies, some other female informants are also mentioned. This therefore is a book that is exclusively based on the intimate circle of Elisabeth's female friends whose words were, it seems, accepted as important and valuable testimonies of the holiness apparent in her life from her early years. The *Book* was compiled during the second phase of submissions to the pope in 1233 to expand on a very brief *Life* written by her confessor Conrad of Marburg and considered not substantial enough. Interestingly, he did not refer to Elisabeth's visions, which are mentioned in some detail in Isentrud's account as reproduced in the *Book*. It seems that by the 1230s, the papal curia's extreme suspicion of female accounts of visions had somewhat relented.

Church authority's suspicion of female visionaries and unauthorized explanations of their accounts resulted in greater scrutiny of reports of visions in the twelfth century. The miracle collection from Coutances, discussed above, hinted at the approval given by two priests to acceptance of Daria's visionary state. She was a lay woman whose visions were accepted because of her connections with a family whose members were officers at the episcopal court. From the twelfth century come several famous cases of visionary abbesses. Elisabeth of Schönau (d. 1164) and Hildegard of Bingen (d. 1179) stand out amongst them. Their work became known because their chaplains, who acted as their secretaries, vouched for the truth of the visions which the abbesses claimed were revealed to them directly by God. Their own words were not sufficient to have their state accepted, but the written version, authorized by priests, was acceptable to the Church authorities.

Abbess Hildegard of Bingen claimed that one of her visions was witnessed by a young woman of notable repute, as well as by her priest Volmar.[27] Referring to her friend, the nun Richildis, as having been present when she related her vision suggests that in Hildegard's opinion a woman could act as a reliable witness. That Volmar was there as well certainly added to the veracity of her account in the eyes of the Church authorities, who presumably would have been more sceptical if she had only put Richildis forward. Abbess Elisabeth of Schönau employed her brother, the priest Ekkehard, as her secretary.[28] He gave up a promising career at the court of the bishop of Bremen to join his sister and help her publish her revelations. It is a common feature amongst all mystical women that their writings were 'published' by male secretaries, who were invariably priests and therefore could vouch for their clients' true inspiration. If women were accepted as witnesses, the nuns themselves could have acted as female amanuenses for the mystics and the male intervention would have been superfluous.

The use of male secretaries to announce the words of visionary women raises another problem that needs our attention. One of the reasons that Elisabeth and Hildegard needed male writers was that they needed the latter's accomplishment in Latin. Both abbesses knew enough Latin to read the Church fathers and other religious texts, and they mastered the language in a pragmatic way for their administrative responsibilities. However, their Latin skills fell short of publishing their religious ideas with the sophistication needed to persuade the Church authorities. Hence the involvement of the priest-secretaries who possessed a profound grounding in Latin. In practice both Elisabeth and Hildegard would occasionally dictate in Latin which would then be adapted into literary Latin of high quality. Normally, however, the women would relate their visions in the vernacular language to their secretaries, who in turn would translate the information into Latin. We have, of course, no idea to what extent this rewriting by men of women's oral communications resulted in the reshaping of the contents of the nuns' visions. As we saw, Conrad of Marburg left St Elisabeth's visions out of his account of her life, however, they were later separately collected at papal request as evidence for her sanctity, but on the basis of exclusively female witness accounts,. The overwhelming amount of evidence and its compelling nature had dented ecclesiastical defensiveness in this case.

Another aspect of the use of the vernacular comes from hagiographers who acknowledge the help they received from women who spoke in their mother tongue. A good example comes from the vernacular *Life of Thomas of Becket*. In the epilogue the author, Guernes of Pont-Sainte-Maxence, expresses his gratitude to Archbishop Thomas's sister Marie, abbess of Barking (d. after *c. 1173*).29 The precise nature of his indebtedness, whether it was information on Thomas or financial help, is unclear. Guernes acted as Lisiard of Soissons had done before him: both hagiographers contacted sisters of a saint (Thomas Becket and Arnulf of Soissons) for information about him and perhaps paid money necessary for the spread of the cult. As we have seen at the beginning of this chapter, the tradition goes back a long time to Hugeburc who wrote about her relative Willibald. Sainthood in the family presumably enhanced the reputation of the family and so added to its value. Women played an important part in its transmission from one generation to another.[30] That there were other ways in which a family could increase its reputation and safeguard its memory, and how men and women co-operated to achieve this, is the subject of the next chapter.

Part II

Remembrance of the Past

4

ANCESTORS, FAMILY REPUTATION AND FEMALE TRADITIONS

In the previous chapters we have seen how relatively few historians and hagiographers acknowledged women as their informants about the past. Some, like Goscelin of Saint-Bertin, even found it necessary to defend their use of female sources against the implicit criticism of readers who seemingly demanded an all-male cast. On the other hand, we have also seen that men and women collaborated in the process of preserving the past. Both lay women and nuns helped with the collect-ion of historical data and their role is most clear in the context of personal histories rather than institutional histories. An extension of this role can be found in the abundance of implicit evidence that exists outlining the role of women close to the historiographical endeavour. Some of this evidence can be found in the chronicles, annals, saints' lives and other hagiographical texts discussed in Chapters 2 and 3.

Importantly, however, other sources exist which are as informative about the role of women and the way in which men and women collaborated in the memorial tradition. Charters, letters and fictional literature provide additional clues to the place occupied by both genders. On the assumption that literary fictional texts, like *chansons de geste* and romances, reflect attitudes of contemporary society which can help to elucidate the historical reality of the memorial tradition, we should not overlook them. And since many of them were commissioned by women or dedicated to women, they, like the histories and saints' lives commissioned by women, form an important part of our evidence. In contrast to the previous chapters which discussed the explicit references to men and women as informers or witnesses of the past, this chapter will focus primarily on their 'hidden' activities as preservers of knowledge about the past. The aim to find out especially what women contributed in this 'hidden' existence justifies the predominant attention paid to women.

Snippets of information showing women as commemorators date from the Carolingian period. Amongst the most famous are those concerning two lay women, both of whom were mothers who saw it as their task to remind their children of their ancestors. In 841 the noble woman Dhuoda, wife of Bernard of Septimania (d. after 844), left behind in charge of the estate in the south of France while her husband had taken her sons away from her, wrote to her 16-year-old son William who was a hostage at the royal court. Reminding her son of her own mortality she admonishes him to remember to pray for their relatives, and in particular, his paternal ancestors from whom one day he would inherit his estates:

> Pray for your father's relations, who handed down their goods to him in legitimate inheritance. You will find written down at the end of the chapters of this book who they were and what their names were. Although Scripture says one man will rejoice in the goods of another their legacy has not gone to others, as I have said before, but your lord and father, Bernard, has charge of it. Pray for those who possessed this legacy to the extent that they have left it behind; and pray that you who are living may enjoy it long and happily.

In Book Ten Dhuoda added eight names of her husband's ancestors, four male and four female. As far as we know, none of her own ancestors are listed.[1] Her reminder to her son of his Christian obligation to commemorate his paternal ancestors was clearly induced by a more practical and down-to-earth concern, namely to give him the names of his ancestors just in case he ever had to defend the legitimacy of his holdings after his parents' death. In an age of endemic violence and warfare, when for long periods the whereabouts of warrior fathers could remain unknown, it was up to the mothers to make sure that the children knew about their fathers, grandparents and great-grandparents.

It was in the same vein that Bishop Frechulf of Lisieux (d. after 852) dedicated his *World Chronicle* to Empress Judith with the suggestion that she read it to her son Charles, the future emperor Charles the Bald (b. 823, king/emperor 843–77). He sent her Book II of his *Deeds of the Emperors* to show her son which examples he should follow and which errors he should avoid. Although the focus here is on the office of emperor, the commemoration of ancestors is not forgotten. For were not several of Charles's immediate predecessors also his forefathers? What Frechulf did for Judith and Charles, offering them the world with all its emperors as ancestor cum predecessor, was on a larger scale than what Dhuoda had done for her son. But the principle was the same: keep their names in your heart for one day, when you have to prove yourself as their legitimate successor, you may need to reproduce them. Moreover, Bishop Frechulf felt that it was as a mother and in charge of his education that Judith ought to initiate Charles in writings about the past.

The immediate use of literacy for the purpose of commemoration is clear from both cases. Dhuoda and Judith were members of the highest aristocracy and the mothers of male heirs who one day would succeed to real estates, and therefore needed to know the names of previous owners. Whether at aristocratic levels or lower down the social scale, oral tradition in itself was too unreliable, and information handed down that way could easily get lost. The Carolingian kings were well aware of this and one reason for their literacy programme was to provide Christian society with an alternative means of remembrance. They targeted the parish as the unit where literacy could be spread through the co-operation of parish priests, but also perhaps because through the parish priests the mothers at home looking after their children could participate much more easily than their husbands. Did these women, like Dhuoda and Judith, only involve their sons or were daughters expected to participate as well? Carolingian sources have not been explored to the extent that we can answer this question. However, slightly later evidence from Germany shows a preponderance of the involvement of daughters rather than sons.

The clearest evidence comes from tenth- and early-eleventh-century Germany, where the Ottonian queens and their daughters were the most active members of the community to encourage the conservation of knowledge about the family. They were the prime movers behind the surge in commemorative writing. Hagiography, historiography and documentary memorials were the products of their task to preserve their family's memory. Queen Matilda I of Germany (d. 968), widow of King Henry I (d. 936), whom we have met already as the subject of the two *Lives* written about her at the instigation of her former maid Abbess Richburga of Nordhausen, formally discharged her own responsibility to her granddaughter Abbess Matilda of Quedlinburg (d. 999). On her deathbed she is said to have handed over a roll with the names to the 13-year-old girl with the request to pray for the souls of herself, her husband and those of other German nobles.[2] The roll itself has disappeared but similar documents have survived from several German monasteries. They are the memorial books or necrologies kept mostly by monks and nuns in their monasteries to commemorate the names of benefactors and those who belonged to the confraternity of the house. The people whose names were listed were commemorated in prayers for ever.

Whereas the monastic copies that still exist are all in the form of codices or books, the reference to Queen Matilda I's roll is fairly unique. Presumably, a list of names in the form of a roll was more handy for family use and could be stored more easily than the heavy bulk of a bound book. The contents of Matilda's list is thought to have been similar to the lists we have of her and her husband's family that survive from the nunnery of Gandersheim, ruled by another of her granddaughters, Abbess Gerberga (d. 1001). In fact, several necrologies of the Liudolfing family are known, each slightly different from the other, but combined they provide the only evidence for our knowledge of the names of Queen Matilda's mother, Reinhild, and her sisters, Bia and Friderun (or Friderim). That the information ultimately derived from Matilda herself is clear and that it was passed on in the female line through more than one granddaughter is proven by the reference to Abbess Matilda of Quedlinburg in her *Life* and the necrologies of the nunneries of Gandersheim, Essen and Trier.

As in Carolingian France, historical works too were dedicated to the women in charge of their family's memory. Widukind of Corvey addressed his *History of the Saxons* to Abbess Matilda of Quedlinburg, the granddaughter who one or two years earlier had been charged with safeguarding the family memory.[3] Widukind's chronicle provided her with a context and background against which she could set the names of the individuals for whom she had to pray. In order to distinguish between the ancestors, many of whom in subsequent generations had identical names, it was absolutely necessary to have a narrative context for stories attached to the different Ottos and Henrys. Against this background women's patronage of historical works is self-explanatory.

The Ottonian abbesses also commissioned works celebrating the deeds of their menfolk. Abbess Gerberga of Gandersheim asked her nun Hrotsvitha (d. *c.* 1000) to write the biography of her uncle, Emperor Otto I (d. 973). Hrotsvitha is one of the most famous women authors of the Middle Ages.[4] A formidably learned woman, she was exceptionally skilled in the liberal arts. Her Latin is impressively sophisticated and shines through in her plays and poetry. Apart from the laudatory verse biography celebrating Otto's achievements, she also wrote, no doubt at

Gerberga's request, a history of the nunnery of Gandersheim. In this verse chronicle she highlighted the role of the women of the Liudolfing dynasty, going back four generations to Oda (d. 912), wife of Duke Liudolf of Saxen (d. 866), who had founded Gandersheim and enlarged its possessions continuously.

Presumably, Hrotsvitha relied on Gerberga and her other relatives for information about the nunnery's history, which must have come down to her generation as much in the female as in the male line. Three of Oda's daughters, Hathumoda (d. 874), Gerberga (d. 896) and Christina (d. 919) had been abbesses of Gandersheim, and some of their young contemporaries would have been able to pass on personal memories to the nuns of Gerberga's and Hrotsvitha's generation. The relative longevity of the Ottonian abbesses and their nuns, as highlighted by Karl Leyser, helps to explain the continuous chain of informants on family history within the Ottonian dynasty.[5] However, the chance of long life was greater for nuns than for lay women whose lives were under constant threats because of the danger of childbirth.

One such death in 946, that of Queen Edith the first wife of King Otto I, left a gap in the family memory that in due course could only be filled with information from England. Edith herself was the sister of King Aethelstan of England (d. 939) and gave Otto I two children, Liudolf (d. 957) who became duke of Swabia, and Liutgard (d. 953) who married into the ducal house of Lotharingia. After Edith's death, Otto remarried Adelheid of Italy (d. 999) by whom he had two more children: Matilda, abbess of Quedlinburg, the one of the death roll and Widukind's history, and Otto II (973–83). Edith's son Liudolf in turn had two children: another Matilda, who became abbess of Essen (d. 1011), and Otto, duke of Swabia. When this Otto died without issue in 982, Abbess Matilda of Essen was the sole survivor in the male line from the marriage of Edith and Otto I. As a nun it was unlikely that she would marry and produce offspring so Edith's line would die out with her. And unless she took action, the family memory in oral form would end with her.

Though we do not know how, Abbess Matilda did manage to contact her distant English relative Aethelweard, who is almost certainly the same person as Ealdorman Aethelweard, one of the most powerful magnates of King Aethelred II of England (978–1016), and author of the Latin adaptation of the *Anglo-Saxon Chronicle*.[6] Aethelweard dedicated his chronicle, translated from Old English into Latin for her sake, to her and the full text of this can be found in Appendix 1. In it he traced Queen Edith's ancestry and so linked the Ottonian East Saxon family with the West Saxon family of the kings of Wessex. In his dedicatory letter to her Aethelweard writes that the chronicle is a follow-up to an earlier initial response to her request for details on their common ancestry. He relied on his own memory for the genealogical information, as well as on stories told by his relatives.

This complex of personal and family-oriented information, transmitted orally, he included in the formal royal Wessex genealogy as contained in the written *Anglo-Saxon Chronicle*. Aethelweard then proceeds to set out the genealogy of their family over the past six generations, tracing their blood relationship back to the brothers King Aethelred I (865–71) and King Alfred (871–99), ancestors respectively of himself and Matilda. Writing in the late tenth century, his knowledge stretches back more than 120 years to King Aethelwulf (839–58), father of these two brothers and the oldest mentioned member of the line. Despite his formidable knowledge of the English side of the family, he had to admit that he had lost track of the whereabouts of the sisters of Queen Edith (Matilda's grandmother) who had married into several Continental royal families. He in turn ends his dedicatory letter by asking Matilda whether she had any details on them, stressing the fact that it was her task as a woman to keep the rest of the family informed 'for you have not only the family connection but the capacity, since distance does not hinder you'.

Aethelwaerd's letter is a most illuminating piece of evidence for the commemorative task of noble women to keep track of the whereabouts of their relatives, alive and dead. It also shows very clearly how oral and written traditions could bridge a gap of six generations in one's own country, while family details could get astray within the space of two or three generations if contacts were not kept up, as in the case of the princess 'near the Alps' who lost touch because of the distance. Note, also, that Aethelweard admits that a gap of three generations, in this case between the early 920s, the date of the arrangement of the marriage, and the 980s was thought of as a 'not inconsiderable lapse of time'. In other words, 60 years was thought to be a long period. Matilda's role in the process of family commemoration can only be explained with reference to her cousins, the other German abbesses who commissioned histories, saints' lives and other commemorative writings. Viewed only from an English perspective, as used to be the case, the dedication of the *Anglo-Saxon Chronicle* to a German nun makes no sense whatsoever.

No other time within the period covered by this book presents us with such a consistent picture of female commemorative activity as the Ottonian tenth century. But this does not mean that after the year 1000 women ceased to fulfil this role any longer. On the contrary, even though the evidence occurs more widely and thinly spread over the rest of Europe, a woman's task as informant of the past continued unabated to judge by the many examples of female patronage of historiographical works.

In England Queen Matilda II (d. 1118), first wife of King Henry I (d. 1135) turned to William of Malmesbury, asking him shortly before her death for a history of the kings of the English. Ironically, her involvement is known only through two letters, written by William to her brother King David of Scotland (d. 1153) and to her daughter Empress Matilda (d. 1167).[7] As a direct descendant of the Anglo-Saxon kings, through her mother St Margaret (d. 1093), Matilda had a particular interest in them as a member of the second-generation of post-Conquest queens of England. Although there is no explicit statement about her own contribution as to the contents of the history, it is not improbable that Matilda herself helped to fill in gaps in the genealogical information. Her successor Queen Adeliza, as widow of King Henry I, commissioned a now-lost life of her husband written by a certain Bishop David, presumably the man who after a career in Germany came to England and became bishop of St David's.[8] Adeliza's step-daughter Empress Matilda was in turn probably the person who persuaded Robert of Torigni, monk of Le Bec in Normandy, to write the only surviving history of Henry I.[9] Earlier, Empress Matilda had been the dedicatee of Hugh of Fleury's *History of the Recent Kings of France*, replacing her aunt Countess Adela of Blois (d. 1137), daughter of William the Conqueror, who had been the original dedicatee.[10] Towards the end of the twelfth century the first wife of King Philip Augustus, Isabel of Hainault, received a copy of André of Marchiennes's chronicle of the kings of France.[11]

In none of these cases do we know for sure whether the female commissioners of chronicles also acted as informers about the men whose deeds they wished to be recorded. Common sense suggests that they did, but that the historians never explicitly acknowledged their contribution. On the assumption that they contributed information about their husbands, fathers and grandfathers, what might they have said and what stories might have been included? The most likely aspects are those referring to personality, family life, marriages, wives, daughters and children. In other words, the meagre information in chronicles on private matters might have come from women. Their contribution on more public and political matters depended on their own involvement and their own access to sources.

As we have discovered in Chapter 2, there are few references to women's

direct role as informants in the chronicles themselves. But what about
the indirect evidence? If we read between the lines of the text of chronicles
and annals, we can certainly find information that might have come from
women. In his history of the dukes of Normandy, Dudo of Saint Quentin,
who wrote c. 1000, praises Countess Gunnor (d. 1031) the wife of Richard
I (d. 996) and mother of Richard II (d. 1026), the very dukes who jointly
commissioned him as ducal chronicler. Since one of Gunnor's qualities,
that is singled out is her memory, it is tempting to see this remark as an
indication of her, presumably oral, contribution to Dudo's work. Born in
c. 960, she can be expected to have passed on memories going back to
the mid tenth century and, through stories related to her by others, to
the beginning of the century. Viewed from this perspective, she was an
important witness for the Danish family she represented within a Norman
elite that celebrated its Scandinavian ancestry as much as its connections
with the Frankish princes. With many of the Danish settlers wounded or
killed during the Viking settlement of Normandy, the few Scandinavian
women left were a precious source of information to tap. Her active
contribution may also reflect a more ready acceptance of female
informants in Scandinavia if we remember the Icelandic woman Thorid
who is quoted as one of the informants of Ari, the author of the
Islendingabók.[12]

From a slightly later date in the eleventh century comes the Flemish
anonymous author of the *Life of King Edward the Confessor* praising
his patron Queen Edith. She had requested him to write what is in fact a
family history of her father, Earl Godwin, and her brothers, King Harold
who died at Hastings and Earl Tostig who was slain at Stamford Bridge.
The author praises her intellect and especially refers to Edith's wisdom.[13]
As in the case of Gunnor, she must have been one of the most important
informants on which the story was based. In Chapter 2 we came across
the case of Petronilla of Susa, the woman who was reputedly more than
200 years old when she told the anonymous author of the *Chronicle of
Novalesa* the history of the monastery's site. As a female informant, her
role is singled out in what we have seen is a fairly unique situation. The
Novalesa story is important for another reason in the context of the
commemorative role of women. When the chronicler introduced
Petronilla as the main source of his information, he pictured her as sitting
on a large stone on the edge of the town surrounded by women (*femine
circuitu*) and then pointed out that the people from Novalesa who
consulted Petronilla comprised both men and women, thereby
involuntarily acknowledging not only that women were curious about

the past, but also that they participated fully in the transmission of information about it.

There are numerous indications of women telling stories about the past in other sources. Most of them concern family relationships, but occasionally one finds a story that links the family to an office like that of queen. In 1143–44 a striking English example was reported in a letter from Abbot Gilbert Foliot of Gloucester (d. 1187) to Brian fitz Count, one of the supporters of Matilda, the empress, on the authority of her mother, Matilda II.[14] According to this story Queen Matilda I (d. 1083), wife of William the Conqueror (d. 1087), had stood godmother to Matilda II in the early 1080s. While bending over the baby, the little girl grabbed a corner of Queen Matilda's veil and pulled it over her little head. This was seen as a good omen that one day the baby would become a queen herself, as indeed happened when Matilda II married King Henry I and became queen consort. Having become a mother herself, Matilda II presumably passed on the gossip to her daughter when she went to Germany as the fiancée of King Henry V (d. 1125). Originally the story was told with reference to Matilda's impending German queen-consortship, but its occurrence in Gilbert's letter concerned with her new role as pretender in her own right in England gives the story added poignancy. Whatever the political circumstances were, this charming tale is revealing of a gossipy tradition about the role of queen passed on through three generations of women.[15]

There are other areas where we may look for women's actions to preserve the past by passing on information orally. What happened in cases where women were the sole heiresses to their father's or mother's estates? Surely they must have been told from a young age onwards about the significance of their position, the importance of marriage and the birth of a child, preferably a son, in order to pass on the family inheritance. Although we know of many cases, listed by Jane Martindale in her article on family and succession in the romance-speaking world for the Continent and by James Holt and Judith Green for twelfth-century England, it is difficult to find explicit evidence of women's awareness of their position, their thoughts and opinions.[16] The many heiresses in the eleventh- and twelfth-century history of the counts of Boulogne left an interesting and diverse trail of their memorial guardianship. Some passed on information orally, some commissioned biographies of women in the family and some acted as patrons of vernacular written texts on the family.

Any discussion of the role of the Boulogne heiresses must begin with the observation that several of them married into the English royal family.[17] These marriage alliances are unsurprising given the position of the county of Boulogne in the extreme northwestern tip of France, which is situated nearest to the British Isles. Long-standing trading contacts and involvements of the counts of Boulogne in England facilitated these connections. In the 1030s Count Eustace II (d. 1086/8) married Godgifu, sister of Edward the Confessor, but had no children by her. This family link, however, accounted for Eustace's interest in the English throne and his support for William the Conqueror's invasion of 1066. His son by his second wife Ida of Bouillon (d. 1113) was Count Eustace III (d. 1125), an important landholder in England who married Mary of Scotland (d. 1115), daughter of King Malcolm of Scotland. Both Mary and her sister Queen Matilda II of England had been educated at the English nunnery of Romsey, an important literary centre with a tradition of strong hagiographical interest in female saints. It cannot be entirely accidental that both the sisters commissioned saints' lives of women, very much in the same tradition as the ones from Ottonian and Salian Germany discussed above. Queen Matilda II, probably in consultation with her sister Mary of Boulogne, commissioned the *Life* of her mother St Margaret, written by Turgot of Durham, later bishop of St Andrews (d. 1115), which contains an exaltation of royal motherhood as well as an illuminating contribution to the historiography of queenship.[18]

From a political point of view the *Life* is significant because it stresses Margaret's, and therefore also her daughters', descent from the old Anglo-Saxon royal line, a highly sensitive topic during the Norman occupation of Britain. Queen Matilda II in turn passed on historical interest to her daughter the Empress Matilda, for it was she who probably persuaded the Norman historian Robert of Torigni that he should add a *Life* of Margaret and Matilda II to the history of the dukes of Normandy, if only to emphasize the legitimacy of the Empress's children as future heirs to the English throne by pointing out that they combined Norman and Anglo-Saxon blood. As far as we know, this plan was never executed and no *Life* of Matilda II has survived.[19] Mary of Boulogne in turn passed on a similar idea to her daughter Matilda (d. 1152), another heiress of Boulogne, who in due course became wife of Stephen of Blois and king of England (1135–54). Matilda of Boulogne was not interested in her own mother and instead commissioned a *Life* of her grandmother Ida. Between 1130 and 1135, she asked a monk of the monastery of Waast to compose the *Life of Countess Ida*. This work too became a tribute to motherhood, with an account incidentally of the benefit of breast-feeding one's own children, and saintly selflessness.[20]

In the next generation, it was Queen Matilda and King Stephen's youngest daughter Mary who became the centre of attention. In 1160 after the deaths of her brothers Eustace and William, she was left as the sole surviving heir to Boulogne. Only one snag, seemingly, prevented her from succeeding to the county: her status as a nun. As a child oblate she had spent her time in a series of English nunneries before she was promoted abbess of Romsey, the same nunnery where 100 years previously her great-grandmother and great-aunt had lived, presumably after her father Stephen had become king. By the orders of her cousin King Henry II (d. 1189), she was forced in 1160 to resign as abbess and to renounce her monastic vows in order to marry Matthew of Flanders, younger brother of the count of Flanders, and to produce an heir for the Boulogne dynasty.[21] This she did by following a family tradition and giving birth to two daughters and no son, so that once again Boulogne was held by an heiress. However, the marriage itself failed and Mary returned to Romsey leaving it to her daughters to keep up the family history.

Ida, the eldest daughter and heiress, with her third husband Rainald Dammartin, commissioned one of the translations into French of the Latin *Pseudo Turpin* text, a twelfth-century history of Charlemagne's victory at Ronceval. They had a genealogy appended to it showing the counts of Boulogne's descent from Charlemagne. Although Ida's blood relationship with the Carolingian family is beyond doubt, the genealogy is wrong in several places; but whether Ida and Rainald knew this is impossible to tell.[22] Their younger daughter Matilda (d. 1210) in due course married into the house of Brabant. This Matilda and her husband Henry count of Brabant (d. 1235) are associated with the Old French romance *Le Chevalier du Cigne*, which is a legendary account of the Knight of the Swan, who was allegedly Count Geoffrey the Bearded of Bouillon, father of Ida of Bouillon/Boulogne and grandfather of Godfrey of Bouillon the Crusader.

Though the vernacular text can be linked firmly with the patronage of Matilda and Henry of Brabant in the early thirteenth century, the story of the Knight of the Swan was known 50 years previously, as early as the 1170s when it is alluded to, in Latin, by Bishop William of Tyre, the famous historian of the kingdom of Jerusalem, who had heard it from descendents of the Bouillon/Boulogne family in the Middle East.[23] Clearly, the story of the Swan Knight had been passed on through Ida's descendants in the female line in Boulogne, but also through the male line represented by her younger son Baldwin, who founded his own dynasty in the East. Duchess Matilda of Brabant continued the strong

Boulogne tradition in which mothers and daughters kept closely in touch during their lives and in death.[24] Matilda of Brabant arranged for her daughter Mary, who until 1207 was the heiress in Brabant, to marry Otto IV of Brunswick, later king and emperor.

When in 1260, 50 years after her mother's death, Empress Mary died, she requested to be buried with her mother in St Peter's at Louvain where she had a new tomb built with beautiful effigies of Matilda and herself. In Brabant mother and daughter were remembered as having been descended from Charlemagne and related to the kings of England, as well as to the counts of Flanders and Boulogne. There is no doubt here about the women's involvement in passing on knowledge about their family's past. Mothers, daughters and granddaughters as well as sisters and aunts can be found in the Boulogne family as transmitters of family traditions and stories of ancestors in a uninterrupted line from *c.* 1060 to the mid thirteenth century. Their example shows that literary images of women sitting together and telling each other tales about the past must bear relation to what happened in real life. It is easy to picture any of the Boulogne sisters from any generation in a similar setting to that proposed by the author of *Le Conte de Floire et de Blancheflor*. In the prologue written in the 1160s the author explains how he came across the story he was about to tell:

> I entered a chamber the other day, a Friday after dinner, to amuse myself with the damsels, of which there were beauties in the room. In the room there was a bed which was adorned with a spread. The spread was beautiful and costly, no better ever came from Thessaly. The cloth was worked in flowers, of blue silken bands and corders, I sat down to listen to two ladies I heard speaking. They were two sisters: they were speaking about love. The ladies were noble, each was beautiful and wise. The elder spoke to her sister about a love affair between two children which had happened a good 200 years ago.[25]

The sisters' high birth and their education, the elder sister's knowledge of a story that had occurred over 200 years earlier and her oral transmission of it to the younger woman would all seem to support the view that an oral female tradition of story-telling among learned courtly ladies was one of the 'sources' of courtly romance. In the eyes of the male author of this text this was not necessarily the case, for a few lines further on at the end of the prologue he tells us: 'But a good clerk had told her, who had read it in writing. It begins in an agreeable fashion. Now hear its beginning.'[26] Thus the author cleverly destroys the fiction of female oral story-telling and replaces it with the reality of male written culture. The case is even more complicated if we accept that the passage describing the sisters' discussion is a late-twelfth-century interpolation in the prologue. In its original form the prologue sets out a fictitious Carolingian genealogical origin for Floire and Blancheflor as part of the male author's introduction. This literary example, however, shows how real the image of sisters talking about the past was. That the female oral tradition of story-telling is subsequently mocked by the male author does not alter the evidence of women exhibiting a commemorative role and possessing interest in the past.

Thus far we have seen the ways in which women were involved in the historiographical process by commissioning chronicles or saints' lives of close relatives, reading them and by actively passing on information about the past. We have also seen how in Germany abbesses helped the dynastic interest not by producing children themselves, but by supporting a written tradition that preserved memories of the past. The Boulogne noble women, many of whom became English queens produced not only children, usually daughters, but also written works to maximize the remembrance of the ancestral feats of both women and men. All these women belonged to the upper echelons of the aristocracy in England and on the Continent. Their dynastic stakes were high and one can imagine the enormous importance attached to remembering what they thought were the most important events of their ancestry. But what about the lower aristocracy or, indeed, the people belonging to groups of the population lower down the social scale? Can we know what the women, and in particular the heiresses amongst them, thought about their role as preservers of information about the past? Two late Anglo-Saxon cases can illustrate the persistence of female historical tradition covering up to six generations.

The first is a short written tract, which traces the descent of land from one heiress called Ecgthryth, daughter of Bishop Ealdhun of Chester-le-Street and Durham (d. c. 1018), through six generations to the end of the eleventh century.[27] Known as *On the Prowess of Earl Uhtred and the earls who succeeded him*, the document has been discussed from different points of view studying the incidence of Scandinavian names in the large kin group, tracing the history of the various estates mentioned and as a source for the history of the earldom of Northumbria.[28] Little attention, however, has been paid to the narrative in so far as it illustrates the inheritance of the lands through several generations of women, and how this may have affected the women in their role of carriers not only of

land, but of knowledge of the family history. The main inspiration behind
the tract was the attempt by a monk of Durham Cathedral to reconstruct
the history of six manors which had originally been leased by Bishop
Ealdhun to his daughter's husband Earl Uhtred, but which formed part of
the episcopal estates. According to Durham, the lease of the estates was
given to Uhtred for his lifetime as long as he remained married to
Ecgthryth. He, however, broke the marriage and thus, as far as Durham
was concerned, the estates ought to have been handed back to the cathedral.
Instead, Ecgthryth took the six manors with her to her next husband Kilvert.
When this marriage also broke down, she returned three manors to Durham
while the other three remained with Kilvert.

During the subsequent generations, claims to all six manors were
lodged with Durham by the husbands of the daughters, granddaughters
and great-granddaughters of Ecgthryth. The tract was obviously finally
written to show (from Durham's point of view) that Ecgthryth, great-
granddaughter of Ecgthryth and Uhtred, and her husband Aelfsige had
no right to any of the property. As far as the rights to the land were
concerned, all leases were made out to the husbands and not to the wives,
even though in this case the inheritance went through the female line.
In other words, historians argue, no doubt correctly, that despite the fact
that the women were the vehicles for the inheritance claims, it was usually
their husbands or other male relatives who pursued the claims in court.
This was purely a practical matter because any claim had to be made in
the shire court to which no women, either as witnesses, claimants or
defendants, were admitted.

Do these circumstances mean therefore that women had no notion of
their property and its history, or that they did not participate in the
handing down of knowledge of the claims? What does the text tell us
about the women's perception as heiresses? I believe that they were aware
of their role and 'value' and that from generation to generation an heiress,
having become a mother, would have explained this to her daughter, the
next heiress. And in those cases where in generation after generation
only women were born, the heiress's awareness of her value must have
increased rather than decreased. To argue, as is conventionally done,
that only the male relatives or the church, in this case Durham from which
the land was leased, knew the history of the estates potentially
underestimates what women knew of their family and the history of their
estates. Firstly, the church depended for its information on its estates
entirely on the information from the family about the descent of leases.
Within the family, both men and women were aware of the way in which

the lands descended, even though the further back one went the hazier the knowledge about the precise circumstances became. Secondly, the men who married the successive heiresses of these estates might have known something, but ultimately they too must have received the details from the women. Overall, the combined efforts of the men and women amongst Ecgthryth's descendants provided the oral history of the family lands, which was ultimately recorded with a bias in favour of Durham by one of its monks.

That behind every dispute over land lay an oral story, even though with regard to women's property it was recorded in writing in a male environment, is beautifully illustrated by the second Anglo-Saxon text, a lawsuit from the time of King Cnut (1016–35) noted down in one of the gospel-books of Hereford cathedral.[29] The case concerns a man called Edwin who claimed his mother's land. He had gone to the sheriff's court where he was faced with Thurkil the White, the husband of his mother's kinswoman Leofflead, who represented her. Thurkil appeared not to know enough details and three thegns were then sent to Edwin's mother to ask for more information:

> And when they came to her, they asked her what her case was concerning the land which her son was claiming. Then she said that she had no land which belonged to him at all, and she became extremely angry with her son, and called to her kinswoman, Leofflaed, the wife of Thurkil the White, and spoke thus to her in front of them: 'Here sits my kinswoman Leofflaed, to whom I grant after my death my land and my gold, and my clothing and my raiment, and everything I possess.' And then she said to the thegns: 'Act like thegns and announce well my message to the meeting before all the good men, and inform them to whom I have granted my land and all my possessions, and to my own son never a thing; and ask them to be witness of this.' And they did. They rode to the meeting and announced to all good men what she had charged them with. Then Thurkil the White stood up in that meeting, and asked all the thegns to give to his wife clear from the claim the lands which her kinswoman had granted her, and they did so. And Thurkil then rode with the permission and witness of all the people to St Ethelbert's minster [Hereford cathedral] and had it entered in a gospel-book.

The precise nature of Edwin's claim against his mother and Leofflaed is unknown, but the interesting thing is, of course, that information about the status of the land and, presumably, its history was well known to Edwin's mother and Leofflaed. That in the end Leofflaed benefited must have something to do with her husband's eagerness to have the record made in writing. Thus, again, we encounter a case where on the surface only male witnesses are knowledgeable (or not, as in this case Thurkil displays his ignorance), but underneath the surface their knowledge depended entirely on what women had told them.

Edwin's mother was a widow who knew details of the lands involved going back some while. From two centuries later we have an example of a widow's knowledge about her late husband's affairs which went back 60 years. In 1265 when she was well into her eighties Loretta, dowager countess of Leicester, was approached by King Henry III (d. 1272) with the question 'what rights and liberties are attached to the stewardship of England with regard to the honour and earldom of Leicester'. She was requested to give evidence to the abbot of St Augustine's and the prior of Christ Church at Canterbury. The stewardship had been held by her late husband Robert who had died 60 years earlier in 1204, but at the time was claimed by his nephew Simon of Montfort. He, through the king, addressed Loretta in a letter appealing to her memory, presumably to establish precisely how and when the prerogatives of the stewardship had become attached to the earldom of Leicester. Her age and her circumstances – she lived as a recluse near Canterbury – pleaded in favour of her status as a witness to a particular custom going back in time beyond other people's memory. Except for this letter no other evidence of Loretta's old age nor about her reaction to it is known. Clearly, in cases when all male avenues of knowledge had been explored a woman's testimony about a public office might be sought.[30]

Knowing the history of one's estates and the history of one's family was as much a benefit as a curse. For some women with landed property and knowledge about its past found themselves being married off to men without any land and thus 'without a past'. Their complaints, recorded in a variety of sources, implicitly confirm what the evidence set out in this chapter tries to prove, namely female interest in and knowledge about the past. No woman would complain about a marriage below her own standing or nobility if she had no idea about her family background, her nobility going back several generations or her value in terms of land attached to her. The very existence of complaints about *mésalliances* are evidence of some notion of family history and family memories which justified the women in their complaints. Women did not moan because their prospective husbands were poor, they complained because these men had no history.

In late-eleventh-century Bavaria, the chronicler Frutolf of Michelsberg

accused King Henry IV (d. 1106) of many shortcomings, one of which
was that he married the daughters of illustrious families off to those of
obscure lineage.[31] Displaying an attitude widespread in western medieval
Europe, Henry used the lands of rich heiresses or widows to reward poor
men who had served him well. One such case can be illustrated,
exceptionally, from the point of view of a mother who was about to lose
her daughter to one of them. In the early 1070s the widowed Beatrix
wrote a letter to her brother Udo, the newly appointed bishop of
Hildesheim, the text of which is printed in Appendix 3. In it she asked
his help in dissuading her daughter's suitor from marrying her on the
grounds that he was of inferior rank and would thus harm the family's
reputation:

> As for my daughter Sophia, who is hidden like a concealed theft, a certain
> person dares to hope that she will be his wife, though he is totally unworthy of
> this ambition; and while he considers our misfortune rather than our ances-
> try, strives to compensate his low birth at the cost of our nobility. Thus the
> fruit of my womb, formerly my pride, is now my disgrace, and I who seemed
> to have given birth to joy, have now brought forth sorrow.

Later on in the same letter she appeals to her brother's help once again
and repeats the sense of shame the young man would bring not only to
her but to the bishop as well:

> . . . and ensure, since I cannot, that she does not marry beneath herself to the
> disgrace of her family; for just as an increase in her honour reflects the shared
> honour of her family, so her dishonour is our common shame.

Beatrix is clearly knowledgeable about her family's history which she
does not set out in great detail because her brother does not need
reminding. For us, however, the lack of detail is frustrating because we
would like to know how far back the reputation of the family went. Her
Latin is as good as that of Hrothsvitha of Gandersheim's and Bertha of
Vilich's, and she displays her learning in a quote from Virgil's *Aeneid*
and in her articulate explanation of her dire circumstances. Significantly,
her letter is the only letter sent by a woman which survives in the collection
of about one hundred episcopal letters from Hildesheim.

Germany was not the only country witnessing the 'loss' of noble
heiresses to newcomers without any background. Like Frutolf of

Michelsberg, the Anglo-Norman historian Orderic Vitalis (d. *c.* 1142)
accused King Henry I of England 'of raising young men from the dust'
by marrying them to rich heiresses.[32] Henry even promised his own
daughter, the Empress Matilda, to the son of his one-time rival in Europe,
Count Fulk V of Anjou (d. 1143). Matilda was so appalled at being married
off to Geoffrey, the son of a mere count that she asked her friend Robert
of Torigni, monk and historian of Le Bec, to include a genealogy in the
Deeds of the Dukes of the Normans showing, wrongly we now know, that
the kings of France were descendants of the counts of Anjou.[33] If kings
could descend from mere counts, her own predicament was not as awful
as it seemed. Yet, there was no way in which women, it seems, could
prevent their sons as kings from prolonging this custom of marrying off
rich women to poor men. Empress Matilda, who otherwise often
succeeded in influencing her son Henry II's behaviour, could do very
little in this respect. He had lists made of widows and heiresses for the
sole purpose of knowing their exact availability for the marriage market.
One of these, the so-called *Roll of Ladies and Boys and Girls* dated to
1185, has survived and lists the details of 128 women and their children.[34]
As a written record it is based on the women's own testimonies relayed
indirectly at the shire court to the royal judges. In only a few cases did
the women's own sentiments trickle through male censure and do we
hear of forced marriages and heavy fines paid to remain a widow or as
punishment for remarriage without the king's consent. A study of this
fascinating document as a source of women's history remains to be written,
particularly in view of the women's perception of their origins since many
list their father's, grandfathers' and great-grandfathers' names.

Italy too, recently occupied by the Normans, provides many cases of
mésalliances recorded in the 1090s by Geoffrey Malaterra. For example,
Count Roger I of Sicily (d. 1101), faced with an impecunious knight
called Ingelmarius and the dependency of his nephew Serlo's widow,
decided that a marriage between them would solve both his problems.
Once married Ingelmarius would benefit from his wife's large estates
while she would have someone, other than the count, to protect her.
Geoffrey, however, shrewdly observed that this Lombard lady was not at
all keen to be married off to a Norman for the second time:

> For this reason, and despite the latter's [the knight's] low birth, he [Roger]
> gave him in marriage to the widow of his nephew Serlo, who had been killed
> in Sicily by the Saracens, along with all the dower which belonged to her. She
> was extremely reluctant for she was a woman of most distinguished ancestry,

the daughter of Count Rodulf of Boiano, but the count [Roger] did this precisely so the social status of the knight amongst his companions might be, at least to some extent, enhanced.[35]

Modern historians have often underestimated the strong feeling amongst women destined to be exchanged like chattels and given to whomever provided their fathers or uncles with the best political deal. Professor James Holt in his article on heiresses went so far as to deny the historical reality of women's feelings, arguing that this was a purely fictional theme with no link to real life.[36] It is far more convincing, however, to turn this argument up-side-down by pointing out that such a fictional theme can only work for an audience of fiction on the very strength of its resonance in reality. Moreover, much eleventh- and twelfth-century fiction was written for women as much as for men and therefore the potential reflection of women's real feelings cannot be ignored. The twelfth-century romance *Havelok* deals with the topic by creating a happy ending to a story in which Princess Argentille had not ultimately been degraded by having been forced to marry her cook Cuaran, because he turned out to be Havelok, the prince of Denmark.[37]

The Latin romance called the *Ruodlieb,* in which we are told of the preparations for Ruodlieb's marriage from his mother's point of view, originates from a slightly earlier date: 'Find for yourself a wife, a woman who you know is of such noble lineage on both sides that on either side your offspring will not be deficient.' To this end she organizes a family gathering where all members of her family are urged to think of a good candidate. Since Ruodlieb himself is of noble but poor origins and collected riches abroad by fighting for a foreign king, it is interesting to note that his mother is urging him to marry a woman of noble background on her paternal and maternal side so that their children can boast nobility going back two generations.[38]

Women's fear of being married to someone of low social origins did not, however, mean that they all hoped for or aspired to a marriage to a person ranked higher in society. For some the price to be paid in order to become queen was simply too high. This at least is the conclusion one can draw from the case of Constance, the daughter of Duke Conan III of Brittany, who in 1160 was promised in marriage to King Malcolm IV of Scotland (d. 1165). She objected on the grounds that Scotland was too far away and appealed to King Louis VII of France (d. 1180) to put a stop to the marriage contract. Constance was successful and although she had asked the king to provide her with a husband of equal rank to

Malcolm, seven years later she accepted Alan III of Rohan, one of her brother's officials and of distinctly poorer background. Despite his relatively low birth Constance's acceptance of him enabled her to stay in Brittany.[39]

Thus far this chapter has traced the hidden ways in which women contributed to the preservation of knowledge about the past. Whether as commissioners of chronicles about their menfolk (deeds of fathers, grandfathers, husbands, brothers or sons) or worrying about *mésalliances*, the prime focus has been on women remembering the deeds of men or male offices. There is, however, some even more hidden information which can reveal how women passed on information in the female line about their female ancestors. This information comes from genealogical tracts incorporated in chronicles and letters. Most of the texts are written by men on the explicit information of men, as we shall see, but ultimately deriving mostly from women.

The first example of genealogical information disseminated by a male chronicler, but deriving from women as much as from men, concerns the cluster of Norman genealogies preserved in Robert of Torigni's revision of the *Deeds of the Dukes of the Normans* and printed in Appendix 4.[40] At the end of his biography of King Henry I, Robert of Torigni explains that it is important to say something about the king's brothers and sisters. He therefore gives a potted history of their exploits and then proceeds with giving details on Henry's kin group. Whereas his paternal ancestors, the Norman dukes, had been the subject of Books I–VII of the *Deeds of the Dukes,* relatively little is said about relatives further removed from the main line. It is in the chapters concerned with kin several degrees removed from the patrilinear line that we find the first information about Countess Gunnor's sisters and nieces as ancestors of several distinguished Anglo-Norman families, like the Clares, the Beaumonts, the Warennes and the Montforts. Historians, including Georges Duby, have not always reacted kindly to Robert's genealogical information by rejecting it as fanciful fiction. Careful comparison with surviving charter information proves that in the majority of cases Robert of Torigni is correct. Where he goes 'wrong' is when he accidentally conflates a father and son, or indeed, a mother and daughter, with similar names. Most of the families whose genealogy Robert presents had close ties with the abbey of Le Bec as benefactors, monks and general well-wishers. Clearly, the monks themselves as issue from these families told Robert about their family origins. But men were not the only informants.

In Chapter 3 we met the three famous widows of Le Bec – Eva Crispin (née de Montfort), Basilia of Gournay (née Fleitel) and Basilia's niece Ansfrida.[41] The three women died in January 1099 when the two eldest, Eva and Basilia, were well into their nineties. Surely these women, like their male relatives, were likely sources of information about their family history? Their old age would have helped them, individually or collectively, to dig up details of long-lost relatives stretching back well into the tenth century. In other words, the Bec widows acted as living links in the genealogical chain connecting the Countess Gunnor, her sisters and nieces with their descendants, who were the widows' contemporaries. Their collective knowledge of their own families, and the families into which they married, lingered long enough for Robert of Torigni to have written it down in the 1130s, while his younger contemporary and colleague, Milo Crispin, drew on the same tradition a decade later when he inserted a short history of his own family in a collection of miracles.[42] His information too derived from the widowed Eve and stretched back about one century. Thus while the men recorded the family histories in writing, the women provided the raw material in oral form.

From Germany comes the example of the chronicle of the Bavarian monk Ekkehard of Aura. He incorporated a short genealogy of two families, the *Aribi* and the *Immidingi*, from which his contemporaries Count Aribo of Kärnten (d. 1102) and his brother Boto (d. 1104) descended. The genealogy stands out because it is the only one included in the chronicle and its presence has given rise to the plausible suggestion that Ekkehard himself was related to the families concerned. Having stated that on the paternal side their ancestor was Aribo, whose hunting feats were still remembered in vernacular songs, on the maternal side he gives their mother Friderun's descent from Immid, brother of Queen Matilda I and thus maternal uncle of King Otto I. Ekkehard himself does not mention Matilda's sister Friderun, whose name, as we have seen above, is listed in the Ottonian memorial books and is passed on to her namesake Friderun, mother of Aribo and Boto. Clearly, Ekkehard's wish to underline the illustrious maternal connections of the brothers must go back in part to oral information given to them by their mother.[43] Furthermore, it is highly significant that Ekkehard 'confirms' this oral female tradition by pointing out that Widukind refers to Immid as Queen Matilda's brother in his *History of the Saxons*. This, then, is yet another striking example showing how oral female traditions and written male traditions converge in family history.

Female input in genealogies also brings us back to the *Life of Adelheid*, abbess of Vilich, by the nun Bertha which we discussed in Chapter 3. No doubt using information relayed by Adelheid herself to her contemporaries, including her servant Engilrada whose help she noted, Bertha included a one-page account of Adelheid's ancestry. On the paternal side there is only the name of Adelheid's father, Meningoz, whom she says was a rich and noble man. In contrast, however, the family of the mother, Gerbirga, is given in great detail, covering three generations back in time to Adelheid's grandparents. There seems no doubt that Gerbirga was of more important ancestry than her husband and that she had impressed her status on her daughter. The main reason why Adelheid made sure that the history of her descent was well known, especially on her mother's side, was to orally safeguard the origin of the nuns' estates brought in by her maternal kin. Moreover, Adelheid herself made sure that the Vilich nuns knew precisely not only her mother's ancestry, but also her illustrious descendants, the children and grandchildren of her sisters who were related to the Ottonian royal family through marriage. For the same reason, Adelheid also had to keep track of her family's lateral ramifications in order to ensure her kin's continued acceptance of the bequests made by her parents to the nunnery. Vilich survived beyond her death and was still protected by male members of the family.

That arrangements for the community's protection were part of the original endowment of a nunnery to be recorded either orally or more permanently in writing is suggested by the parallel case of the Westfalian nunnery of Geseke. In 1014 Abbess Hildegund placed herself and her nunnery under the protection of the archbishop of Cologne because, as she says, she was the last of her kin (*cognatio*) who could rule the convent. As Karl Leyser has pointed out, by this she meant her direct descent from her paternal grandfather Haold through her father Bernard.[44] At Haold's founding of Geseke on 26 October 952, the abbacy had been reserved for the women of Haold's lineage, while the advocacy, that is the protection of the nunnery in case of litigation and military defence, went to his own and his brothers' sons. When 70 years later Hildegund noted the lack of eligible women in her family for the position of abbess, she turned to the archbishop so that he could rule who else might be the next abbess. The point of this story is that in order to know that there were no more women, Hildegund must have made sure that she knew the whereabouts of her relations.

Other historical narratives from the twelfth century confirm the picture of family history and genealogical detail passed down the generations by men and women. In Herman of Laon's biography of Bishop Bartholomew of Laon (d. 1158), which itself is enshrined in a collection of miracles devoted to the Virgin Mary, Herman traced the extended family of Bartholomew. They were all members of his mother Adelada's kin, herself being one of the seven daughters and two sons of Count Hilduin of Roucy and his wife Adela, the couple at the head of the genealogy. Herman related not the history of Hilduin's and Adela's sons, but the history of each of their daughters' marriages and their descendants. From this we must deduce that the information collected ultimately derived from the female members of the family. We can be more precise than that. Herman was a contemporary of Bishop Bartholomew's younger cousins, another Bartholomew and Richard, who were both archdeacons of Laon. Their great-grandmothers were sisters of Bishop Bartholomew's mother, and thus daughters of Hilduin and Adela. Both archdeacons traced their connection with them through the female line which suggests, once again, that the information came from their mothers, grandmothers and great-grandmothers. Interestingly and importantly therefore, the male author of a male biography was deeply indebted to the information about his subject's family as provided, indirectly and presumably orally, by the women of the family.[45]

Herman of Laon's younger contemporary was Lambert of Wattrelos, who similarly included an important account of his family's origin in the *Annals of Cambrai* which he wrote in the years between 1153 and 1170; the family history is printed in Appendix 5. Although both Fernand Vercauteren and Georges Duby have studied his genealogical inform-ation and stressed the importance of Lambert's maternal origins (in terms of family wealth and landed possessions), neither of them was particularly interested in the sources of his knowledge.[46] According to Lambert, he was told 'the genealogy of my ancestors according to truthful oral reports'.[47] Unfortunately, he does not specify who these informants were. Apart from the obvious candidate, that is his maternal uncle and patron Abbot Richard of Mont-Saint-Eloi (d. 1129) who was responsible for his education, his own mother Gisla (d. 1145) is the most likely source for the story of her ancestry. Perhaps, she entertained him in the 1120s when he was sent home from the monastery to recuperate from a serious illness. A fact that incidentally reminds us how loosely defined the segregation of the lay and monastic worlds was.

On Gisla's paternal side, the most famous event was the death of ten of her uncles on the same day in the same (unidentified) battle, a disaster of epic proportions which in Lambert's day was still commemorated in

the vernacular songs of jongleurs. But Gisla's greatest pride was in her
own mother Resindis's noble Flemish origin and her kinship with many
of the contemporary Flemish ecclesiastical authorities, including the
Abbots Lambert of Saint-Bertin and Lobbes and Abbess Gisla of
Bourbourg. If neither Lambert nor, for that matter, Herman of Laon,
Robert of Torigni, Milo Crispin or Ekkehard of Aura mentioned their
female informants by name, this was purely a reflection of the general
reluctance to mention women as witnesses of the past. It was clearly not
a true reflection of reality, which shows them to have received crucial
information about their forebears from their female relatives.

Besides historical narratives, correspondence is another source of
genealogical information. In an appendix to Flodoard's *Annals* known
from only one manuscript, a mid-eleventh-century letter survives
detailing the relationship between the ducal families of Aquitaine and
Burgundy; it is included amongst similar sources as Appendix 2. Probably
written by Rainald of Burgundy (1027–57/8) to his sister's son William
VIII of Aquitaine (1058–87), it discusses their descent from two sisters
Matilda and Albereda, daughters of Gerberga and King Louis IV of France
(d. 954). The four links in both lines of descent are all women. Thus,
although the letter was written by one man to another, the contents
concern the female lines within the two ducal families and thus the details
must have come at least in part from the women concerned.[48] Lauer
speculated that the letter was concerned with a succession case or with
plans for a marriage between the two houses for which the precise degree
of blood-relationship needed to be established. Women's knowledge of
their descent was vital in the case of inheritance through the female line.
Here, again, we are reminded of the case of the heiresses who know their
family history because the inheritance of their estates was at stake.

Other epistolary examples of this kind are the famous letters of Bishop
Ivo of Chartres (d. 1115) and Archbishop Anselm of Canterbury (d. 1109)
tracing the degrees of consanguinity linking the children of King Henry
I (d. 1135) with potential spouses.[49] Bishop Ivo, citing written genealogies
he had seen, dissuaded King Henry I from marrying one of his
(illegitimate) daughters to Hugh fitz Gervase of Châteauneuf-en-
Thimerais, a descendant of the Montgomery family, because Hugh was
apparently related in the sixth degree to Seufrida, a sister of Countess
Gunnor of Normandy (d. 1031). She in turn was the great-great-
grandmother of King Henry's daughter. Since the blood relationship
depended on descent through the female line on both sides, one would
assume that the women of the family had been the vehicles for the

knowledge on which the genealogies were based.[50] A similar case was discussed with Anselm in *c.* 1107 following the royal proposal that another of King Henry's daughters might marry William II of Warenne. Anselm surely had a genealogy at hand when he pointed out that: 'he and your daughter are related on one side in the fourth degree and on the other side in the sixth degree'. As in the previous case the blood relationship originated in a sister of Countess Gunnor.[51]

The most striking example of male and female collaboration in the preservation of genealogical material, both in writing and through oral tradition, derives from Gui of Bazoches's letters. Gui was a younger son of a local aristocratic family in northern France who, from a young age, was destined for an ecclesiastical career. He became a priest in the mid twelfth century and his career was advanced by his paternal uncle Bishop Haimo of Châlon (1151–53), in whose church he eventually rose to the position of chanter. He died in 1203. He was known to his contemporaries as a historian, wrote a now lost *Apologia* at the request of his mother Hadwich and left us the autograph copy of his correspondence. These letters offer a fascinating demonstration of the pride felt in a family's illustrious origins. Several of Gui's letters to his mother Hadwich, his sister Alice and his nephew, Alice's son Archdeacon Rainald, allow us to piece together the family's knowledge of their ancestry. In the latter, printed partially as Appendix 6, Gui described the maternal line covering four generations from his mother Hadwich, who had married the lord of Bazoches, via her mother Alice, wife of Nicholas II of Rumigni and Florennes, to her grandmother Ida of Lower Lotharingia, the wife of Baldwin II of Hainault (d. 1098).

Gui knew that Ida was the daughter of Henry of Louvain and sister of Godfrey of Louvain. Although he did not explicitly acknowledge the tradition as an oral one, it seems obvious that the family history had been handed down orally by the women concerned. From his great-grandmother onwards, he traced the ancestry back in the male line to Charlemagne on the basis of 'histories'. Clearly, the women had kept alive knowledge of the maternal genealogy, which was ultimately grafted onto the written chronicle material known so well by Gui, for the instruction of his nephew Rainald. Again the interaction between a female oral and a male written tradition is self-evident.[52] Gui deftly deployed this same material in his dealings with Count Henry of Champagne, for whom he acted as historical adviser. At least two letters to the count trace his origin back to the Carolingian kings quoting a mixture of oral information (from his own family) and written chronicles, amongst which we find the *Deeds of the Dukes of the Normans.*

The material surveyed thus far also illustrates the frequency with which we see uncles and nephews actively writing down the oral information given to them by their mothers, grandmothers and aunts. We have seen how Gui de Bazoches informed his sister's son Rainald, Count Rainald of Burgundy informed his nephew Count William of Aquitaine, the archidiaconal cousins told Herman about their uncle Bishop Bartholow's ancestry, while Lambert of Wattrelos got some details from his mother's brother Abbot Richard. To this material we can add the examples, discussed in Chapter 2, of Count Geoffrey of Anjou who informed his nephew Count Fulk le Réchin, Walter of Clusa who informed his nephew Arnold of Ardres, and Otto of Freising who wrote for his nephew Emperor Frederick Barbarossa. In these cases the explicit evidence comes from men, who presumably in turn were informed by their female relatives as well. And it cannot be entirely accidental that in all cases where the blood relationship is known precisely, the uncles concerned are maternal uncles. This surely suggest that the mother and her brother(s) played an important part in relaying family traditions to the younger generation. Furthermore, this chapter also showed that sisters formed bonds which resulted in the passing on of details and gossip about family matters. Unlike the brother-nephew relationship, however, these links were purely oral.

The examples of noble women passing on stories heard from their mothers and grandmothers represent an oral historical tradition which is hidden within the public histories of their male relatives. However, their existence demonstrates the sense of identity felt in the transmission of stories from one generation to another. One of the few cases where this task is described in relation to family remembrance in particular comes from the *Deeds of Hereward*, which illustrates in considerable detail how an heiress was in charge of her family's *memorabilia*.[53] The text in question is a biography of Hereward 'the Wake', the most famous Anglo-Saxon rebel in the struggle against William the Conqueror. The Latin text was composed by Richard, a clerk at Ely during the reign of Bishop Herbert of Ely (1109–31), on the basis of a now lost Old English biography written by Hereward's priest Leofric, and supplemented by oral information from two of Hereward's companions, Siward and another Leofric. The extent to which Richard elaborated upon and altered the vernacular narrative cannot be known. However, his careful acknowledgement of the different written and oral traditions he used should be taken seriously.[54] For the purposes of the present discussion, historical reliability as such is not at stake, but rather that his picture of an heiress in charge of the family treasures is resonant and significant.

According to the biography, shortly before 1066 Hereward had been exiled by Edward the Confessor and hired himself out as a soldier in Cornwall, Ireland and Flanders before returning to post-conquest England in an attempt to recover his patrimony. While in Flanders, at Saint-Omer, he met the noble Turfrida, a girl 'greatly devoted to the liberal arts and particularly skilled at handicrafts'. After their first meeting, full of the intention of impressing him with her family's wealth, she leads him into her parents' house:

> . . . showing him all her father's wealth of gold, silver and other materials and many things of her mother – and also a mail-coat of great lightness and very fine workmanship, and much brighter and purer than any iron or steel, and a helmet of similar beauty and strength. Speaking of these she added: 'There have been many rich and powerful men that have asked about these, making lots of inquiries as to their whereabouts and promising people rewards for their production, wanting to get them for themselves by trickery, threats, force, bribes or any stratagem whatever. But up to now I have kept their heirlooms, always the most treasured among my great-grandfather's, grandfather's and father's things, so that I could present them to my bridegroom. Now I favour you above all men for your bravery and courageous spirit; and it would give me great pleasure if my love should tell me he is glad of the gift.'[55]

The imagery of Turfrida impressing her poor suitor with her (movable) inheritance is something which can easily be imagined. The objects put on display covered four generations. The many things inherited from her mother, though unspecified, presumably included jewellery, while the military artefacts were passed down in the male line. That an heiress would show these to a prospective husband does not seem out of place. They were expensive items which were passed on from father to son, or as the case may be, son-in-law. The historical Hereward probably married an heiress and the history of his estates, listed in *Domesday Book,* strongly suggests inheritance through the female line to a granddaughter who was a contemporary of Richard of Ely. Living not far from Ely on the estates of her husband Richard de Rullos in East Anglia, she may have known her grandfather's biographer and told him about these Flemish treasures which, for all we know, might have survived.[56] If they did, would they have helped to reconstruct her grandparents' history? Did she label them or mark them in any way so that future generations could rely on them as pegs for the family's history?

Turfrida's case may or may not be fictional, but the questions it raises are important ones for they point to the role family heirlooms played in the memorial process. The next chapter deals with these questions and discusses artefacts and the way they helped men and women to remember the past.

5

OBJECTS AS PEGS FOR MEMORY

In the previous chapters we have occasionally signalled how memories of persons and places are linked with objects and sites. Objects such as jewellery, sacred vessels or cloths were passed on from one generation to the next and carried with them stories of their donors. That material evidence helps to trigger memories has been shown conclusively in anthropological studies of primarily oral cultures in modern times. The use of photographs, especially, has been found to be enormously effective in helping to recall the (recent) past.[1] In the Middle Ages the use of pictures and objects to recall past events, and stories in general, was well known and advocated by the clergy as a means of teaching the illiterate.[2] Today we have to rely on written references to ways in which medieval people were reminded of the past by looking at sites and objects. Few of the actual sites and objects which are mentioned in the sources have survived. Of the surviving material evidence, only objects from ecclesiastical institutions remain because churches and monasteries had archives and treasuries built in which to keep their heirlooms for ever. Very few objects from a secular background have survived, however, because family possessions if not stored in institutions, got dispersed and lost. Buildings and sites were more durable and they, like objects, had stories of their founders or later events attached to them. They too functioned as pegs for collective memory as well as being symbols for the transmission and memory of rights. In this chapter we will explore the function of objects and sites as triggers for stories about the past more fully.

The object on which memorial tradition was most immediately focused was the body of a dead person. Once buried, the burial place and tomb became the centre for the family tradition of mourning and commemoration. Although modern scholars have paid attention to the development of family burial churches, often in monasteries, and the ensuing political importance attached to these centres, little thought has been given to the period between the moment of death and the moment of burial. This period is important, particularly for those people who died far away from home or who were killed in battle. If the distance involved was great, the procedure normally followed involved the removal of the heart and entrails which were buried in one place, while the rest of the remains, often after some form of embalmment, were taken home to the family church. Women played an important role in the burial procedures, though our knowledge of their precise activities is scanty.

The bodies of aristocratic fighters and military leaders were normally collected by male relatives or servants who arranged for a proper burial. Though women would not normally be present on a battlefield, there is evidence that in some cases they were near enough to take on the role of undertaker. In 1066 Countess Gytha of Wessex implored William the Conqueror (d. 1087) to hand over the body of her son, King Harold, and presumably also those of his brothers Leofwine and Gyrth who were killed alongside him during the Battle of Hastings.[3] William apparently refused Gytha's request, ordered one of his men to temporarily bury the English king, and only at a later stage allowed the canons of Waltham Abbey the privilege of reburying him. Due to the passage of time they had to call on Harold's mistress, Edith Swanneck, to help them identify the body.[4]

When Count Odo II of Blois was killed in the battle of Bar in 1037, Bishop Roger of Châlons-sur-Marne (d. 1042) and Abbot Richard of Saint-Vanne-de-Verdun (d. 1046) recovered his mangled body from the carnage and handed it over to Odo's wife, Ermengard. She then took the corpse and sent it to Tours for a proper burial next to his father in the abbey church of Saint-Martin at Marmoutier.[5] Sickelgaita, the second wife of Robert Guiscard, was with him when he died while campaigning in the Balkans against Emperor Alexius Comnenus in 1085, off the coast of southern Italy. She took the body back to Italy by sea because she did not wish it to remain on hostile soil. During the return journey, the ship was shipwrecked and the body, having fallen overboard, was almost lost:

In order to prevent a noxious stench, Robert's wife, ever endowed with provident counsel, ordered his entrails and heart to be buried in Otrante. She embalmed the rest of the body with much aromatic material. From there she arranged for its transportation to the city of Venosa where the tombs of his elder brothers had been constructed. Robert was buried close by with great ceremony.[6]

Robert Guiscard's wife arranged for both transport to and burial in the new family church at Venosa, and presumably made the necessary finances available to care for the funeral costs and the long-term preservation of his memory afterwards. When King Henry I of England died on 1 December 1135 at Lyons-la-Forêt in Normandy, his entrails were taken out and buried at the priory of Notre-Dame-des-Prés near Rouen. His body was then embalmed at Rouen and taken by ship to England, where it was buried at Reading Abbey on 4 January. His wife, Queen Adeliza, had remained in England and was not therefore at her husband's side when he died. However, her charters for Reading offer us a glimpse of her involvement at a later stage. She instructed the monks to keep 'continuous lights burning in front of the body of my lord Jesus Christ [Holy Sacrament] and the body of my lord the most noble King Henry'. On the first anniversary of his death, she granted the manor of Aston to the monks as well as 100 shillings annually at Christmas, again to celebrate the anniversaries of his death. Moreover, she added another 100 shillings-worth of land to pay for the convent and other religious persons to attend the abbey on the king's anniversary.[7]

Women's care of the bodies, the funeral service and the commemoration took place in collaboration with priests and monks of the church or monastery where the dead people were buried. To what extent the men and women involved in this macabre business exchanged stories about the events leading up to the death, we do not know. Common sense and knowledge of human emotions might lead us to suppose that the period immediately after death, and in particular violent death in battle, would have been a moment when stories and gossip about such events were exchanged. We have no way of assessing how long the monks observed the commemoration of the king, or how long the money lasted to pay for such services. They were meant to last in perpetuity, but the passage of time and lack of finances usually meant that after three or four generations, someone else took the dead person's place.

The fact that women normally provided the care for bodies after death and commemoration after the funeral should not disguise another fact, namely that some women were actually glad to see father or husband gone forever. In such cases the sense of relief and guilt would have produced mixed feelings, and the resulting commemorative care might show sufficient ambiguity to leave later generations baffled. One such case has recently been highlighted by Janet Nelson. She draws attention to the fact that in 814 Charlemagne was buried at Aachen, where his body was entombed in a splendid marble Roman sarcophagus. The recycling of Roman antiquities in the Carolingian period was nothing new and the scenes depicting the rape of Proserpina could be explained in Christian allegory. Contemporaries say that Charlemagne's children, that is his daughters because none of his sons were present, organized the funeral and oversaw his burial. These unmarried daughters, Nelson suggests, chose the Proserpina sarcophagus to leave posterity the message that their father had kept them 'at home', forbade them to marry and may even have sexually abused them. In this way they exercised power behind the throne and became a danger to Charlemagne's successor, their brother Louis the Pious (d. 842), who removed them from the court. Thus the Rape of Proserpina may have been thought a proper symbol, emasculating the virgin daughters of Charlemagne by sending them away from the imperial court. The story has to be pieced together, but the symbol – the Roman sarcophagus – still remains in the cathedral at Aachen.[8]

For a memorial tradition involving a daughter and her mother, we have to turn to the late twelfth century where something clearly went wrong between Eleanor of Aquitaine (d. 1204), estranged wife of King Henry II (d. 1189), and her daughter Matilda. This particular example is the more poignant because it involved a memorial case during the queen's lifetime. In *c.* 1188 Matilda and her husband Duke Henry the Lion of Saxony (d. 1195) presented a splendid Psalter produced at Helmarshausen to the Cathedral of Brunswick. The dedication leaf of the manuscript is an elaborately illuminated page showing the young couple with three generations of family besides them. On the left-hand side, beside Duke Henry, we see his father and mother, Duke Henry and Duchess Gertrude and his maternal grandparents, Emperor Lothar II (d. 1137) and his wife Empress Richenza. Each of these persons is identified by inscriptions above their heads. The emphasis on the duke's maternal side can be explained because Henry had inherited his lands through his mother and maternal grandmother, who were both rich heiresses. On the right-hand side Matilda is flanked by her father King Henry II of England, her grandmother Empress (here called Queen) Matilda, the former widow of Emperor Henry V, and an unidentified lay woman. There is no sign of Matilda's mother Queen Eleanor, unless one assumes that the lay woman, without crown or royal insignia and tucked away in the corner without an identifying label is Eleanor. The date assigned to the Psalter leaf is the year between two lengthy visits the couple made to England. It seems inconceivable that the artists would not have known about Matilda's mother, and I can only suggest that she was either omitted on purpose or disguised as an insignificant lay woman on the instructions of Matilda herself. Political expediency prevailed and forced her to cast the memory of her mother, at the time incarcerated by Henry II, to oblivion.[9] If it had not been for the strong pro-mother sentiment on Duke Henry's side, Matilda's act of *damnatio memoriae* would not have been nearly so obvious.

Such an attitude was, presumably, not very common. Normally, aristocratic commemoration was a festive affair with no expenses spared, an occasion which needed careful planning by the dead person's relatives and the church where he or she was to be buried. Patrick Geary argues that although women were the chief mourners and the benefactors who financed mourning in the short and long term, it was the monks who took the initiative in procuring bodies and money, and thence they monopolized the growth, spread and importance of the remembrance. As we have seen in the previous chapters, there seems insufficient evidence to argue in favour of a monastic monopoly of remembrance. The survival of monastic sources is biased in favour of the monks (or nuns) at the expense of the role undoubtedly exercised by lay women. Evidence for the role of women from non-ecclesiastical sources in the central Middle Ages is more difficult to find. However, there is enough to show co-operation between men and women and that their roles in commemoration were complementary. The memorial stones from tenth- and eleventh-century Scandinavia are a case in point.

The runic memorial stones from Scandinavia are between one and two metres tall with inscriptions engraved most often on the flat side. They were mostly positioned in public places on roadsides, near bridges or on parish and farm boundaries. A considerable number of them were commissioned by women who wished to commemorate their dead fathers, brothers, husband or sons.[10] Most are relatively short stories expressing grief about the loss of loved ones, usually during Viking expeditions abroad. A good example is the stone erected by a woman called Tola in memory of her son Harald, brother of Ingvar:

> They went gallantly
> far for gold
> and in the east
> fed the eagle.
> They died in the south
> in Saracenland.

Two sisters, Holmfrid and Hedinfrid, were responsible for the stone at Fagerlöt (Sweden) in memory of their father Eskil:

> He offered battle
> on the eastern route
> before the war-fierce one
> had to fall.[11]

A widow called Sigrid built a bridge to commemorate her husband. The bridge itself, over water or marshy land, has not survived, but the inscription, known from a stone in Ramsundberget (Norway) announcing its construction, has survived: 'Sigrid, Alrik's mother, Orm's daughter, had this bridge built for the soul of her husband Holmger, Sigröd's father.' Sigrid had a stone not only for her son Alrik but also for her husband and his father, a Viking chief. Since this is so, Sigrid may well have used some of his spoils collected abroad to build this expensive, but very practical monument to his memory. This particular inscription has an added interest in that it is part of an elaborate composition that includes scenes depicting some episodes from the Völsunga-saga. Inscription and 'illustrations' together suggest a careful, though difficult to interpret, memorial from a wife rich enough to pay for an expensive art object as well as a bridge.[12]

Another bridge epitaph from Bro, Uppland (Sweden), is carved on a big granite slab in an elaborately decorated inscription. Again the commissioner was a woman commemorating her husband:

> Ginnlaug, Holmgaeir's daughter, Sigraud and Gaut's sister, had
> this bridge made and this stone set up after her husband Assur,
> son of Earl Hakon. He was guard against Vikings with Gaeitir.
> Now may God help his spirit and soul.[13]

The last line puts the Christian setting of the memorial beyond any doubt. Quite a number of purely Christian memorials survive which contain biblical scenes carved in stone with appropriately religious images. For example a Norse bridge stone from Dynna in Hadeland (Norway) shows an Epiphany scene with the three Magi, a star and an angel. The setting was commissioned once again by a woman. This time it was a mother mourning her dead daughter: 'Gunnvor, Thrydrik's daughter, made the bridge in memory of her daughter Astrid. She was the handiest [most skilled] maid in Hadeland.'[14]

Very often the texts contain information about family relationships and the division of the inheritance. The latter in itself provides one of the clues for the erection of such public monuments. They were announcements, permanently carved in stone, for the division of lands and goods among the different branches of the family and bear witness to the knowledge of men and women about the family's past, sometimes going back three or four generations. In Sweden a woman called Inga had at least four stones erected at Snottsta and Vreta that between them contain precious information about her husband Ragnfast, his sisters Gyrid and Estrid, his retainer (*huskarl*) Assur and that he was the sole owner of his farm after his father Sigfast. The most elaborate information of this kind comes from a stone in Hillersjö (Sweden) which actually complements the family story provided by Inga's four monuments. Unlike other stones it does not begin with the usual phrase: 'X made this monument in memory of Y'. Instead the text plunges straight into the complicated, and sad, family circumstances:

> Geirmund married Geirlaug when she was a girl. Then they had a son before he [Geirmund] drowned and the son died later. Then she married [Gu]drik . . . . Then they had children, but only one girl survived. She was called [In]ga. She was married to Ragnfast of Snottsta, then he died and [their] son [died] later, and the mother [Inga] inherited from her son. Then she married Eirik. She died there, and there Geirlaug inherited from her daughter Inga.[15]

The combination of all the details shows how Inga, an heiress who twice married, commissioned memorial stones for her first husband Ragnfast, whose heir she became after the death of their son. After the death of Inga's second husband Eirik, and Inga's own death, Inga's mother Geirlaug, herself probably a sole heiress, inherited all that Inga possessed. The information on the Hillersjö stone is carved in the form of a serpent. Details of the stone carver, 'Thorbjørn skald carved these runes' can be found outside the serpent's body. The stones prove that women played an important part in commemorating the dead and as part of that task, they had family traditions carved in stone and thus preserved for future generations. These secular and religious memorial stones provide us with the evidence that women sometimes collaborated with their male kin, but also often acted quite independently from them. They also show that in Scandinavia, monks (or nuns) only gradually found a role in the process of commemoration.

The Scandinavian stones find no parallel in the rest of Europe. There the memorials to those who fell in battle are mostly church buildings. The most obvious place for the memory of battles was the actual site of the military encounter. Long after such events, physical remains reminded people of the bloodshed, even though such material evidence was not, as far as we know, left there for a specific memorial reason. Normally, the victims of war would be buried either on the site or in nearby churches. However, if the bodies were too numerous, on-site burial might be rapid and careless so that bones remained visible for long periods. This at least is the implication of Otto of Freising's remark in the mid twelfth century that there were still heaps of bones visible on the Italian battlefield near Civitate, where in 1053 the soldiers of Pope Leo IX (d. 1054) had fought against Norman troops led by Robert Guiscard.[16] His contemporary Orderic Vitalis described how, in his time, the physical remains of the victims of the Battle of Stamford Bridge in September 1066 were still visible for anyone to see.[17] In these cases the reference is specifically to the remains of the ordinary soldiers, which one supposes would disappear in due course. But there were, of course, also other reminders of battles left on site. William of Malmesbury, for example, describes how the wrecks of ships, which had taken part in the abortive invasion of England in 1033, acted in the early twelfth century as visible reminders at Rouen.[18]

In some cases the memory of a battle was preserved because a sign was erected on the spot in perpetual commemoration of the victims. Such war memorials varied from a simple wooden cross to larger buildings, like abbeys or churches. In England the most famous was Battle Abbey, founded by William the Conqueror on the very spot where King Harold had died during the battle at Hastings. The monks of Battle Abbey remembered where some actions during the battle had taken place because they had attached themselves to the monastic memory. For example, Hedgeland was allegedly the place where the Normans first spotted the Anglo-Saxon formations and the Malfosse was the ditch where, near the end of the battle, several Norman horsemen died in pursuit of the fleeing English fighters.[19] In Flanders, Count Robert the Frisian

(d. 1093) followed William the Conqueror's example by building an abbey at Cassel where, some years previously in 1071, he had won an astounding victory over his young nephew which controversially earned him the title of count.[20] A well-known example from France is the abbey of Beaulieu-les-Loches, established by Fulk Nerra in commemoration of his victory at Conquereuil in 992; though in this case the abbey was not built on the exact site. Perhaps to ensure the survival of the collective memory, in *c.* 1011 a frieze was unveiled which showed Fulk's triumph over his brother-in-law Conan of Rennes.[21]

The evidence on objects as pegs for memory and the survival of oral tradition is much more substantial. If we stick to the topic of war memorials, the most impressive object to commemorate a battle is of course the Bayeux Tapestry, which depicts William the Conqueror's victory. It was probably commissioned by William's half-brother Bishop Odo of Bayeux (d. 1096) and made by English artisans. The story represents the Norman version of events, even though there are some sympathetic scenes of Harold. The interpretation of the narrative is fairly straightforward despite a few scenes which are opaque. The enigmatic picture of an otherwise unknown woman, named as Aelfgifu, with a priest cannot be illuminated by any written tradition and must therefore represent some aspect of the story which survived exclusively in oral tradition.[22] The Bayeux Tapestry is unique on account of its survival. We know of other tapestries that have not survived, but which are interesting because they can be connected with women in their roles as rememberers of the past.

In a lengthy poem Baudri, abbot of Bourgueil and later bishop of Dol (d. 1130), addressed Countess Adela of Blois (d. 1137), daughter of William the Conqueror, describing four tapestries which allegedly hung in her chamber. One of these forms the framework of Baudri's verse narrative of the Norman Conquest of England in 1066. Did Baudri use a well-known literary device, projecting a tapestry or sculpture or painting as a fictional setting for a historical narrative, or did he describe real hangings which portrayed William's' deeds – in which case might he be describing the Bayeux Tapestry itself? There is no way that we can establish the truth of the matter. But even if we could prove that the setting was fictional, it could only work as fiction if the image of a woman sitting in her chamber with pictorial hangings, some of which represented her father's deeds, made sense to the poet's audience. In other words, fiction must bear some resemblance to reality to make an impact. Countess Adela's position as patron or potential patron is clear from the final verses in which Baudri asks for suitable payment for his poem. There is nothing implausible in the possibility that she actually commissioned Baudri to commemorate her father's most famous battle in the form of an embroidered hanging, that this was the Bayeux Tapestry seems extremely unlikely. Perhaps we should follow a recent suggestion that Baudri had seen the Bayeux Tapestry and followed its story, but used a literary fictional setting of Adela's chamber.[23]

It is generally thought that in the Bayeux Tapestry, Anglo-Saxon embroidery skills were used to erect a monument to the Anglo-Saxon defeat. Very few Anglo-Saxon tapestries have actually survived, but we know of the existence of many through written references to them. The most rewarding sources for our knowledge of them are Anglo-Saxon wills from the tenth and eleventh centuries. Approximately 30 are known, of which one third concern women as testators. For our purposes, it is significant that the female wills provide us with evidence for the material objects, including tapestries, they possessed and were free to bequeath after their deaths. In c. 950 Wynflaed bequeathed to Aethelflaed, daughter of Ealhhelm, amongst other objects: 'a long hall-tapestry and a short one and three seat coverings'.[24] No details are given about the patterns on the tapestry or whether they depicted any war scenes. A similar lack of details frustrates us in our knowledge that Wulfwarn, an unidentified widow who lived c. 1000, promised her hall tapestries to her two sons:

> And I grant to my son Wulfmaer a hall-tapestry and a set of bed-clothes. To Aelfwine my second son I grant a tapestry for a hall and tapestry for a chamber together with a table-cover and with the cloths which go with it.[25]

A third widow who owned tapestries was Aelfflaed, the widow of Brihtnoth who died at the battle of Maldon in 991. Surprisingly, her will does not refer to the tapestries, but the chronicle of Ely, the monastery that ultimately received them, does. This chronicle is also the most rewarding text explaining the representations on it. The *Book of Ely* mentions that the tapestry was commissioned by Aelfflaed, wife of Ealdorman Brihtnoth, depicting his deeds 'in memory of his bravery'.[26] The hanging must therefore have been similar to the Bayeux Tapestry in that it commemorated military activity. We must not jump to the conclusion that it recorded Brihtnoth's participation at Maldon itself. It has been suggested that the hanging represented some of his earlier fighting against the Vikings, embroidered while he was still alive and put on display at his home before it was given to Ely at his death. Obviously, his widow was concerned that this record of her husband's brave actions should be kept in an institutional environment to safeguard its survival rather than to bequeath it to other members of her family. It is unclear from the account in the *Book of Ely* whether it was still in existence when the author wrote in *c*. 1170. Since the note of the gift is based on genuine documents incorporated in the cartulary-chronicle and since it follows a two-page biography of Brihtnoth, it is likely that the author recorded a mixture of pictorial (the hanging), documentary (the wills and charters) and oral tradition. If this was not enough, the golden ring presented by Aelfflaed together with the hanging might also have helped to preserve the memory of Brihtnoth.[27]

Like tapestries, vestments were precious objects that were kept, so serving to keep stories of their makers, their commissioners or their donors alive. Like tapestries, they were vulnerable so that not many medieval ones have survived and for information about them we must rely on written descriptions. In 1097 the Canterbury historian Eadmer accompanied Archbishop Anselm to the council of Bari, where he met the archbishop of Benevento who was wearing a splendid cope. Eadmer, recognizing the English origin of the mantle, wondered whether it might in fact be the cope which he remembered had been given by Archbishop Aethelnoth (d. 1038) to the then bishop of Benevento in exchange for a precious relic. Three of Eadmer's older colleagues, Edui, Blachman and Farman, had in the past told him how as adolescents they had witnessed Queen Emma (d. 1051) checking the authenticity of the Italian relic that was offered in exchange for the cope, before she made the money to pay for it available. When Eadmer told the bishop of Benevento this story, he confirmed that he was wearing the very cope that had been given to his see by the monks at Canterbury.[28] It is clear that the vision of the cope triggered Eadmer's memory of the relic, unless of course he had been reminded of the story at home and told to be on the look out for the cope, which could reasonably be expected to show up in Italy. Another aspect of the story is important, namely Eadmer's reliance on a story told to him by three old monks about an event they had witnessed as young men before 1038, the year in which Archbishop Aethelnoth died. Eadmer therefore relates a tradition that was more than 60 years old.

The Canterbury cope was clearly a spectacular piece of embroidery which one did not easily forget. But what about the ordinary clothes people had? Cloaks in good condition were not thrown away. Noble people, including women as we shall see later on in this chapter, passed on their ceremonial vestments to monasteries in order to be refitted as liturgical vestments. But what did they do with less spectacular clothes ? The purpose of passing them on was probably purely practical, but the effect was that the garment preserved the memory of its original owner. Again Anglo-Saxon wills provide us with some good examples. The mid-tenth-century widow Wynflaed left precise instructions about what should happen to her clothes after her death. They all went to women in her household. The main beneficiary was a(n) (unidentified) woman indicated to be daughter and granddaughter: Aethelflaed, daughter of Ealhhelm, Aelfhere's younger daughter, received Wynflaed's double-badger-skin gown, as well as a linen gown. Most of her garments, however, went to her granddaughter by her son Eadmer, called Eadgifu. Two other women, Ceolthryth and Aethelflaed the White, were to share between them her nuns' vestments.[29] Although the will is informative and enables us to trace Wynflaed's memory to her granddaughter's time, we cannot be absolutely sure beyond Eadgifu's time what happened to the memories of Wynflaed associated with her clothes. Presumably, there was no living memory attached to the gowns due to their disintegration. For vestments, southern European wills, the only ones to have survived from the same period in western Europe as the Anglo-Saxon ones, are a rewarding source.

From the Languedoc a cluster of late-twelfth-century charters survives with details of the bequest of the noble woman Galburga, widow of Pons of Montagnac. In 1174 she had her wishes recorded in the presence of her mother, her four daughters, a god-daughter and several servants, including her chaplain. The women in due course would divide her furs, cloaks and clothes except for those that were outworn. One of the cloaks is described as having been handed down to Galburga by one Bruneta, daughter of Ferrande. The men, on the other hand, were to receive respectively a foal, a horse, a donkey, while the chaplain would be rewarded with twenty lambs and sheep, one bed and its furnishings for himself. As in the Anglo-Saxon wills, the division between male and female spheres is clear.[30] This is not, however, the case in the Italian wills that have survived.

Italians, it seems, were less gender specific in their bequests, for we find mothers and fathers bequeathing clothing of cotton and silk to their sons and daughters. In 1035 Atenolf, son of Balsamus, left his daughter Letitia 100 'modia' of grain to be sold in order to buy silk clothing, in 1054 Mele, son of Martin of Monopli, left his daughter Specia silk and cotton clothing, while the widow Gemma of Taranto in 1049 gave cloths to her nephews and Ulita, presumably her servant. From a late-tenth-century Salernitan dispute we learn that two brothers-in-law, Peter, son of Truppoald, and Maio, son of Autari, disputed the goods of Peter's wife Marelda, the sister of Maio. They consisted of a blouse, a linen face cloth (perhaps a veil?), a linen head cloth and a necklace. Peter claimed them for his daughter Miranda, and Maio, admitting that he had kept them illegally, returned them to his niece.[31] These examples pertain to ordinary clothes that people passed on and which were not expected to last more than two or three generations. In contrast to these day-to-day clothes, ceremonial vestments were preserved due to their value, status and political significance. Coronation robes in particular stand out for their longevity and, thereby, memorial value.

One of the most striking characteristics of medieval ceremonial vestments is that most of the ones that have survived have signatures attached to them. They contain inscriptions detailing their makers, their commissioners and the circumstances under which they were made. These labels were therefore clearly produced with posterity in mind and were meant to prevent knowledge of the owner/benefactor disappearing into oblivion. This is how we know that Emperor Henry II's so-called 'star mantle', preserved at Bamberg (Bavaria), was made for his coronation in 1002 – an embroidered inscription implores the Eternal King to increase the rule of King Henry II. A second mantle attributed to Henry's wife Kunigunde, but probably made for Henry's dedication of Bamberg cathedral in 1012, has also survived although without an inscription.[32] The Ottonian tradition of coronation mantles was preserved in Italy, where the Norman kings took it over. Amongst the coronation vestments of the Habsburg emperors, inherited from their Sicilian ancestors, is the coronation mantle woven for King Roger II of Sicily in 1133–34. Along the seam of the mantle an embroidered text records the occasion for which it was made and guarantees memory of its makers and first owner:

[This mantle] belongs to the articles worked in the royal workshop in which fortune and honour, prosperity and perfection, merit and distinction have their home. May the king rejoice in good acceptance, thriving magnificently in great generosity and high splendour, renown and magnificence and the fulfilment of wishes and hopes; may his days and nights be spent in enjoyment, without end or change; in the feeling of honour, dependency, and active participation in happiness and in the maintenance of well-being support and suitable activity: in the capital of Sicily in the year 528 [of the Hegira].[33]

This mantle at least provides a date and a text, albeit in Arabic, which might have helped people to remember its origin. Through King Roger's grandson Emperor Frederick II it passed, with other imperial vestments, to the Holy Roman Emperors and is now kept in the *Schatzkammer* of Vienna.[34] Some liturgical vestments were later used as coronation mantles. A splendid example comes from Hungary where in 1031, King Stephen (d. 1038) and his wife Gisla presented a silk, embroidered mantle to Székesfehérvár Cathedral, which was used for royal coronations over the following century. Both their portraits are embroidered on it including, in a touching gesture, the picture of their small son Emeric who had died in the same year.[35] All this information is given in an inscription embroidered along the edge of the garment. It is tempting to see this memorial to their dead son as partly inspired by the queen herself. She might even have taken part in the embroidery herself, for there is enough evidence to suggest that most noble women knew how to embroider, and the gift to a relative of one's own craftsmanship would add an extra emotional edge to such activity. Queen Edith (d. 1075), wife of Edward the Confessor (d. 1066), was a skilled needlewoman who, according to her husband's biographer, had embellished his garments with golden embroidery.[36] Apart from these ceremonial, and even emotional traditions attached to garments and clearly instilled by their patrons and makers, their life beyond the first generation took on an additional memorial significance. Many sumptious vestments given to churches and monasteries were refurbished for liturgical use, as will be clear from the examples we find in the wills of three noble women discussed later on. They were far too valuable to pass on to relatives and for this reason they often ended up in an ecclesiastical institution. On account of their later liturgical use and written references to them from the monks and priests, we know many of the vestments' original purpose.

Besides vestments, and in particular liturgical ones, jewellery survived with stories attached to it. As mentioned above, Aefflaed, the widow of Brihtnoth, gave the monks of Ely a tapestry and a golden ring in memory of her husband's courageous fighting against the Vikings. While still a young and unmarried girl, that is before she married King Louis VII of France in 1140, Eleanor of Aquitaine (d. 1204) for unknown reasons gave a golden ring to a friend called Richard Animal, whose initials R. A. were engraved on the ring. He in turn gave the ring, perhaps as a pledge of some sort, to the monks of St Albans. The ring is now lost, but we know the story of its original owner and her gift through a drawing made of it in 1259 by Matthew Paris, the chronicler-monk of St Albans, as part of a pictorial survey of the treasure of the abbey.[37] Clearly, the monks of St Albans were not simply interested in the value of the ring as a jewel, but also in its interesting origin and the royal connection with Queen Eleanor, whose second husband was King Henry II of England.

A story told by Abbot Suger, of Saint-Denis near Paris (d. 1151), about the origin of one of the jewels in his abbey's treasury dates from a century earlier. On his deathbed in 1137, King Louis VI of France handed over a great many treasures to Suger amongst which was the jewel in question: 'the very costly hyacinth that had belonged to his grandmother, the daughter of the king of the Russians'. The king's grandmother was Anna of Kiev, who herself was naturally the source for the story about the jewel's origin.[38] In order to preserve traditions about the origin of such splendid pieces, the safest thing to do was to engrave the name of its original owner on to the object. Another example from the abbey of Saint-Denis shows how well its monks, and particularly Abbot Suger himself, were at keeping such records.

In his account of the refurbishment of Saint-Denis, Suger tells us how he had ordered the engraving of the names of the illustrious owners of a beautiful rock-crystal bottle given by Eleanor of Aquitaine as a wedding gift to her first husband King Louis VII:

As a bride Eleanor gave this vase to King Louis
Mitadolus to her grandfather, the king to me, and Suger to the saints.

This verse was engraved along the bottom rim of the bottle's metal base studded with precious gems. Along with other royal possessions the bottle ended up in the abbey's treasury, presumably as one of the many precious objects this king mortgaged to the abbey although, in this particular case, Suger says that the king had given it to him as 'a tribute of his great love'. The owners go back to Mitadolus, who has recently been identified by George Beech as Abd al-Malik ibn Hud 'Imad aldawla (1110–30), the Muslim king of Saragossa, the last representative of the Hudid dynasty before the Spanish Reconquista. He gave the bottle as a token of friendship to Eleanor's grandfather Duke William IX of Aquitaine (d. 1126) after their victory in the battle of Cutanda on 17 June 1120.[39] It is interesting to note that the earlier history of the crystal bottle must have been relayed to Suger by Eleanor herself. This is yet another example of the way in which women helped to preserve knowledge about the past in an oral form which was then recorded by a monk for posterity.

Jewellery was sometimes given as a symbol representing a gift of land and as such, it was much more precious than the average knife or stick normally used for such transactions. Between 1150 and 1160 Earl William of Albemarle gave his niece Eufemia, wife of Robert II of Brus, a ring and money because she agreed to let him use the income of the land of Dimlington, which he had given her as her dowry, for his life only, after which it would return to her or her heirs.[40] Rings or other pieces of jewellery were made of more durable material than tapestries and vestments and could, in principle, survive permanently. Because of their value they were often melted down and used in new, contemp-orary designs. Unless a picture was drawn of the object, like Matthew Paris did of Eleanor's ring, or an account of its history was written like Suger's, it would disappear forever and with it the memory of the transaction it represented. Perhaps for this reason Aelfflaed gave a ring of durable metal, as well as a tapestry, to Ely in the hope that if one got lost, the other would still carry on the commemorative tradition. As it turned out, it was only the written tradition of the bequest that survived long enough for us to know that 900 years ago a widow had gone to great lengths to ensure the permanent survival of her husband's memory.

Thus jewellery has not survived in large quantities, nor do individual pieces often carry with them the story of their origin nor subsequent details of bequest and receipt. A valuable source for information on jewellery which can be directly linked with the women who wore it are the Anglo-Saxon wills which, as we have seen, were so informative about tapestries. The same Wynflaed who in *c.* 950 gave the woman Ealhhelm a tapestry, passed on to her daughter Aethelflaed 'her engraved bracelet and her brooch'; whether the engraving stated the donor or maker of the jewel or whether it was a dedication, we do not know.[41] Aelfgifu, sister of the chronicler Aethelweard, whom we discussed above in connection with Abbess Matilda of Essen, bequeathed to 'my brother's [Aethelweard's?] wife Aethelflaed the headband which I have lent her', and to the queen her necklace and armlet.[42] Finally, the unknown widow Wulfwaru gave her older daughter Gode 'a band of thirty mancuses of gold and two brooches and a woman's attire complete', while the younger one, Aelfwaru, had to make do with 'all the women's clothing which is left'.[43] Considering that one mancus bought an ox, the value of the [head]band is enormous.

The gender aspect of these bequests is very pronounced, jewellery that could be worn went to the testators' daughters or sisters, while drinking horns, or cups, decorated with gold and silver leaf went predominantly to sons or grandsons. No jewellery is passed on, as far as we can tell, to sons- or daughters-in-law. The assumption must therefore be that jewellery was passed on as far as possible in the maternal, female line. Only in the absence of daughters would necklaces or rings be given to in-laws. The Italian wills are less forthcoming about jewellery. Most do not specify individual items and instead refer to gold or silver, which might have been cash or objects made of such precious metal. Mele, son of Martin of Monopli, whom we mentioned before, gave his daughter Letitia unspecified jewellery, while the two disagreeing brothers-in-law bickered over a necklace which Peter wanted for his daughter Miranda.[44]

Apart from female jewellery there was also jewellery designed specifically for men. Most of the items in this category formed part of the military outfits of high-ranking soldiers. Wills of men, and of women, sometimes list them. Foremost among them are the armbands or armrings which were bequeathed to specific individuals, usually brothers, sons or grandsons. A good example comes from the widowed Wynflaed from Hampshire, whom we met earlier. She left her grandson Eadwold a wooden cup, not apparently for him to drink from, but to recycle its golden decoration: 'in order that he may enlarge his armlet'.[45] The bequest and the subsequent wearing of the armrings carried the memory of the previous owner with it. This, at least, is what the poem *Beowulf* suggests in lines 3015–16 when describing the victor's reaction to his enemy's possessions:

> No man shall wear an ornament in his memory
> and no beautiful woman a necklet about her throat.[46]

These wills give us very rare examples of jewellery possessed by lay people and bequeathed to their loved ones. From military jewellery it is but a small step to military weapons; they too carried the memory of famous fighters and sufficient examples have survived suggesting that they were widely kept as physical memorabilia of great events. The very fact that fighting was a male activity causes most of the references to concern gifts from men to men, though we have seen in Chapter 4 that it was the heiress Turfrida in the *Deeds of Hereward* who acted as the keeper of her male ancestors' weaponry. A sword of King Offa (d. 796) turned up more than 200 years later amongst the treasures of the aetheling Aethelstan, son of King Aethelred (d. 1016), who drew up his will in 1015. In it he bequeaths Offa's sword to his brother Edmund, together with another sword, a blade and a silver-coated trumpet. To his father he left 'the silver-hilted sword that belonged to Ulfketel', whose identity is not further revealed, as well as 'the coat of mail which Morcar has'.[47]

Presumably, Offa's sword was handed down from one generation to the
next with the name of its original owner attached to it. We have, of
course, no way of checking now whether it really was one of his many
swords.

Nor do we have any idea whether other famous weapons, recorded as
being in the possession of the Wessex kings, came from their alleged
owners. In 926, only 112 years after the death of Charlemagne, Duke
Hugh of the Franks may well have been right in thinking that he handed
over the great king's lance to King Aethelstan of England. As the son of
the first Robertian and non-Carolingian king of France, it was in his
interest to 'dump' Carolingian memorabilia abroad and there would have
been no point in inventing the story. However, the historical origin of
his other gift, the golden sword of Emperor Constantine is more open to
doubt, simply because of the length of time between Constantine's death
in 337 and Hugh's embassy 600 years later.[48] In the thirteenth century
the then earl of Warenne claimed that he still possessed the sword with
which his ancestor had come over to England in 1066. He presented it
as evidence of his right to hold his land when he came to see King Edward
I as part of the *Quo warranto* procedures, proving title to land:

> Asked by what warrant he held [his land], he produced an ancient and rusty
> sword and said: 'Look at this, my lords, this is my warrant! For my ancestors
> came with William the Bastard and conquered their lands with the [this?]
> sword, and by the [this?] sword I will defend them from anyone intending to
> seize it.[49]

As in the case of Charlemagne's lance and the swords of Constantine
and Offa, the authenticity of the Warenne sword is impossible to deny or
confirm. What matters here, however, is the memorial value attached to
these weapons and the stories they generated. These objects of war were
passed on from generation to generation as symbols of ancestral prowess.
They were put on display, exchanged as valuable presents or used for
ceremonies to make a point about the history of a family and the land
occupied by them. The arms themselves were worn or used exclusively
by men, but the guardianship of the objects and their memorial value could
be exercised by men and women. Indeed, in the absence of male heirs it was
up to the women to dispose of them to the next generation.

Another category of jewels associated with political displays of power
and ceremonial occasions deserves attention in the context of memory
and tradition, namely the regalia. The objects which represented secular

power were the crown, sceptre and the orb. Each medieval ruler, whether emperor or king, had a collection of such royal belongings which varied in size and splendour according to his wealth and position. Thus the German emperor had a more impressive collection than, for example, the king of Burgundy. Despite their symbolic importance, few of the regalia from the early and central Middle Ages have survived. We are best informed about crowns and the following examples will not only show how easily they became lost for a variety of reasons (disrepair, melting of gold and break-up of royal treasuries), but also how the memory of their existence survived due to the recording of their, often adventurous, whereabouts. In this context, once again the role of women in the preservation of knowledge about their historical significance was of the utmost importance.

In order to understand the dispersal of crowns all over Europe, one has to realize that the regalia formed part of the royal treasure that belonged to the king. Since no distinction was made between private and state property, the king was free to dispose of the insignia of his power. In practice, however, it seems that kings handed over the main crown (and sceptre and orb), with which they had been crowned, from one generation to the next, so that we can often trace the history of a crown from king to king within one dynasty. We also know that kings usually had different sets of crowns which they wore for different ceremonial occasions. The English kings, for example, had a crown for coronation ceremonies and other ones for the liturgical festivals of Christmas, Easter and Whitsun. As part of the royal treasure, the regalia travelled with the king wherever he went, adding to the risk of accidental loss. One of the most famous examples is the loss of King John of England's luggage in the Wash near King's Lynn in the early thirteenth century, resulting in the loss of most of the royal treasure at that time.

If a king had time to make a bequest before he died, he would normally decide what happened to his treasury. William the Conqueror made bequests, even though the account that lists them is modelled word for word on the bequest made by Louis the Pious two centuries earlier.[50] Both kings bequeathed their regalia to their royal successors and thus it follows that William Rufus became the new owner of the English regalia. Another tradition, however, recorded in a charter of the monastery of Saint-Etienne at Caen, maintains that the Conqueror gave his crown, orb and sceptre to the monks of this monastery. It is conceivable, however, that William the Conqueror was inspired in his gift to Saint-Etienne by his wife's bequest four years earlier of her crown and sceptre to Sainte-

Trinité at Caen. That this must have been her English regalia is clear because the Norman dukes did not have ducal crowns. After 1066 when in Normandy, they wore their English crowns symbolizing their status as king of England. In Normandy, a province of France, only the king of France had the right to wear a crown. As seems likely in the case of William and Matilda there must have been more than one set of regalia available for each of them: one to be give away and one, at least, to be kept in England for William Rufus's coronation in 1087.

These bequests also clearly show that it was the king's and queen's prerogative to dispose of regalia at will. An early-twelfth-century example from Germany, involving this same couple's granddaughter Empress Matilda, shows that regalia could be taken across the border. After the death of her husband King Henry V in 1125, Matilda was handed several items from the German treasury. As royal widow she was entitled to the king's movable possessions, which included the regalia. Some sort of trade-off seems to have taken place by which the childless Matilda left most of the regalia in Germany for the next king, but took two crowns home with her to England. Ultimately, in 1134 the two crowns ended up in the Norman monastery of Le Bec after Matilda had recovered from a serious illness due to the birth of her second son (by Geoffrey count of Anjou). The monks recorded her gift starting with an elaborate description of the imperial crowns:

> One crown of solid gold and with precious stones with which King Henry [II of England], son of the emperor [Empress?] was later crowned; it was so heavy that it had to be supported with two silver rods when the emperor or king was crowned. The 'arms' [brachia] could be taken apart for storage in the treasury; when put together it bore on the front a jewel of great size and value with a golden cross superimposed. The other one was small and gold and had been used by the emperor on solemn occasions.[51]

It is interesting that the larger of the two crowns was later used by Matilda's son Henry in 1154. Clearly, a crown therefore could be used in a different country from the one for which it was originally designed. Otherwise, the importance of Matilda's ownership of the crowns lies in the fact that she told the monks of Le Bec of their origin and they recorded her story for posterity. Finally, there was at least one more crown, a third one, dispensed by the empress. Abbot Suger in his account, which we used earlier, of the splendours of Saint-Denis refers to 'some flowers from the crown of the empress' which he had acquired for his abbey. Unfortunately, the circumstances of this particular donation remain unknown.[52]

Thus far, we have encountered descriptions of objects from monasteries whose monks were informed by men and women about the origin of precious gifts. Some information came from men whereas other information came from women. Gender clearly played a part in the source for information on the cash gifts related by Leo of Ostia, the chronicler of the abbey of Monte Cassino in Italy. Towards the end of his book on Duke Robert Guiscard (1087) in the abbey's history, he records the numerous cash donations and gifts of precious objects he and his wife made. The cash, usually in coins of different denominations, was a man's (Robert's) gift and was recorded on the basis of his own information. The money formed part of the booty collected during raids and paid as a penance for the sins committed in the process of acquisition:

> When he (Robert Guiscard) marched against Aquino he sent 500 bezants here. When he recaptured Bari, he gave 12 pounds of gold to [Abbot] Desiderius. On a following occasion, when he marched against the city of Tivoli, he deposited twelve pounds of gold in the chapterhouse and 100 'skifati' and a precious cloth on the altar. On a third occasion, when he returned from Rome with Pope Gregory, he deposited 1000 amalfitan 'tari' in the chapter house and one hundred bezants on the altar; and as he was leaving he sent here 190 blankets [*farganae*] for the brothers in the dormitory.

The reference to blankets suggests that some cash might have been spent on other practical objects. Some of the cash money might have been spent on liturgical goods such as reliquaries. An earlier example from England illustrates that the monks of Abingdon used royal cash for precisely such a reason. Their reliquary for the remains of St Vincent of Spain bore an inscription recording that it had been financed from '230 gold coins purified by fire and two pounds of silver' presented to them by King Cnut and his wife Emma.[53] Somehow the monks of Monte Cassino had kept better records of the circumstances under which the cash had been given than for the numerous precious objects which Robert and his wife Sickelgaita gave, for Leo only occasionally gives details about the latter. In an impressively long list, he enumerates the golden and silver altar vessels decorated with precious jewels which could all be displayed during the Mass and other celebrations. Besides the metalwork, the other category of gifts consisted of textiles with an emphasis on liturgical vestments. Silk, gold embroidery and sewed on jewels were the norm and illustrate the enormous wealth spent on the abbey.[54] Significantly, however, no jewellery of any personal nature was given, nor the sort of vestments which one person might pass on to another in the fashion described in the Anglo-Saxon wills. Such items must have been reserved for Robert's and Sickelgaita's relatives, even though no written record of such gifts have survived.

This brings us to the important issue of the role of objects in the memorial tradition. In the absence of any wills of the sort that we have seen were made in Anglo-Saxon England and Southern Europe, it is impossible to assess what people in post-Conquest England, or elsewhere in Europe, passed on from one generation to another outside of the monastic sphere. Sometimes, we catch a glimpse of the history of an object which allows us to trace its route from one individual to another in a series of bequests. Orderic Vitalis (d. c. 1142) a monk at Saint Evroult gives the precise details of the provenance of one of his monastery's great Psalters, tracing its history back through more than three generations of owners, male and female:

> Abbot Robert procured for the monks of Saint Evroult a great Psalter richly illuminated which is still in almost daily use by the choir as they chant psalms to the glory of God. This is the book Emma, wife of the English king Aethelred gave to her brother Robert, archbishop of Rouen. His son William carried it off from his father's chamber as sons do and gave it to his beloved wife whom he sought to please in all things.[55]

The string of owners started with Queen Emma, daughter of Duke Richard I of Normandy, who first became the wife of King Aethelred of England (d. 1016) before then marrying King Cnut (d. 1035). She must have given the Psalter, which had been made in one of the Anglo-Saxon scriptoria, to her brother Archbishop Robert of Rouen before he died in 1037. According to Orderic, it was Archbishop Robert's second son William who took the Psalter from his father's room (library?) and gave it to his wife Hawise of Giroie. Hawise's first husband had been Robert of Grandmesnil, by whom she had a son Robert, the abbot referred to by Orderic. It was this Abbot Robert who in turn presented the book to the monks of Saint-Evroult. What Orderic does not mention is under what circumstances Hawise passed on the Psalter to her son, whether this was during her lifetime or whether it was part of her will. Ultimately, she must have been the source of information about the story of the Psalter's origin and its famous first owner. Her and Orderic's knowledge was probably boosted by a note in the Psalter giving details of Queen Emma's gift. Several other liturgical manuscripts given by her to Continental friends bear inscriptions which identify her as the donor. The Saint-Evroult Psalter has not survived, but the interesting way in which it arrived at the monastery is a memorable story in its own right.[56]

Bequests and wills are known from monastic sources but they usually record only gifts made to the monastery and do not contain information about the other possessions of the testator. A few examples will illustrate the limitations of these documents compared with the Anglo-Saxon wills discussed earlier. They also serve to show how three noble women, Matilda I of England (d. 1083), Judith of Flanders (d. 1094) and Empress Matilda (d. 1167), used male and female monasteries as repositories for their, mostly public, possessions on the assumption that their belongings would act as memorials to their lives.

The bequest of Queen Matilda I of England, wife of William the Conqueror, to her own abbey of Sainte-Trinité at Caen in Normandy, was drawn up shortly before her death in 1083 and contains a strikingly 'impersonal' list:

> . . . a chasuble made at Winchester by the wife of Aldreth and the cloak made of gold [thread?] which is in my chamber and which is to be made into a cape and two golden hangings which contain crosses, and a lamp with engraved emblems to be hung in front of the holy altar, and the very large candlesticks made at Saint-Lô, and the crown and the sceptre, and the chalice and the vestments made in England and all the trappings for the horses and all the vases, except for those which I have already given away on earlier occasions.

Amongst these possessions only the English cloak and the horse trappings can be described as 'personal' belongings. Matilda had already foreseen that her cloak would be of no use unless it were to be reshaped as a liturgical vestment and this is what she requested be done. The trappings for the horses would probably be useful for the abbess or prioress during visits away from the abbey. Amongst the other items, her crown and sceptre stand out as public objects over which Matilda had complete authority of disposal as we have pointed out above. To what extent her daughter Cecilia, then a nun at Sainte-Trinité in her early twenties, influenced her mother to leave these particular items to the nunnery, we do not know. The charter listing the gifts was kept at Sainte-Trinité and served as a record alongside the bequest, thus keeping alive the memory of Matilda as the founder of the nunnery long after the actual objects had perished or been lost.[57]

The second bequest is that of Judith of Flanders, Duchess of Bavaria, who in 1094 together with her husband Duke Welf IV (d. 1101) had her will recorded listing her gifts to the monastery of Weingarten. Several lists detailing the bequest have survived. Though they are all slightly different, they agree that the donation was a most substantial and generous one:

> . . . reliquaries, two of which were of gold, three missals, and one gospelbook, three altars, four gilded and two golden chalices, two golden portable altars, two precious golden crosses with inlaid stones, three small crosses with others even smaller, three silver precious and heavy candelabras, two copes decorated with gold thread and a third without, two dorsals of which one is extremely long, five precious chasubles of the best goldwork, six capes of which five were decorated with goldwork, three golden dalmatics, two subdeacon's garments, two 'phano' of gold and inlaid with stones.

Among the gifts are two relics which, recorded in another document, testify to Judith's interesting history. One was the relic of Christ's blood, which had once belonged to Emperor Henry III (d. 1056) who had presented it to her half-brother Count Baldwin V (1035–67). According to a twelfth-century narrative about the relic written at Weingarten, and thus presumably based on Judith's own information, it was given by Baldwin to his sister on the occasion of her second marriage. The relic of St Oswald came from England and is a reminder of Judith's first marriage to Earl Tostig of Northumberland (d. 1066). This same background accounts for the splendid Anglo-Saxon gospel-books which Judith bequeathed on this occasion.[58] One of them is particularly interesting because it preserves the only known portrait, however stylized, of Judith herself as commissioner and patron of the book's scribe.[59] A more intangible, but no less interesting part of Judith's legacy is formed by her stories relating to her time in England as the wife of Tostig, one of the pretenders to the English throne in 1066, which will be discussed in the next chapter.

For the third and last example of a monastic bequest to a monastery from a woman, we return to Empress Matilda's donations to Le Bec. Apart from the crowns which, as we have seen, were said to have come from the empire none of her other gifts can be explicitly associated with her life in Germany and Italy. That some of them must have been produced in Continental workshops seems to be beyond doubt and is indeed confirmed, as we shall see, by Robert of Torigni, her father's biographer. As in the case of Matilda I and Judith, the empress gave items suitable for use in a monastic liturgy:

> Two golden chalices, a gold cross decorated with precious stones, two gospelbooks bound in gold studded with gems, two silver censers decorated with gold, a silver incense box and spoon, a gold pyx for the Eucharist, three silver flasks, two portable altars of marble decorated with silver.

Besides these liturgical objects she gave numerous vestments like chasubles, dalmatics, copes and a vestment that did come from Germany and is described as an 'imperial cloak sprinkled with gold to make albs from'. Like Matilda I, the empress gave a secular garment that would be of little use unless it could be remade into liturgical vestments. All these items were given to Le Bec on the occasion of her illness in 1134. Thirty years later, after her death and burial at Le Bec in 1167, a final bequest of treasures reached the monastery comprising the empress's books from her chapel, a gold chalice, four chasubles, two tunics and two silver censers and two silver basins. The most spectacular present she gave was two boxes, described as 'eggs of griffins whose legs and claws gripping the eggs were made of silver'. The shape of these boxes suggests an original secular use for them, which Marjorie Chibnall has suggested may have been inspired by the legends of Sybil or courtly romance.

Unlike Queen Emma's and Countess Judith's gospel-books, none of Empress Matilda's books have survived, due to the looting and subsequent dispersal of most of Le Bec's library at the time of the French Revolution. Neither have any of the relics nor other liturgical objects from this list survived, so that our only knowledge of them depends on the lists drawn up by the monks of Le Bec in memory of their most generous patron. Apart from these inventories, we have a little bit of more circumstantial knowledge about the first part of her gift in 1134 based on what Matilda herself discussed with Robert of Torigni. In a section full of praise for the empress, he refrains from listing her gifts because: 'it would be superfluous to describe them individually or give their names in order to impress the memory of this perfect and illustrious lady upon the hearts of the monks'. He then gives a hint that her gifts were put on display for noble visitors to view when they came to Le Bec, not least as an invitation for others to follow in Matilda's footsteps. Robert's concern is not so much with the memorial value of her donation because, after all, he wrote in *c.* 1139 when she was still alive and in excellent health. Nevertheless, as a historian he must have realized the future importance of the inventories and of his chronicle as part of the commemoration of the empress at Le Bec. Moreover, Robert of Torigni has also preserved an almost hagiographical note in this context, according to which Matilda donated her silk mattress on which she had slept during her illness. The buyer is unknown but the proceeds went to a charity for lepers.[60]

The three women's bequests are important examples of the way women used monasteries as repositories for their belongings, and consequently as a place where their memory would be kept alive. Matilda I at her own nunnery of Sainte Trinité at Caen, Judith at her second husband's family monastery of Weingarten and Empress Matilda at the monastery of Le Bec. But what is so striking about the lists of their gifts is the almost complete absence of any personal belongings like the contents of their wardrobes, except for the cloaks bequeathed by the two Matilda's to be remade into liturgical garments. There is no trace of jewellery like necklaces, headbands, rings nor bracelets nor any sort of personal jewellery, nor is there any reference to bed hangings, bedspreads, tapestries nor other items of furnishing. In other words, precisely those objects which make the Anglo-Saxon wills so important for our knowledge of what women handed on to their children and grandchildren, and by which they presumably were remembered, are lacking from these bequests. Not knowing who received the jewellery, bed hangings or tapestries robs us of the possibility of tracing the survival of memories about individuals attached to such objects within the private sphere of the family. Instead, we have to be content with what the monasteries have preserved by way of a more official memory of the person in his or her public role.

Thus the nature of the surviving memorial traditions attached to gifts and objects, which derive almost exclusively from a monastic environment, presents a profound paradox. Men and women provided the monks with memories of themselves and their families in their official roles. This resulted in bequests of land, property and objects in so far as the monks and nuns could use them for their own life. Other items, like Matilda's silk mattress, were sold and the cash used for more liturgical items. But the personal and individual objects of jewellery, furnishings and clothes did not reach the monastic world. The main reason was their unsuitability for reuse in what was supposed to be an austere environment. The other reason was probably a reluctance on the part of lay people to see their belongings being depersonalized. Why give your grandmother's precious necklace to a monastery if it is being used as yet another string of beads around one of their saints' relics? This might help the fame of the saint but does not help the memory of you as a donor. Therefore, in order to be remembered as an individual, it was better to pass on one's own personal objects to one's children and grandchildren. Such a conclusion is very important in its implication for the differences between men's and women's options.

Men led public lives and were commemorated in monasteries for their public roles. Little was necessary for their private roles to be remembered. Women, leading private lives to a much greater extent, perpetuated their private lives through oral bequests of their potential memorials to their daughters and granddaughters who simply perpetuated this tradition. The paradox therefore is more striking for the women involved in the task of preserving the past. They informed the monks and nuns of monasteries about their menfolk's public lives, they contributed in the public role of mourner and fund-raiser to finance the family's memorial tradition. On the other hand, they maintained a private memorial tradition by handing down objects and I believe, with those objects, private stories to their daughters and granddaughters. This by its very nature was an oral and not a written tradition.

A corollary to this conclusion is that oral tradition does not forever record stories associated with objects unless some form of identification of the original owner is attached to it in written form. Thus many objects that survived 'loose', that is without a context that could identify its origin, received a new history or a new life. Reliquaries in particular were prone to this process, as has been shown by Amy Remensnyder. For example, at the abbey of Conques reliquaries of the eleventh and twelfth centuries became associated with legends alleging that Charlemagne or his father Pepin had given them to the monks. In a gradual process called 'imaginative memory', the monks began to associate their saints' relics with a Carolingian past which fitted in with the current revival of interest in the Carolingian kings, particularly after Charlemagne's canonization in 1172. A similar process went on at Saint-Denis where Suger argued that many of the objects in the monastery's treasury had Merovingian origins. In the absence of knowledge of historical styles in the Middle Ages, such anachronistic reasoning was quite common and led to missidentifications. The examples I mentioned earlier, such as Offa's sword, Constantine's sword and Charlemagne's lance, may well belong to this category. But does it matter for our investigation into the ways medieval men and women remembered the past? Such 'false' memories attached to objects are as illustrative of medieval perceptions about the past as real memories. For the ways stories and objects interacted with regard to memories of the Norman Conquest of England, we have to turn to the next chapter where I shall focus on how a single event became memory.

Part III

One Event Remembered

6

THE MEMORY OF THE NORMAN CONQUEST OF ENGLAND IN 1066

After the thematic approach of the previous chapters where we looked at the acknowledgement of oral witnesses in historiography and hagiography, at women's unofficial role in commemoration and the significance of objects as pegs for memories, we turn now to the memorial tradition of one event. The occasion of the arrival of the Normans in England was a sudden event which caused the death of the ruling class of the English nation and its consequent replacement by another elite. No other event in western European history of the central Middle Ages can be compared for its shocking effects: the carnage on the battlefield, the loss of life and the consequent political upheaval. Apart from the social, economic and cultural consequences, the event caused an explosion of historical writing that finds no contemporary parallel. It is through the pages of the four generations of chronicles, annals, saints' lives and vernacular poetry that we can sense the shockwaves of horror, pain, regret and grief.

From the initial raw shock to the more restrained polished expressions of regret later on, we can follow how, on the victims' side, the English came to terms with defeat and how, on the conqueror's side, the victors' initial euphoria turned to a slow realization of the misery they had caused. Various themes discussed in the previous chapters will re-emerge and illustrate the memorial process: the interaction between oral and written traditions, the reliance on women for the transmission of eyewitness and second-hand reports; the patronage by women of the vernacular texts on the conquest; and the role played by objects as *memorabilia* of the event. Before we turn to them, a short introduction to the factual history of the Norman Conquest is necessary.

In January 1066 King Edward the Confessor of England died without issue. He was succeeded on the day of his burial by Earl Harold of Wessex, who claimed that he had been chosen as his heir by Edward himself on his deathbed. Harold ruled for just over nine months till his defeat at Hastings. Harold was the eldest surviving son of Earl Godwin of Wessex and his wife Gytha, and had successfully pushed aside his brother and rival Tostig, whom we have met as the first husband of Judith of Bavaria. Almost immediately after Harold's accession to the English throne his action was contested by William, duke of Normandy and later to be the Conqueror. He claimed that Edward the Confessor had chosen him as his successor, first in 1051 and thereafter in 1064 or 1065. On the second occasion, so the Norman version maintained, it had been Earl Harold himself who had conveyed the king's wish. Harold had even sworn an oath, so well illustrated on the Bayeux Tapestry, on the relics of Bayeux Cathedral. Duke William argued that Harold's accession was a flagrant breach of his oath of fealty and from this the charge of Harold's perjury was born.

With backing from Pope Alexander II and Cardinal Hildebrand, later Gregory VII, William recruited an army of several thousand soldiers and had a fleet of about 700 ships assembled. At the end of September 1066 he crossed to England and on 14 October he faced Harold at the Battle of Hastings. Unfortunately for Harold, at the time of William's invasion he was on his way back from the north of England where he had just defeated the alliance of his brother Tostig and King Harold of Norway, both of whom were killed. He and his troops were exhausted and this was a major contributory factor to the English defeat at Hastings. After the battle, where indeed many on both sides had been killed, the Norman duke received the surrender of the English and at Christmas he was crowned at Westminster Abbey in London. Another four years of resistance from small groups of Englishmen followed before the country was finally subdued. The long Norman rule of England had begun and with it the memorial tradition of the Conquest of England.

The anonymous author of the *Battle Abbey Chronicle*, writing in the 1170s, records that on his deathbed the Conqueror bequeathed the amulets he used to wear to Battle abbey.[1] He does not explicitly say that these were the amulets which William had with him at Hastings and which, according to William of Poitiers,[2] the duke had worn around his

neck, but we can assume that this was the case. Since he founded Battle
in atonement for the bloodshed during the battle and out of gratitude
to God for victory, it seems reasonable to assume that that is where the
relics he had worn on that very day ended up.[3] No precise description of
the objects has survived, but we know that they were of metal, that they
were precious and that they joined others hanging round a larger relic
shrine. Within a decade of the bequest, however, the monks of Battle
parted with this souvenir and the chain of events which then unfolded
illuminates the way in which medieval traditions, oral and written,
emerged.

As part of a fund-raising expedition aimed at rich post-Conquest
England the monks of Saint-Germer at Fly, a small Benedictine house
just a few miles across the border of the French Vexin, pursued King
William Rufus (1087–1100) through England and Wales in their quest
for money to buy a new chasuble for their church. After several attempts
to rid himself of them, Rufus became fed up and directed them to Battle
Abbey with an order to Abbot Henry (d. 1102) to pay them. Henry
protested poverty to the king but in vain, whereupon he felt obliged to
convert the Conqueror's amulets into cash. With the money thus acquired
the monks of Fly purchased purple cloth out of which the chasuble was
made. About a year later lightening destroyed the garment, but the others
lying immediately above and below were left unscathed. The miraculous
loss of the garment was seen, both at Fly and at Battle, as punishment by
God. A written account of the misfortune was apparently published at
Fly and about two decades later, during the abbacy of Abbot Warner (d.
1138) but before 1133, Abbot Odo of Fly and his monk Richard, who
was the man who had originally approached William Rufus, came to
Battle to perform a public apology. It was witnessed by the Battle Abbey
chronicler as a young monk, who wrote in his account that he relied
upon what he heard on that occasion rather than on the earlier Fly text.[4]
Sceptics may argue that the amulets had disappeared for other reasons
and the chronicler's story was invented to explain the loss, but it was
confirmed at the time by the French historian Guibert of Nogent, a former
monk of Fly, in his autobiography.[5]

We do not know who orchestrated the public apology and it is possible
that it was motivated on the French side by political considerations. It
took place after the defeat of King Louis VI (1108–37) of France at the
battle of Brémule in 1119, and it may represent an attempt to achieve
reconciliation by bringing monks from a French house to a prestigious
royal monastery in England. It is, however, on the attitude of the Battle

community that I wish to focus here. I link the apology with the death in 1124, at the age of 84, of perhaps the last survivor of the generation of monks who had experienced the Conquest, Abbot Ralph of Caen.[6] I link it with the efforts to collect and record 1066 *memorabilia* which followed Abbot Ralph's death – efforts which resulted in the copying of the *Ship List* of William the Conqueror and the early histories of Battle Abbey.[7] The monks of that time, it seems to me, were acutely aware that 50 or 60 years after the Conquest they were losing touch with the past. In that climate, the loss of a relic dating from the Conquest seemed a much more serious matter than it had seemed to Abbot Henry in the late 1090s. There is a pattern here which can be traced elsewhere. First comes the epic event, a moment of triumph or disaster according to one's point of view. About two generations later comes the realization that aspects of the event which were once common knowledge are common knowledge no longer; hence the urge to collect information and pass it on, usually by oral communication to younger people, but sometimes in writing. About two generations later still come the first attempts at detached historical analysis, such as the account which the Battle chronicler set down in the 1170s.[8]

Likewise at Waltham Abbey, about a century elapsed before crucial information about the true burial place of its one time patron, Earl Harold, was written down, though that information had been collected orally about fifty years earlier. In this case the writer was an elderly canon, who composed his history of the abbey in about 1177 in order to ensure that the memories of his community would not be forgotten if Henry II carried out his threat to close it down. Almost incidentally, he included a number of stories going back to the Norman Conquest, some of which had been told to him in the 1120s by the sacristan Turketil, then about eighty years old. Turketil had witnessed King Harold's visit to Waltham on his way back from his victory at Stamford Bridge after he had been told of the Norman invasion, and he was probably the source of the story, undoubtedly true, that King Harold's remains had been buried in a proper tomb in Waltham by two canons who had brought them back from the battlefield.[9] The anonymous author who recorded these stories *c*. 1177 was probably unaware of the Norman accounts which claimed that Harold had been buried on a hilltop in Sussex, but he evidently knew of other rumours in circulation to the effect that: 'Harold dwelt in a cave at Canterbury and that later, when he died, was buried at Chester'.[10] It was to kill off such unfounded speculation that the Waltham canon put the record straight in writing.

At Westminster in the late 1130s, meanwhile, Osbert of Clare took up the cause of King Edward's sanctity as yet another means of preserving in a positive and very personal way the memory of 1066. On evidence which was distinctly meagre, as Frank Barlow has pointed out, he waged a tireless campaign for almost 30 years. Like the chroniclers of Battle and Waltham, Osbert claims to be using oral information from people who witnessed, shortly after Edward's death in 1066, miraculous events attributed to his holiness. Edward's canonization was approved in 1161 and was followed two years later by his solemn translation to a new tomb in Westminster Abbey. King Edward's death, an event which had led to the Norman challenge to the English throne and hence, indirectly, to the bloodbath of 1066, was thereby transformed: having been a fateful tragedy for the English in 1066, it became for Osbert and the Westminster community in the 1160s a triumph of saintly commemoration.[11]

In Normandy, the main fourth generation contribution to the analysis of 1066 took place in the form of Wace's *Roman de Rou*.[12] Wace was a canon of Bayeux Cathedral and had been educated at Caen. In the 1150s and 1160s he began to translate and adapt the already considerable body of Latin historiography into Anglo-Norman verse. He collected oral stories for the pre- and post-Conquest history of Normandy and built these around the centrepiece of his work, the longest narrative account of the Conquest. I have argued elsewhere that although several stories are clearly anachronistic and of little historical value, his list of the Conqueror's companions is based on what we now would call an oral history project. Most of the people he lists had connections with Bayeux Cathedral or the abbeys at Caen. I believe Wace to have combed through the archives of those institutions and supplemented this material with stories collected orally from his contemporaries, both men and women, about their grandfathers and great-grandfathers. The most striking of them is the story of William Patric, who shortly before the Conquest witnessed Duke William in the company of Earl Harold riding through his village of La Lande Patry on his way to Brittany.[13] The duke's expedition is well recorded in contemporary chronicles, but without the charming eyewitness account passed on by William Patric's grandson and namesake to Wace.[14]

Abbot Ralph and Sacristan Turketil, on whom the chroniclers of Battle and Waltham relied, were quite old in the 1120s and had been grown men at the time of the Conquest. There must, however, have been others still alive at the same period who had been teenagers in 1066. Among those who undoubtedly had stories to tell would have been Robert of

Beaumont and William of Evreux on the Norman side, both of whom died in their late sixties in 1118, and Edgar the aetheling on the English side, who died in about 1125.[15] But from, say, 1130 onwards it was up to the children of the 1066 generation to pass on the stories. Robert of Beaumont's twin sons Waleran and Robert, for example, who died respectively in 1165/6 and 1168, may well have informed Wace about their father's deeds.[16] William the Conqueror himself died in 1087, but several of his children survived until the mid 1130s and may as pensioners have told stories about their father to third-generation historians.[17] Such details concerning age and longevity should be borne continuously in mind when we discuss the transfer of stories from one generation to the next. We need to tread carefully, however, because although the reconstruction of a chain of informants may help to assess how memories are formed, it cannot guarantee that particular memories were accurate.

So far I have concentrated on stories of 1066 which were transferred two generations later by oral means and not written down until the fourth generation. Some stories, however, were written down in the second generation. The first accounts of the Conquest to be written down in England, all of them brief and all of them written by monks, took the form of additions to the *Anglo-Saxon Chronicle*: the contributions made by Eadmer of Canterbury (d. *c.* 1124), John of Worcester (d. after 1140), Symeon of Durham (d. after 1126) and William of Malmesbury (d. *c.* 1143) are the most significant. In recent years Richard Southern, James Campbell and Antonia Gransden have argued that one effect of the Conquest was to turn English monks back to their Anglo-Saxon past in an attempt to salvage what they could of it.[18] They sought to link that past with the present by interpreting the defeat of the English by the Normans as God's punishment for English sins. In effect, they presented a theological rationalization of the collective national shame, a common enough literary reaction to defeat in battle.

The English monks who first attempted to chronicle the events of 1066 pay some attention both to King Harold and his two brothers, who were all three killed with him at Hastings, and also to members of the English resistance, such as Eadric the Wild, Hereward and Earl Waltheof, but on the whole they are surprisingly silent about individual disasters. In an age of liturgical commemoration, when monasteries were normally scrupulous in recording deaths in memorial books, obituaries or other documents, why did no English monk write down the names of the victims of 1066? All we have is a handful of names preserved by accident in *Domesday Book*, in charters or in later cartulary chronicles. Perhaps this is due to the fact that monks were writing history. Janet Coleman, in her study on ancient and medieval memories, has argued that the rule of St Benedict aimed at persuading monks to forget their families and personal histories, to live a communal life and to think of themselves as part of a community. Little space was left for any attention to individuals.[19] However, complete disassociation from one's own family is impossible for most of us. In my view, in the two generations which followed the Conquest, English monks experienced a very deep sense of loss and shame which had a national dimension, an institutional dimension and a personal dimension as well; it permeates even their brief accounts which, unsurprisingly, are all pervaded with gloom. Yet, by introducing the theme of national sin and divine punishment, and by depersonalizing their subject matter, they contrived to some extent to counteract the trauma from which they were suffering.

A few fragmentary remarks about 1066 are to be found in sources which predate the monastic versions of the *Anglo-Saxon Chronicle*, and those which reflect the English point of view are bleaker still. The earliest such source is the *Life of King Edward*, written at the request of his wife Queen Edith in the years 1065–67. The queen lost three of her brothers in the battle at Hastings and her mother Gytha and other relatives were obliged to flee to Flanders to escape the wrath of the Normans,[20] yet the battle is only hinted at in the *Life*. The catastrophe was too appalling and too recent, I suggest, for an author to face it. The various entries in the *Anglo-Saxon Chronicle*, all condemning the invasion, are equally brief. Version 'D' may have been written as contemporary comment on events immediately after the Conquest, but due to interpolations, it is difficult to distinguish what was written when in the only available copy, itself known to have been written after 1100. Version 'E', copied at Peterborough, is based on Canterbury material up to 1120, and here too, it is impossible to tell what the annalist wrote in 1066. In both versions revisions therefore date from a time when England was firmly under Norman control.[21]

Amongst this meagre harvest, the E-version of the *Anglo-Saxon Chronicle* is unique in expressing the anguish and frustration of the English; it seems to have been focused on the aetheling who appears everywhere, but without being able to rally effective groups of resistance fighters around him. The most evocative expression of grief comes in a poem written by the skald Thorkill Skallason for his master Earl Waltheof after he had been executed for treason in 1076. It is written in Old Norse, but may have been based on an Old English version used much later by

William of Malmesbury.[22] The most intriguing aspect of this poem is its theme of Waltheof's betrayal by William the Conqueror, which neatly reverses the official Norman charge of treason against the earl:

> William crossed the cold channel
> and reddened the bright swords,
> and now he has betrayed
> noble Earl Waltheof.
> It is true that killing in England
> will be a long time ending.

Here, Thorkill may be avenging Waltheof's death by hinting at the fact that it was Waltheof's wife Judith, William's niece, who betrayed her husband.

The shortage of information about the Conquest in English sources which date from the decades immediately following it, a shortage which I have attributed to the traumatic effects of national disaster, can to some extent be made good by looking at Continental sources. Most of these express horror and moral indignation at the bloodbath and loss of life. English authors would surely have expressed the same sentiments had they been less stunned.[23]

There is, however, one exception to the rule of the *tabula rasa* of post-Conquest personal commemoration in England and that is the *Deeds of Hereward*, the biography of Hereward which we have already discussed several times in this book. The Latin text was written between 1109 and 1131 by a clerk at Ely, probably called Richard. He used a now lost Old English biography by Hereward's chaplain Leofric, which he claims to have combined with the reminiscences of several of Hereward's companions, two of whom he names as Siward of Bury St Edmunds and Leofric the Black. Bearing in mind that 1066 veterans survived well into the twelfth century, as has been shown above, there can be absolutely no doubt that Richard of Ely consulted these elderly eyewitnesses. Hereward's adventures cover two distinct phases. During the first in the 1060s, he fought as an exiled mercenary for a variety of masters in Cornwall, Ireland and Flanders, while during the second phase, he led the uprising in the Fenland and the siege of Ely in 1071. His *Deeds* contains the fullest account we have of these events: the kernel of it is substantially corroborated by details from the *Anglo-Saxon Chronicle*, John of Worcester and documentary texts.[24]

Hereward's biography is based on a series of eyewitness reports which

Richard of Ely linked together as best he could. The linking is clumsy, but I take that to be a sign of authenticity, for no forger would have produced something so full of 'contradictions'. The *Deeds of Hereward* is very much an attempt to cope with the trauma of defeat, not by theological rationalization and depersonalization, but by romanticizing heroic behaviour and honourable surrender through the medium of epic narrative. Its personal nature may be partly due to the original version having been written by a secular priest in the vernacular, the language in which most of the oral stories must have been told. Richard, the author of the Latin text, must have been bi-lingual, or even tri-lingual, if he was able to translate the original Old English into Latin and supplement it with vernacular reports.[25] He may himself have been a member of the secular clergy attached to Ely rather than a monk and may have felt freer on that account to tell the story of an Anglo-Saxon defeat in personal terms.

If he were a secular clerk, Richard may be compared profitably with two other secular clerks who were responsible for later off-shoots of the *Anglo-Saxon Chronicle*. Archdeacon Henry of Huntingdon extended the chronicle into the 1150s, rewriting and revising his text continuously.[26] His struggle to reconcile the demands of a military society full of worldly vanity with God's plan pervades his brief account of the Norman Conquest. Yet his secular background enabled him to be much more forthcoming about the actual organization of the Conquest. His views on the vital role of William fitz Osbern as the brain behind the logistics of the invasion predates the same opinion held by Canon Wace of Bayeux. Henry is, however, the first historian to focus his thoughts on the military aspects and achievements of the Conquest. He too thought that moral lessons needed to be learned, not in the form of one nation repenting its sinful past, but by soldiers and other groups of population each contemplating their own past. Henry of Huntingdon's contemporary was Gaimar who in 1137–38 translated the *Anglo-Saxon Chronicle*, not like the others into Latin, but into Old French.[27] Though he does not contribute much new material to the topic of the Norman Conquest, he includes the longest account of Hereward outside the *Deeds of Hereward*, albeit in a slightly different version.[28]

There is, of course, considerable irony in the fact that a French clerk appropriated the language of the conquerors in order to present them with a history grafted upon the *Anglo-Saxon Chronicle*. This is surely a sign that by the third generation, some grandchildren of the Conquest were prepared to learn the history of their new country from an English perspective. Henry's and Gaimar's place in society as secular clerks meant a much more intimate contact with the people in England and the effects of the Conquest on the common population than, I believe, the monk historians had. It also meant closer contact with women and their view of the past. Gaimar wrote in response to a request from a lay woman, Constance wife of Ralph fitz Gilbert, who may have had access to members of Hereward's family. Henry of Huntingdon was almost certainly married and one just wonders to what extent his wife's views influenced his account of the Conquest. The down-to-earth tone, attention to the practical side of life and willingness to move away from abstract theological moralizations are surely due to a non-monastic environment.

Thus far I have concentrated my analysis on England and the historians writing in that country, and I have shown how an initial shocked silence was followed by two parallel perceptions of the past: oral stories which were more personal and emotional were circulating at the same time as abstract writings theorizing national guilt. But what was the historiographical development like in Normandy? How did historians writing in the duchy perceive the past during the first four generations? The literature generated by contemporaries, that is first-generation Norman Conquest, is not surprisingly dominated by the Norman view. William of Jumièges added a brief account of the Norman Conquest to his history of the dukes of Normandy, but firmly declined any possibility of writing about England after 1070; instead he promised a future sequel about William the Conqueror's son Robert Curthose.[29] William of Poitiers wrote a biography of the victorious duke which contains the Norman story of the Conquest, concentrating on the invasion, battle and subsequent campaigns in England.[30] He highlights the careers of the Conqueror's 12 main advisers, but is silent on the 3000 to 5000 participants in the Conquest. His account of the raids in northern England show a particular degree of detail not easily matched elsewhere.

Although his story has survived incomplete, we can reconstruct its last chapters through the *Ecclesiastical History* of Orderic Vitalis who copied the end, but supplemented it with his own comments.[31] Some aspects of this mixture, normally attributed to Orderic, may in fact have come from William of Poitiers. One of the central characters of the immediate post-Conquest period was Earl Morcar. He had been captured in 1071 during the siege of Ely and brought to Normandy, where he was entrusted to the care of Roger of Beaumont.[32] The following 15 years were spent in Normandy, where in 1086 he witnessed one of Roger's charters for the abbey of Saint-Wandrille.[33] In 1087 he was set free as part of a general amnesty issued by William Rufus.[34] William of Poitiers himself knew the Beaumont family intimately and his sister was the abbess of the Beaumont foundation, Saint-Leger at Préaux,[35] so it is not at all improbable that he had access to Earl Morcar's memories, in particular for information about his family and the military campaigns in which Morcar and his brother had been involved. An exchange of some sort between the English Morcar and the Norman William may have generated a certain understanding for the English victims and led to William's surprisingly well-informed account with its mild but emphatic flavour.

Thus we cannot exclude an oral exchange between Normans and Englishmen for the specific purpose of historical writing in the immediate post-Conquest period. In this context, we need to remind ourselves that in 1067 several aristocratic Englishmen, who presumably exchanged views with their Norman 'hosts', were in Normandy as the Conqueror's hostages: Archbishop Stigand, Edgar the aetheling, and Earls Edwin, Morcar and Waltheof.[36] Even Bishop Guy of Amiens in his celebratory poem on the Conquest, which is our most detailed but not necessarily most trustworthy account of the battle, may have consulted some English informants for his intriguing story about the English negotiators before their surrender.[37] Like William of Poitiers, his occasional empathy with the English position could emerge alongside vituperation against the English leader Harold. The passionately negative terms in which he denounces him have recently been characterized by Giovanni Orlandi as typical in writing as an immediate victorious response to a battle.[38] The other contemporary source for the Norman Conquest is the Bayeux Tapestry, which alone gives a glimpse of a more positive portrait of Harold, carrying one of his men on his shoulders during the Breton campaign, before he acceded to the throne. But this may simply be an artistic trick to emphasize his later arrogance and fall in terms of sharp contrast. The overwhelming reaction of first-generation Normans was one of legitimizations and justifications which were, in fact, abstract moralizations to bury any sense of guilt or shame.

This tendency to moralization did not stop with the death of the 1066 survivors. If anything it became much stronger. The most important representative was Orderic Vitalis, a monk born in England of mixed Anglo-Norman origins, who worked in Normandy. He interpolated William of Jumièges's *Deeds of the Dukes of the Normans* with details on King Harold's brothers Tostig and Gyrth, the battle and, in general, a revision of William's text aimed at toning down some of the more explicit pro-Norman sentiments.[39] Orderic not only fitted the account of 1066 more firmly in a Norman context, but he also expressed empathy with the English losses. At the same time he began his *Ecclesiastical History*, where he transformed a local history of his monastery into a large-scale chronicle of western Europe. For his account of the Norman Conquest, he used William of Poitiers's biography and some passages from his own interpolated version of the *Deeds of the Dukes of the Normans*. He also wove the famous condemnation of William the Conqueror's harrowing expeditions in the north into this account.[40] Even at an early stage of Orderic's career in 1114–15, he bore witness to the fact that some people on the Continent had refused to accept land or spoils from England on the grounds that they had been gained at the expense of too much bloodshed. He puts into the mouth of Abbot Guitmund of La Croix-Saint-Leufroi words to this effect:

> After carefully examining the matter I cannot see what right I have to govern a body of men whose strange customs and barbarous speech are unknown to me, whose beloved ancestors and friends you have either put to the sword, driven into bitter exile, or unjustly imprisoned or enslaved. Read the Scriptures, and see if there is any law to justify the forcible imposition of God of a shepherd chosen from among their enemies.[41]

It has long been thought that Orderic put forward these sobering thoughts because of his English origin. But some purely Norman writers certainly shared his ideas. Canon John of Coutances, the author of the biography of Bishop Geoffrey of Coutances written at about the same time, defended his father Peter, who had been Geoffrey's chamberlain, against implicit accusations of greed for English spoils. Having set out Peter's acquisitions for the new cathedral of Coutances, he assures his readers:

> . . . that the venerable bishop had not, as some people believe, acquired all this from the copious abundance of England's bounty . . . but that most of the abovementioned lands had been acquired before the English war.[42]

As a good historian he then proceeded to give evidence by pointing out that the cathedral was dedicated in 1056 and that the English war did not take place until nine years later. John's indignation at the thought that some believed the bishop enriched himself at the expense of the English sounds a little hollow if we read the next paragraph, where he lists the 'precious ornaments, embroideries and goldwork with smaragds and gems' which the bishop had brought over from England after the

Conquest.[43] Like the young Orderic and John of Coutances, the anonymous Norman author of the *Short Account of William most noble Count of the Normans,* which was written at Battle Abbey between *c.* 1114 and 1120, makes moral comments with regard to that English war. He contrasts the haughty Harold, who did not recognize that God was on the side of the humble, with William as a paragon of humility by developing the bible quotation 'pride comes before the fall'.[44] The author also develops William of Poitiers's story of the Conqueror inadvertently putting on his hauberk back to front and laughing the matter off saying it was not a bad omen. Here he has Duke William say:

> If I believed in magic I would not today engage in battle. But I have never put faith in magicians nor loved witches. In all I have ever undertaken I have always commended myself to my Creator.[45]

This emphasis on God's predisposition as opposed to the workings of magic may well be an implicit stab at the Battle monks – mourning at that very moment the loss of the Conqueror's amulets – who thought that the relics did swing the outcome of a battle in favour of the Normans. These three Norman historians all wrote within a decade after the Battle of Tinchebrai, fought on Norman soil in 1106 almost 40 years to the day after the Battle of Hastings, as William of Malmesbury pointed out.[46] The theme of God and not military prowess or magic deciding the outcome of battles had a curiously topical value.

An entirely different approach to the story of the Conquest can be found in the so-called *Hyde Chronicle,* written in Normandy towards the end of the reign of Henry I by someone, perhaps a chaplain, attached to the Warenne family.[47] Although there is no doubt about the author's Norman point of view, he is remarkably well informed about the family of King Harold, much more than Orderic was, with the result that the account of 1066 is set in a much more 'English' context than any of the other Norman chronicles. The author clearly knew a great number of sources, including English ones, considering his frequent references to oral and written testimonies which he, unfortunately, does not identify. His sources require further investigation, but suggest a Flemish or northern French link with the community of Saint-Omer, which offered shelter to King Harold's mother Gytha and which had been the home of Gundreda of Warenne. The details on the two families of Harold and Warenne introduce a personal element in an account that is far less moralizing than that of Orderic or the author of the *Brevis Relatio.* The chronicler's exceptional military information on the battles of Eu and Brémule suggests that he might have been William of Warenne's chaplain. His Latin style is poor and suggests that it came from the pen of someone better versed in vernacular French. As such his work prepares us for the writings of Wace, another secular clerk.

Wace single-handedly transformed writing on the Norman Conquest from a series of moralizations to a triumphant account of the achievements of the Norman soldiers. He used the Latin sources with great ingenuity, but left out all moralizing justifications and legitimizations. Like Henry of Huntingdon, he paid attention to the logistic organization of the Conquest, in the process of which he unwittingly introduced certain anachronisms, and like the author of the *Deeds of Hereward,* he commemorated the names of those who took part in the Conquest. Not only did he list William the Conqueror and his 12 leaders, whom William of Poitiers had compared with Julius Caesar and his senate, he added more than 130 names of local Norman lords, whose achievements had not yet been recorded in writing. Their deeds had survived in the oral tradition, which was the single most important source for Wace's reconstruction of the actual Conquest.

Wace was not interested in the Norman nation or the collective Norman memory, he was a local historian writing the history of the Cotentin soldiers, based on interviews and historical archival research. In fact, he put into practice what two English chroniclers described as the task of a historian. The Waltham chronicler and Walter Map, as we have already seen, stipulated that memories handed down from father to son and from son to grandson constitute valid alternatives in cases where prime eyewitness accounts had been lost. Any information handed down along a recognizable chain of informants within a period of 100 years, so Walter Map says, is admissible evidence for 'our own time'.[48] Thus, according to this rule, the historians of the fourth generation were the last able to record the memories of 1066 and employ them as substitute eyewitness accounts. At the same time, Henry II's lawyers, for the same reasons, stopped people pursuing land claims going back beyond the Conquest. Officially, no one could go back beyond the reign of Henry I.[49]

The study of the formation of oral and written memories of 1066 clearly shows the circulation of stories about the Conquest down several generations into the reign of Henry II (1154–89). The stories were local, centred on specific aspects of the Conquest and were quite personal. This oral tradition for a time ran parallel to a written tradition which attempted to cope with the past by seeing the defeat of 1066 in terms of

God's punishment for the sins of the English nation. By the reign of Henry II, the theme of 'national guilt' had evaporated and made place for discussions of military matters. Tales of military defeat and resistance survived. But what strikes the modern historian most is the almost total amnesia in the long term of individual loss and grief. Trauma as a psychological reason is as likely an explanation for the complete lack of a memorial to the English dead of 1066[50] as any other which blame the abbots' fear of being associated with the memory of rebels or the lack of patronage for literary activity in general. In Normandy the situation was different. The written memories concentrated first on the victorious leader, his legitimization of the use of force and the justification of military action. The second and third generation continued and expanded the moral justification of their actions. Meanwhile, oral tradition kept alive memories of fighters lower down the social scale. These were rescued by Wace and incorporated in his vernacular *Roman de Rou*, which became a memorial for those who had fought at Hastings.

Thus far I have occasionally referred to the role of women in the memorial process of the Norman Conquest of England: Queen Edith who commissioned a biography of her husband King Edward the Confessor, the wife of the chronicler Henry, archdeacon of Huntingdon, and Constance fitz Gilbert, the patroness of Gaimar. Edith and Henry's wife were full-blooded English women whereas Constance was probably of mixed Anglo-Norman background. It is worth scrutinizing the position of women in post-Conquest England and Normandy in more detail to see if we can be more precise about their contributions to the formation of memories about 1066.

The most obvious category to look at first is the aristocratic women who lost their menfolk at Hastings. Deprived of the protection of their fathers, husbands and sons, they were in a particularly vulnerable position with regard to the land-hungry newcomers eager to legitimize the acquisition of new land through marriage.[51] A considerable number of widows and heiresses married men of Continental backgrounds, like the heiresses Ealdgyth, daughter of Wigot of Wallingford, who married Robert d'Oilly; Muriel, daughter of Colswein of Lincoln, who married Robert de la Haye; Aelfgifu, daughter of a Warwickshire thegn Leofwine, who married Geoffrey de la Querche; of slightly later date Lucy of Bolingbrooke who married three Continental husbands in succession, Ivo of Taillebois, Roger Fitz Gerold and Ranulf le Meschin earl of Chester; and finally, most famously of all, Matilda II who married Henry I. She was not, strictly speaking, a sole heiress bringing land with her, but she brought with her the vital link with the Anglo-Saxon royal house through which her husband Henry I could establish an extra claim to legitimize his holding of the English throne.

Evidence for Anglo-Saxon widows remarrying Normans is thin and would confirm the evidence from Lanfranc's letter, which we will discuss below, suggesting that many women fled to nunneries in order to avoid marriage. *Domesday Book*, on the other hand, testifies to a considerable number of them holding on to some of their lands; for example Godgifu, widow of Earl Leofric; Aelfgifu, widow of Earl Aelfgar; and unknown women, like Wulfeva widow of Finn; Saewulf's widow; Wulfweard the White's widow; Edric's widow; and many others.[52] Whether the women who married foreigners did so out of free will or were more or less forced to accept marriage, we do not know. If there was a strong element of coercion, one would expect the memory of resentment to have lingered on for some while. Is there any evidence for women passing on stories of forced marriages to their daughter or granddaughters? Not directly on the compulsory element of marriage, but certainly on the loss of land associated with marriage into Continental families.

Paul Brand, in particular, has pointed out that amongst the late-twelfth- and early-thirteenth-century claims for land going back to the pre-Conquest period, a high percentage was based on claims through the female line.[53] One cannot help wondering whether such claims were kept alive because they were associated with strong feelings about the loss of land and kin. Otherwise, English women were instrumental in keeping alive a tradition of English first names for their daughters in particular. Whereas boys' names very quickly became gallicized, girls retained their English names well into the twelfth century. Clearly, a strong sense of historical tradition, perhaps mixed with latent aggression against the Normans, was thereby expressed by the women. As mothers, women had available a variety of ways by which they could influence their sons. Three of the most important Anglo-Norman historians Orderic Vitalis, Henry of Huntingdon and William of Malmesbury were of a mixed parentage: Orderic and Henry had English mothers, whereas William had one parent, probably his mother, of English origin. All three knew English, read Old English source material and used English eyewitness accounts. Having learned their native language from their mothers, common sense suggests that with the language they also received instruction on customs and manners, which in due course inspired them to write down the history of their maternal inheritance. Tracing similar influences amongst daughters of English women is much more difficult. That such influence existed, however, must be concluded from the patronage exercised by the second and third generation of children who could claim English ancestry.

In Chapter 4 we discussed the case of a Romsey hagiographical tradition which inspired women to commission their mother's or grandmother's biography. Queen Matilda II, brought up at Romsey, ordered a *Life* of her mother Margaret, while her niece Matilda was probably instrumental in the commissioning of the *Life* of her grandmother Countess Ida of Boulogne. The mother as the link in a family chain was seen as an important instrument for keeping track of one's ancestry and the *Life* functioned as a shrine encapsulating memories for posterity. These *Lives*, however, were mostly private testimonies of the women involved. On a public level, Queen Matilda II commissioned William of Malmesbury to write the *Deeds of the Kings of the English* which still stands as a monument to archival research and a record of oral tradition encapsulating much of what we now know of Anglo-Saxon England. Through her historical interest and dynastic responsibility – after all she embodied the continuation of Anglo-Saxon royal blood after the Conquest – she bridged the gap between life in England before the Conquest and life under foreign occupation after 1066. As queen consort she was of course in a powerful position to exercise such influence as she could.

There were other, more subtle ways in which the women of the Conquest period left a conscious trail of reminiscences. Take, for example, Tostig's widow Judith, whom we have met before as benefactor of the Bavarian monastery of Weingarten in her capacity as wife of Duke Welf of Bavaria. There is no doubt in my mind that she was a prime witness for the 1066 details we find in late-eleventh-century Bavarian chronicles and annals. One of the most persistent stories circulating there must have been generated by Judith's belief that her first husband Tostig, instead of his older brother Harold, should have succeeded to the throne of England. She is undoubtedly the source for the persistent rumour that she was the widow of the king of England, who brought with her a fabulous amount of wealth.[54] Even her obituary at Weingarten lists the claim of her royal widowhood. The rivalry between Tostig and Harold is independently confirmed by the biographer of King Edward, who says that Tostig was the king's favourite. Clearly, Judith fostered a sense of frustration till the end of her life that her first husband had lost out to his brother Harold in all respects and that he, not Harold, should have been king and she a queen.

Lay women, and in particular mothers, had family links to pass on traditions to their children and grandchildren. But what happened in English nunneries? Did nuns play a role in the transfer of traditions beyond 1066? To avoid union with foreigners, the only alternative for English women was to take up the veil and retreat to a nunnery. This had apparently happened to such a large extent that in the 1080s, Archbishop Lanfranc turned to his Norman colleague Bishop Geoffrey of Coutances for expert advice on canon law.[55] The problem was that many women, who had become nuns not out of vocation, but 'out of fear for the French', wished to leave the convent. Lanfranc, prepared to be flexible, confirmed that his will was also that of the king, and allowed the women to depart provided that their fellow nuns would testify that they had entered under duress. Two decades later Queen Matilda II, in a conversation with Archbishop Anselm, confirmed the story of the women taking refuge in nunneries, hinting that she had been one of them herself. On balance, many women who could afford the nunnery's entrance fee preferred life within the cloister to sharing a bed with a foreigner.

One of the reasons why it is difficult to trace evidence for the manner in which 1066 was remembered in nunneries is the paucity of documentary evidence from such houses. What we have are little more than snippets here and there. On several occasions we have looked at the nunnery of Romsey, where the Anglo-Saxon royal cousins Queen Matilda II and her sister Mary were looked after by their Aunt Christina, a sister of their mother Queen Margaret. They were joined by Gunhild, daughter of King Harold, who was apparently left behind while the rest of her family (her grandmother Gytha, her aunt Gunhild and her aunt Judith) went into exile in Flanders. Did the fact that they belonged to rival royal clans make any difference to the way in which they perceived the Norman Conquest? It is interesting to note that in the end, all three aristocratic women left monastic life for marriage: Matilda married Henry I of England; Mary went overseas to Boulogne as wife of Eustace III; and Gunhild, whose further fate is unknown, eloped with Count Alan the Black of Brittany, a feat for which she was severely reprimanded by Anselm.[56] All three belonged to the category of women who, in a sense, had been forced to retreat to monastic life while the country was in turmoil. Yet the coming and going of these aristocratic women may be explained differently.

As English women they were not alone in the nunneries. They were joined by foreign women, who were established there by fathers and brothers who were busy consolidating their new acquisitions in England.

Having their womenfolk inside rich monastic houses helped to prepare the ground for general acceptance of the newcomers in England. One of them was the unnamed daughter of Stephen fitz Airard, captain of the Conqueror's flagship, the Mora.[57] One cannot but wonder about the conversations that would have taken place at Romsey between the women representing such different political backgrounds. In Wilton we find similar tensions. There Queen Edith, widow of King Edward the Confessor, retired and died in 1075. A few years later Eve, the daughter of a Danish-Lotharingian couple, who had entered the monastery in 1065, left to take up life as a recluse on the Continent at Angers.[58] Did political animosity between rival ethnic groups cloud the atmosphere in nunneries or do we envisage the women serenely living a life of prayer and contemplation together? And what did such tensions do to the memorial tradition in monasteries? It must have been extraordinarily difficult – as we know, for example from the monks' community at Christ Church, Canterbury – to rebuild anything resembling a communally satisfying memorial tradition in these establishments.

At Barking we find the first hints of a more permanent literary memorial revival much later in the twelfth century. At the beginning of the century, the nun Matilda was actively involved in a miracle performed through the intervention of King Edward, while later on a nun, probably Clemence, wrote a verse life of Edward the Confessor in Old French. The sympathies of these nuns were with the old Anglo-Saxon dynasty more than with the new Norman family. This seems to have been the overriding, lasting sentiment in the English nunneries, for at Chatteris, near Ely, the nun Marie reworked a Latin life of St Etheldreda as a *Vie Seinte Audrée* in French.[59]

Nunneries were not the only monastic houses to offer shelter to beleaguered girls and women in the post-Conquest period. At Crowland, Earl Waltheof's memory was guarded by the English and French monks who offered to bury the body of the only Anglo-Saxon aristocrat to be executed for treason by William the Conqueror. Whether the inspiration for his burial at Crowland, one of the last abbeys to submit to foreign rule, came from the monks or from the earl's widow, Countess Judith niece of the Conqueror himself, remains a mystery. Crowland too was the place where a romantic tale of Judith's refusal to remarry was written down. Allegedly, she refused a landless northern French soldier, Simon of Senlis, whom she passed on to her daughter and heiress Maud.[60] Considering the fact that for the next three generations only women passed on her line and kept in touch with the monks of Crowland, it is tempting to believe that the story went the same, female, route before it was committed to writing. It was also Crowland that offered to look after Hereward's Flemish widow Turfrida, if a fifteenth-century tradition is to be believed. Whether or not these late stories are true, they testify to a growing perception in English monasteries that the post-Conquest period took its toll particularly of women. It is therefore no wonder that memories about the conquest, partially fuelled by women's experiences, were kept alive through oral tradition before they were written down three or four generations later.

   This case study of the memory of 1066 shows the various ways in which different generations remember the Conquest and its aftermath. In the first place, there is the oral evidence which was passed on through several generations before it was recorded in writing. We have seen how men and women remembered stories, but that it was mostly, though not exclusively, men who put pen to paper. Virtually all oral stories exchanged by the Normans and the English were part of the social process to come to terms with the momentous change in landholding patterns, new customs and above all the intrusion of a new language. Secondly, the quite exceptional circumstances of a complete take-over of one country by the elite of another resulted in personal memories of people from different ethnic backgrounds (Norman, Breton, Angevin, Flemish, et cetera), from both the victorious and the victimized sides, so that from the first down to the fourth generation, each family had its own version of events to tell. Historians from the second generation onwards began to write, though new stories kept emerging well into the late twelfth century. Thirdly, the evidence presented here shows that gender played an important part in the remembrance of things past. Men *and* women were responsible for passing on stories about the events of 1066 and we should not underestimate the role of at least three English women whose sons, Orderic, Henry and William, became the most famous chroniclers of the Conquest.

7

CONCLUSION

Remembrance of things past is inextricably bound up with family life. Medieval people had parents, grandparents and great-grandparents whom they remembered if not personally, then through the stories told by others. Then, as now, the overlapping circles of the three-generation family, and of their wider kin, generated the stories about the past discussed in this book. The evidence for knowledge amongst the noble classes and literate people, that is those groups who have left documentation about their ancestors, is overwhelming. What are the more specific conclusions we can draw if we remind ourselves of the three broad themes which we have discussed in this book: oral tradition, memory and gender?

Oral Tradition

Much information about the past circulated orally before it was written down. Those people who recorded oral stories did so extremely conscientiously, noting down all the links in the chain of informants they could remember. As far as authority was concerned, eyewitnesses were considered the most trustworthy informants and the value of authority decreased the further away one moved from the original informant. In the absence of eyewitnesses, any person knowing someone linked to the original informant or event was useful. Amongst the informants men, and particularly church men, rated highest followed by lay noble men. Women were only quoted if they could not be avoided. In other words, if the sole available informant was a woman she was heard, but a great deal of scepticism was attached to her story.

Great care was taken to record the links in the chain of evidence, a care which should not be underestimated or ridiculed. The precarious oral links in conjunction with the perishable nature of any written record on wax tablets, scrappy notes or even parchment in single copies meant that documentation remained immensely vulnerable. The vulnerability of any information about the past was therefore well known in the central Middle Ages. It is my firm belief that medieval people were profoundly conscious of this and that for this reason, they did what they could to acknowledge chains of information. We may now consider some of these techniques clumsy, awkward and unsophisticated. In a society where writing was still reserved for the rich and privileged, oral communication was a vital way to pass on information about the past from generation to generation. Descriptions of ways in which knowledge about the past were preserved should be considered as genuine attempts to salvage what was thought to be necessary information for posterity.

Considering the fragile nature of ways of recording oral evidence, the oral evidence itself remained even more fragile and liable to be forgotten in the mists of time. The evidence presented in this book, whether pertaining to historiography or hagiography, or stored in other sources shows that usually, after three or four generations, someone in a community, normally within a family, decided that it was time to write down the information about the past. This means that stories normally circulated orally for three to four generations and that during this period, they were liable to undergo alterations, embellishments and variations. Then, as now, oral stories changed and people were aware of that. In the period under consideration there is a marked increase in the amount of evidence acknowledged in texts as coming from oral sources.

With the development of literacy as a tool of government, administration, and particularly religion, written modes of communication increased. The written word provided more accurate ways of checking what had happened in the past if events or transactions were recorded. The benefits of such records as proof of what had taken place influenced people in the way they increased the recording of other oral information, even if it went back a long time. The urge to capture, or freeze, stories in writing could also be observed with regard to objects. Even material evidence only made sense through stories attached to them, identifying donors, detailing the circumstances of a gift or the chain of hands through which an object had passed. Such information, usually only available orally, was often written down by the monks of the monasteries who ultimately acquired the objects: either on the objects themselves by means of inscriptions (ceremonial vestments, jewellery or precious vessels) or in separate written documents listing the monastic treasures. The increase in evidence of orality is therefore a direct result of the greater frequency with which the written word was applied. The oral tradition, however, was never replaced by a written tradition. Both modes of communications remained in existence, cross-fertilizing each other.

Memory

This book has surveyed how between 900 and 1200 people remembered their past and recorded their experiences in oral and written traditions. As we have seen, most of the traditions recorded were those that pertained to the family, the kin group consisting of a nuclear family of father, mother, children, grandchildren, grandparents and sometimes also great-grandparents. Family stories that were collected normally stretched back three or four generations to the great-grandparents. Alternatively, occasionally we also find stories about grandchildren or great-grandchildren. As far as cousins are concerned, references to second- or third-degree kinship relations are the most one can expect with precise definitions of the degree of blood relationship. Thereafter links become vague.

The increase in that type of literature, often based on oral information written down after the third or fourth generation, can be linked with two major developments in the period under consideration. In the first place, there was the requirement of canon law from the late eleventh century onwards that marriage within seven degrees of kinship was forbidden. In order to know whether one was free to marry, one had to know one's family history back to one's great-great-grandparents and to cousins several times removed. Peter Damian (d. 1072), the brain behind this complicated and totally unworkable scheme, never explained in any of his writings how the counting of degrees of consanguinity should in practice happen.[1] Although he could figure out the blood relationships in theory and the vocabulary appropriate for describing it, there are no hints as to how parish priests and bishops had to cope with the counting in practice.

Nor is there any suggestion in his treatises or letters that people ought to keep a written track of the way their family moved around. That a written record was the only solution to this problem of knowing to whom one was or was not related becomes clear when we take the genealogical literature into account. The episcopal letters and other documents discussed in this book illustrate how men and women had to resort to writing in order to prove the ways in which they were related to other families. In most cases the memorial history of a family before it was written down varied from up to three or four generations to six or seven generations. Thereafter, particularly if the information could be grafted on to an existing document, one could trace ancestors down for further generations. The oral and social memory of a family group normally did not stretch back further than seven at the most. However, the increased written tradition of family records still did not solve the impracticalities of the church's incest prohibition particularly because in small communities all people were related to one another and could not avoid incest according to Damian's definition. At the Fourth Lateran council of 1215, Pope Innocent III was forced to return to the old custom whereby people could marry within four degrees of consanguinity.

The second reason why interest in ancestors, and the past in general, received such a boost in the period between 900 and 1200 is the change in landholding patterns. Georges Duby has argued that the interest in genealogical literature is directly related and, indeed, reflects a major change in ownership of land and offices.[2] On the basis of documentary sources, like charters and the genealogical literature, discussed here in Chapter 4, he concluded that late-eleventh- and twelfth-century family memories do not normally stretch back further than the late tenth or early eleventh century because the memory was attached to the land. Since the land had descended in a more or less straight line from father to son due to primogeniture, the knowledge of family history went in reversed direction along the same route. It stopped where it did in the late tenth century because round about that time the land was held by a large amorphous family clan, who had temporarily been given it by the king. Because central royal authority gave and retrieved land as it suited the king, there was no point in the family knowing the history of the land and therefore people did not record the history of the family. In other words, so Duby argued, the genealogical literature confirms the change in landholding pattern around the end of the first millennium.

This book suggests a different explanation. In the first place, one cannot argue from the absence of written records that social memory of families did not exist. I believe that most families would have exchanged information about relatives in pretty much the same way as they did in the eleventh and twelfth centuries. The evidence from earlier periods and different geographical areas surveyed in this book, for example Ottonian Germany and early-eleventh-century Anglo-Saxon England, suggest a common human pattern of social family memory in oral and written form. Other explanations apart from the one given by Duby are suggested by looking more closely at the gender of those who preserved memories of the past.

Gender

It is with regard to the roles of men and women that this book offers new insights into the ways medieval people preserved knowledge about the past. An impressive amount of evidence from sources ranging from chronicles and saints' lives to objects and wills underlines the important position of women in the passing on of stories and traditions about the past. Much of the transmission of stories took place orally in the context of family history and can therefore only be implicitly found in the sources. Little explicit reference is made to women as witnesses of past events, a result, as we have seen, of women's low status in authority. Since women were not allowed to act as legal witnesses very little public acknowledgement could be given to stories told by them. However, this does not mean that they did not pass on information about the past. On the contrary, women were crucial links in the chain of traditions binding one generation to another.

The role of women as female informants about the past was pretty constant and evenly spread through Europe. The only exception is the wealth of information from Ottonian Germany, where the royal and noble abbesses inspired an impressive array of historiographical and hagiographical literature commemorating their ancestors. But in principle we see the same happening all over Europe, albeit on a smaller scale. There seems to be no decline after the year 1000, nor is there any evidence to substantiate the opinion that, at this same time, a permanent transfer of commemorative responsibilities from (lay) women to monks (and nuns) took place.[3] On the contrary, what strikes us most is the constant interaction between men and women, lay and ecclesiastical.

The collaboration between men and women, however, took place according to more or less defined rules for each gender. Men as persons with legal authority collected stories about the past and wrote them down. They acknowledged primarily male witness accounts and only very rarely and apologetically female reports. They were, however, very happy to use information given to them by both sexes and, indeed, executed commissions for biographies or chronicles given to them by men and women. One interesting characteristic that emerged from the genealogical information shows how men recorded in writing the family traditions which were collected and passed on orally by women. In this context the relationship between maternal uncle and nephew stands out as a significant link between the generations.

Women collected stories about male and female ancestors and passed them on almost exclusively in oral form. The evidence for women as authors and writers remains significantly smaller than for men, even though we have to keep an open mind that in the future more evidence might emerge for female authorship. The oral role of women as transmitters of information about the past emerges, as we have seen, implicitly and by chance, due to the lack of public acknowledgement given to them by men. Nevertheless, their position as vital links in chains of historical information is undeniable. They were important informants for guaranteeing that canonical rules against incest were not breached and that knowledge about land and estates descending in the female line would be preserved. Women's knowledge about the past was not, however, exclusively linked to land they owned or passed on.

One of the remarkable conclusions that can be drawn from the genea-logical material surveyed in Chapter 4 is the amount of information women passed on in the female line, going back through the mother and grandmother to the great-grandmother. In some cases this is because the land owned by the generation responsible for recording the story in writing came from the maternal ancestor, a thesis propounded by Georges Duby. He argued that the family, and in particular the male members of the family who wrote down these texts, was interested in the land and therefore traced back its inheritance, and as a result traced back the female line. Since the social make-up of the ancestry frequently consisted of the higher-born maternal kin versus the lower-born paternal kin, so the argument went, the (male) offspring who were the most politically active had the maternal history recorded. Quite a number of cases, as we have seen, either do not follow the heiress's line but simply record the female line without there being evidence that the land descended through them, or concern women as story-tellers who were daughters or granddaughters of heiresses. In both cases it is the women, not the men, who must have passed on the stories in the female line. It was the women, in other words, who attached political significance to their own ancestry and offered it to their children, male and female, as the (nuclear) family's past.

The fact that the men of the family, usually a son or brother, recorded the stories in writing does not alter the significance of the women as prime movers in the remembrance of things past. The English-born mothers of the three Anglo-Norman historians of the Norman Conquest, William of Malmesbury, Henry of Huntingdon and Orderic Vitalis are the most striking examples in post-Conquest England. Moreover, women's interest in a mother's or grandmother's own personal history and in the whereabouts of cousins seems to have played at least as important a role as (legal) interest in land. Such conclusions neatly parallel Sarah Kay's recent plea to accept the fictional genealogical literature of the twelfth century, the *chansons de geste*, as family 'romances' in which women, and in particular mothers of high-born descent, are dramatically aware of their political role, which they play out to maximum effect.[4]

If this reconstruction is correct, there is another conclusion that can be drawn. A remarkable feature of the genealogical material, both in the genealogies and other sources, traces the female line back through more generations than the male line. Whereas the oral male line often runs out after the (paternal) grandparents are mentioned, the maternal line goes back five or six generations. The evidence of families tracing their origin through the female line to a great-grandmother or great-great-grandmother is significantly larger. In order to explain this we have to bear in mind the ages of the men and women involved. Aristocratic marriage patterns, which were broadly similar all over Europe, suggest that women married from their mid-teens onwards, while men normally waited until their twenties.[5] Such patterns, however, were preserved for the high-status groups and were not the same as those of the lower-status groups for which the, admittedly later, evidence suggests a divide between northern and southern European customs.[6] If they did not die in childbirth but survived, high-status women were close in age to their children, the age difference between the generations being 15 to 20 years. For men who married relatively late and thus had children at an older age, the trend was of a larger age gap between themselves and their children. It follows that if women remembered their ancestors, they remembered mothers, grandmothers and great-grandmothers on the basis of personal knowledge, simply because the age gap between them was much smaller than for men. Men might remember their fathers or grandfathers, but hardly ever their great-grandfather.

This situation might explain why historians like Hugh of Flavigny, the Waltham chronicler, and Walter Map specify that oral tradition is a reliable source of information as long as the chain of informants is limited to the

sons or the grandsons of the men whose events are being narrated. For
Walter Map the maximum span of three male generations was
approximately 100 years, a period he calls the modern times. Although
we have no such explicit statement for female generations, 100 years
could easily comprise five generations of women according to the
calculations given above. It would follow that if 100 years is a notional
period for which oral tradition was considered to be valid, women could
and would cover a greater generation span than men. The evidence
presented in this book certainly supports the view that the men who
wrote down women's stories implicitly accepted that women's memory
stretched back further than that of men.

Finally, this book has stressed the significance of the collaboration
between men and women in the remembrance of things past. This was
neither an exclusive role of men nor of women. Men and women
depended on each other's input to make sure posterity had some notion
of what their ancestors had done. In the seventh century Isidore of Seville
(d. 636) described in his *Etymologies* the degrees of kinship based on
the information set out by Emperor Justinian in his law collection.[7] Right
from the start pictorial evidence was included to visualize the complicated
calculation of consanguinity. It seems fitting to end this book by pointing
out that by the middle of the twelfth century, the illustration for this
particular topic had evolved from a simple graph to a sophisticated
genealogical pyramid showing ancestors, descendants and lateral
relatives. But the most striking aspect of one mid-twelfth-century picture
deserves special mention. The anonymous artist from the monastery of
Zwiefalten (Germany) added a man (Adam) and a woman (Eve),
respectively on the paternal and the maternal side, to the figural
representation of the tree of consanguinity. They are shown with heads
bent and drooping shoulders, clearly burdened by their heavy load of
ancestors. The picture thereby brilliantly visualizes what I have attempted
to show in this book, namely that knowledge of the past in the central
Middle Ages was a shared responsibility and the collaborative task of
both men and women, as well as a set of links between young and old.

APPENDIX 1

The chronicler Aethelweard addresses the prologue of his Latin adaptation of the *Anglo-Saxon Chronicle* in the form of a letter to his distant cousin Abbess Matilda of Essen (Germany) d. 1011, (*The Chronicle of Aethelweard*, ed. and trans. A. Campbell (London, 1962), 1–2)

Ealdorman Fabius Aethelweard [that is noble quaestor] wishes everlasting [salvation] in Christ to his cousin Matilda.

To the most talented Matilda, a true handmaid of Christ, the noble Aethelweard [wishes] salvation in the Lord. Most beloved, I have received the letter I desired from you, and having clasped what you wrote to my soul, I have not merely read it, but have laid it away in the treasury of my heart. Indeed I pray very frequently for the grace of most high God, that he may keep you safe in this life and after departure from the body, conducting you to the everlasting dwellings. Just as we have previously informed you by letter about what is known of our common family and also about the migration of our nation, it is now desirable, with the help of God, employing the annalists from the beginning of the world, to offer a clearer exposition, so that attention may be increased by the gentle voice of the reader and the desire of the listener to hear [may grow]. In the following pages you can very easily find by way of example so many wars and slayings of men and no small wreck of navies on the waves of ocean, especially with reference to the arrival of our ancestors in Britain from Germany, that in the present epistle I dwell in plain style upon our family in modern times and upon the reaffirmation of our relationship, so far as our memory provides proof, and as our parents taught us. Aelfred was the son of Aethelwulf, from whom we are descended; five sons followed him. Of these, I am descended from King Aethelred, and you from King Aelfred, both sons of King Aethelwulf, who has been already mentioned. Aelfred sent his daughter Aelfthryth to the land of Germany to marry Baldwin, who had by her two sons, Aethelwulf and Earnwulf, and also two daughters, Ealhswith and Eormenthryth. From Aelfthryth, as a matter of fact, count Earnwulf, who is your neighbour, is descended.

Aedgyfu was the name of the daughter of King Eadweard, the son of Aelfred, who has been mentioned already, and she was your great-aunt and was sent into the country of Gaul to marry the younger Charles. Eadhild, furthermore, was sent to be the wife of Hugo, son of Robert. King Aethelstan sent another two [of his sisters] to Otho, the plan being that he should choose as his wife the one who pleased him. He chose Eadgyth, from whom you spring in the first place. The other sister he married to a certain king near the Alps, concerning whose family we have no information, because of both the distance and the not inconsiderable lapse of time. But it is your task to bring information to our ears, for you have not only the family connection but the capacity, since distance does not hinder you.

Fare well always and at all times. The prologue ends.

Appendix 2

Letter from Count Rainald of Burgundy/Portois (1027–57) to his nephew Duke Guy-Geoffrey (also known as William VIII) of Aquitaine (1058–89) on their descent from two sisters, the daughters of Queen Gerberga. The letter has survived as an appendix to only one manuscript of Flodoard's Annals, Ms B, Paris Bibliotèque Nationale, Ms lat. 9768, under the year 966 (*Les annales de Flodoard*, ed. Ph. Lauer (Paris, 1905), 158–9, and commentary on liii–lvii).

At that time [966] letters were sent from a certain count to the duke of Aquitaine with these contents: 'Rainald, count of Portois wishes all be best to G[uy], duke of Aquitaine. I have to cancel completely our meeting and my departure on which you advised me, for my age and other impediments have prevented my journey. However the genealogy, or record of our kinship, which you wanted me to give to you during the visit, I have had written down in this letter, as far as I know it: Matilda and Albereda were daughters of Gerberga. Matilda gave birth to King Rodulf and his sister Matilda; Albereda gave birth to Ermentrudis. Matilda, daughter of Matilda, [gave birth to] Berta. Ermentrudis [gave birth to] Agnes. Berta [gave birth to] Gerald of Genève; and Agnes [gave birth to] Guy.'

APPENDIX 3

The noble widow Beatrix writes to her brother Bishop Udo of Hildesheim, *c*. 1079–80 (*Briefsammlungen der Zeit Heinrichs IV*, ed. C. Erdmann and N. Fickermann, *Monumenta Germaniae Historica: Die Deutsche Geschichtsquellen des Mittelalters 500–1500, Die Briefe der deutschen Kaiserreich*, 5 (Weimar, 1950), 64–7: I am very grateful to Dr Neil Wright for his assistance with the translation).

To her most beloved lord and brother Udo, bishop by the grace of the Lord, Beatrix, happy only in name not fortune, [sends] what befits a sister to her brother, a beloved to her most beloved, and only one to her only one.

But I would like to give you an account of my misfortunes – provided I do not seem to burden your mind, which is occupied with many matters – so that, when you have heard the state of my affairs, I may find in you timely aid. The first and foremost of my ills, the misery of my soul, is that my sons live as wanderers and exiles in a land which is not their own; and that a foreign hand, albeit kindly, serves men whose wealth once surpassed, or easily equalled, the richest in their homeland. Their virtue – for virtue excites envy – had stirred up the hatred of the envious against them to the point of civil strife, and, seeing that they could not counter the injuries inflicted by their enemies, they preferred to abandon everything rather than their virtue. My younger children, those who still live with me to be cherished and nourished in the maternal bosom, cannot be [safe] because of their tender years. For both the king's power and the violence of our enemies have usurped for themselves almost all the estates which ought to have gone in inheritance to my son Heriman; thus the fact that he had brothers damages my son in the king's eyes. As for my daughter Sophia, who is hidden like a concealed theft, a certain person dares to hope that she will be his wife, though he is totally unworthy of this ambition; and, while he considers our misfortune rather than our ancestry, strives to compensate his low birth at the cost of our nobility. Thus the fruit of my womb, formerly my pride, is now my disgrace, and I, who seemed to have given birth to joy, have brought forth sorrow.

Finally, to come to myself, the king's authority has constricted the extent of my estates by so narrow, so unjust a boundary that he has reduced me to poverty from great riches. On the pretext of various matters he has taken from me gold, silver, clothes, everything; he was not ashamed to persecute a woman, and for the sole reason that I bore such sons. Those who formerly feared me now despise me, now necessity forces me to approach my enemies and to seek advice and aid from them, with the result that I truly avow that I was born as a parable of Fortune, since from a great pinnacle of power she has cast me down into a pit of misery.

So, you have heard the mournful epilogue of my misfortune; now I beg, hear my request with the ear not only of the flesh but also of the heart. Thus I ask you by the goodwill which you owe me through your brotherly blood that, if by agreement the Saxons surrender themselves to the king's majesty, you remember my sons in exile there; and do not to your disgrace and shame permit them to be excluded from any agreement of reconciliation, seeing that they have borne along with you the burden of the same cause, indeed all the more onerously since they were weaker, being deprived of any allies. Should my son Conrad come to you, receive him graciously and treat him more so. As for my daughter Sophia, who is now ripe for marriage, and whose age and beauty incite against her unworthy abductors because her brothers' protection no longer defends her from violence, try to join her in marriage where it may be honourable and fitting, and ensure, since I cannot, that she does not marry beneath herself to the disgrace of her family; for, just as an increase in her honour reflects the shared honour of her family, so her dishonour is our common shame. If the occasion presents itself, promote the lady Burtgarda, my daughter who is married in Christ, to a respectable position befitting her vows, so that your advancement to high office is also to our benefit, glory and promotion. Further, since excessive requests can be made by a sister without much loss of modesty in her brother's eyes, the need of my own situation begs and demands your help. Finally, I implore you to recognize the justice of my claim to my estates, which my brother, lord H. of blessed memory, took for himself in unbrotherly spirit; and that out of regard for justice you cause to return to me those things which ought by inheritance to be mine.

Please send me a sure and swift report of what I can expect concerning all this. May the Lord grant me that we soon see each other in peace, we who have for so long now been apart in place if not in mind. Amen. Farewell in Christ, dearest brother.

In addition to all this, I most humbly request your grace, as is just, that, if your brotherly love sees fit to send us anything of what we require, it be set out in writing point by point and sealed with your name to avoid deception.

Appendix 4

Robert of Torigni inserted many genealogies of Anglo-Norman families into his version of the *Gesta Normannorum Ducum*, written in the late 1130s. All genealogies ultimately stem from Countess Gunnor of Normandy (*c.* 960–1031), her sisters Sainsfrida, Wevia and Duvelina, and unnamed nieces (her sisters' daughters) (*The Gesta Normannorum Ducum of William of Jumièges, Orderic Vitalis and Robert of Torigni*, ed. and trans. E. M. C. van Houts, 2 (Oxford, 1995), 266–75).

Book VIII, Chapter 36

Because we have referred to countess Gunnor on account of Roger of Montgomery's mother, her niece, I should like to write down the story as reported by people of old of how Gunnor came to be Duke Richard [I]'s wife. One day when Duke Richard was told of the celebrated beauty of the wife of one of his foresters, who lived in a place called Equiqueville near the town of Arques, he deliberately went hunting there in order to see for himself whether the report he had learned from several folk was true. While staying in the forester's house, the duke was so struck by the beauty of his wife's face that he summoned his host to bring his wife, called Sainsfrida, that night to his bedchamber. Very sadly the man reported this to Sainsfrida, a wise woman who comforted him by saying that she would send in her place her sister Gunnor, a virgin even more beautiful than her. And thus it happened. Once the duke perceived the trick he was delighted that he had not committed the sin of adultery with another man's wife. Gunnor bore him three sons and three daughters, as is set out above in the book containing the deeds of this duke. When, however, the duke wished his son Robert to become Archbishop of Rouen, he was told by some people that according to canon law this was impossible, because his mother had not been married. Therefore Duke Richard married Countess Gunnor according to the Christian custom and during the wedding ceremony the children, who were already born, were covered by a cloak together with their parents. Thereafter Robert could be appointed archbishop of Rouen.

Book VIII, Chapter 37

Apart from Sainsfrida, Gunnor had two sisters, Wevia and Duvelina. The latter, with the help of the countess, who was a very wise woman, married Turulf of

Pont-Audemer. He was the son of someone called Torf, after whom several towns are called Tourville to the present day. Turulf's brother was Turketil, father of Ansketil of Harcourt. Turulf had by his wife Humphrey of Vieilles, father of Roger of Beaumont. The third of Countess Gunnor's sisters married Osbern of Bolbec, by whom she bore the first Walter Giffard, and then Godfrey, father of William of Arques. This William was the father of Matilda, who married William of Tancarville, the chamberlain, by whom she bore Rabel, who was his successor. Walter married one of the daughters of Gerard Fleitel. Another of them, Basilia, the widow of Rodulf of Gacé, married Hugh of Gournay, whose succession and offspring have been mentioned above. Walter Giffard had a son called Walter Giffard II as well as many daughters, one of whom, named Rohais, married Richard, son of count Gilbert, who was the son of Godfrey, count of Eu, a natural son of Richard I, duke of the Normans. Gilbert had two sons, Richard and Baldwin. Baldwin had three sons, Richard, Robert, and William, as well as three daughters. Richard, Baldwin's brother, had by Rohais four sons, Gilbert, Roger, Walter and Robert, and two daughters. The second of these married Rodulf of Fougères, by whom she bore Fransvalo, Henry and Robert Giffard. Gilbert acquired his father's lands in England whereas his brother Roger obtained those in Normandy. Gilbert by the daughter of the count of Clermont had three sons, Richard, his successor, Gilbert and Walter, as well as one daughter called Rohais. Richard married the sister of Ranulf the younger, earl of Chester, by whom he had three sons, Gilbert, his successor, and his brothers. Richard met an untimely death, being slain by the Welsh, who once they heard about King Henry's death, started a savage rebellion against the English. When his uncles Roger and Walter died without children, Gilbert, son of Gilbert, by right took over the lands they had conceded to him. He married Count Waleran of Meulan's sister, called Isabel, by whom he had as first-born son Richard. The first-born son by one of the daughters of Waltheof, earl of Huntingdon, succeeded Robert, son of Richard. Waltheof had three daughters by his wife, a daughter of the countess of Aumâle, who had been a half-sister of William the elder, king of the English. Simon of Senlis married another of Earl Waltheof's daughters and received with her the earldom of Huntingdon. He had by her a son called Simon. After the death of Earl Simon, David, brother of Matilda II, queen of the English, married his widow, by whom he had one son. After the death of his brothers Duncan and Alexander, kings of Scots, he became king. Another of Waltheof's daughters, Judith, married Rodulf of Tosny, as we have already mentioned. A third daughter was married to Robert, son of Richard, as we have also mentioned above.

Because we have referred to the sisters of Countess Gunnor, it seems

appropriate to tell something about her kindred to the second degree of
consanguinity, according to the information given by the folk of old. The
countess had by her brother Herfast a nephew Osbern of Crepon, who was
the father of William, earl of Hereford, a man praiseworthy in every way.
Gunnor had many nieces, but I have heard of only five of them who married
husbands. One was the wife of William I of Warenne's father, by whom she
bore William, later earl of Surrey, and his brother Roger of Mortemer.
Another one married Nicholas of Bacqueville, among whose descendants
were William Martel and Walter of Saint-Martin. A third one married
Richard, vicomte of Rouen, father of Lambert of Saint-Saëns. A fourth one
married Osmund of 'Centumvilla', vicomte of Vernon, by whom she bore
Fulk I of Alnou and many daughters, one of whom was the mother of Baldwin
of Reviers. A fifth one married Hugh of Montgomery, by whom she bore
Roger, father of Robert of Bellême.

Book VIII, Chapter 38

Let us return, however, to the events from which we digressed on account of
the genealogies . . .

APPENDIX 5

In 1153 Lambert of Wattrelos (d. *c.* 1170) inserted his family history into his chronicle under the year in which he was born (1108) (*Lamberti Waterlos, Annales Cameracenses*, in *MGH SS*, vol. 16, 511–12).

1108. In this year I was born between Easter and Pentecost. Whose son and descendant I am, I will set out in simple terms for the various readers. I come from the area of Tournai, from the village of Néchin. In that land I received, by the grace of God, these parents: my father, called Alulfus and my mother Gisla. My father was the son of Ingebrand, soldier of Wattrelo and of Havide of Néchin. My grandmother was Havide of Néchin who belonged to a local family of secular standing, for all my grandfather Ingebrand's possessions in Néchin came from her. My grandfather Ingebrand was a relative of Evrard of Wattrelo. This Evrard of Wattrelo had three sons by his wife Disdelde: Elbod, Baldwin and a third one whose name I cannot now remember. Elbod was the eldest and married the sister of Gossuin of Avesnes, the maternal aunt of Walter Puluchet. My grandfather Ingebrand had four sons, namely Ingebrand, Oghot, Gummar, Alulf, and one daughter who died unmarried; any one of them married a woman of secular standing. The eldest son Ingebrand married at Tournai; he, and his offspring, died before his father. Oghot married Gisla, the sister of Rabod of Dossemetz, and their son is Evrard, a soldier and powerful man of arms. Gummar married Mersinde, sister of Gummar of Saméon. She was the niece of the castellan of Tournai. Alulfus, as the youngest of all, married Gisla, the daughter of Radulf of Wattrelo, who bore him six sons and four daughters. I stem from his flesh. Baldwin the eldest of them died during the siege of Soissons. He was already married. My grandfather Radulf, the father of my mother, was a very rich man, a relative of the aforementioned Evrard; he had [gap in text] . . . brothers, ten of whom were slain by the enemy on the same day in the same battle. At home their deeds are still being recorded in an epic poem by jongleurs. My grandfather Radulf had several sisters who were married in the area of Ménin and they bore many children. This Radulf married a noble wife, Resinde, from Ménin-sur-Leie. She descended from ancient nobility in Flanders. She had eleven brothers, of whom four were castellans at the time of Count Robert [II, 1093–1111], the father of Baldwin. She brought with her into marriage male and female serfs, although I say

159

that nobody ought to be a slave unless he has sinned, for the voice of God says: 'He who sins is the slave of sins'. She had so many brothers that it is suitable to say of them: 'The branches extended to the sea and their shoots reached the river'. From this stock many people stem, namely Lambert, abbot of Saint-Bertin and his sister, Gisla abbess of Bourbourg and her nephew Lambert, abbot of Lobbes, and Richard, standard-bearer of Count William the Norman [= Clito], who was killed in the civil war with count Thierry, and the famous soldiers of Lampernisse and the grand people from Furnes, and the other noble people who were blood relations. But let us return to my grandparents. Radulf and Resinde had four sons and four daughters: Tiard and Lambert, who were soldiers, Richard the clerc and Evrard who was the youngest and who died after a fall from his horse. My uncle Lambert together with some of his friends went over to Henry, king of England, who honourable kept him and his companions [in his service]. Tiard, the eldest, later became mayor (alderman) of Wattrelo. He married an honest girl Emma, who bore him soldiers and clercs. The very good king [Henry] handed over to Lambert many estates in Normandy. However, he was wounded in the war between the king of England and Count Balduin of Flanders, took refuge in a church and then died. My brother Baldwin was also present. Richard, of happy memory, having renounced his worldly affairs, went to Mont-Saint-Eloi, where later by God's wish he respectfully became abbot over the brothers and his body was buried there. Of the three daughters of my grandparents, Godelide, the eldest, gave birth to Lambert and Gummar, who both are regular [gap in manuscript: canons?] at Watten. Disdelde gave birth to Radulf, a kind and devout man, who later succeeded his uncle Richard as third abbot of Mont-Saint-Eloi. From Gisla last but not least I, Lambert, spring who by the same uncle Radulf [for Richard] was made a regular canon at the church of Saint Aubert, bishop of Cambrai; [Lambert], who has written down this genealogy of his ancestors according to truthful oral reports and who by the inspired grace of God has inserted this brief account [here].

APPENDIX 6

Gui of Bazoches, chanter of Châlons-sur-Marne (d. 1203), sets out his
paternal and maternal ancestry in a letter (no. 33) to his sister Alice's
son Archdeacon Rainald (*Liber epistularum Guidonis de Basochis*, ed.
H. Adolfsson, Acta Universitatis Stockholmiensis, Studia Latina
Stockholmiensis, 18 (Stockholm, 1969), 141–2).

. . . Remembering who you are and from whom you stem, I beg you
wholeheartedly, that you bend your mind to deal with these matters
pertaining to your family. For you may welcome the special and outstanding
glory of prowess not only because you are born from noble and powerful
counts and magnates on your father's side, but especially because on your
mother's side you stem as a flower equally from imperial and royal stock.
Thus the present historical narrative paints [the relationship] as follows:
the magnificent Clovis, first Christian king of France, had a son Chlothar.
Chlothar had Blitild, who bore the famous man Ansbert Duke Arnold. Duke
Arnold's sons were Duke Arnulf and the holy bishop Ansigisis of Metz.
Ansigisis's son was Pippin II. Pippin's son was Charles Martel. Charles
Martel's son was King Pippin. Emperor Pippin's son was Charlemagne.
Charlemagne's son was Emperor Louis the Pious. Emperor Louis the Pious's
son was Charles the Bald. Charles the Bald's son was Louis the Bald. Louis's
son was Charles the Simple. Charles the Simple's son was another Louis,
who by Gerberga daughter of Emperor Henry and sister of Otto, had Lothar,
Charles and Matilda. Matilda's son was Arnulf II count of Flanders, whose
son was Baldwin with the Beard; he is said to be the fourth or the tenth
count depending on whether he his called of Flanders or of Hainault from
the first to our own time when the seventh [count] was Baldwin of Jerusalem.
[He had] a daughter Alice of Rumigni, whose daughter was Havide of
Basoches, mother of Alice of Château Porcien, your mother, and my most
beloved sister.

The same Charles, son of Louis and Gerberga, father of Lothar, had a daughter
called Gerberga; her son was Duke Lambert, whose son was Henry of Louvain
and his children were Godfrey and Ida. Ida's daughter was the aforementioned
Alice, the grandmother of your mother. Thus as these histories show you stem
as 25th from Clovis, the first Christian king of France, through Matilda, daughter
of Louis and Gerberga, or 24th through her brother Duke Charles and 11th
through him from Henry the first Roman emperor of Saxon origin.

ABBREVIATIONS

AA SS   *Acta Sanctorum quotquot toto orbe coluntur* (Antwerp 1643–1940), 67 vols.

MGH SS   *Monumenta Germaniae Historica* (Hanover, 1826 onwards).

Migne, *PL*   *Patrologia latina* , ed. J. P. Migne (Paris, 1844–64), 221 vols.

NOTES

CHAPTER 1 INTRODUCTION

1. For the modern commemoration of the First World War, see J. Winter, *Sites of Memory, Sites of Mourning: The Great War in European Cultural History* (Cambridge, 1995).
2. R. Thomas, *Oral Tradition and Written Record in Classical Athens* (Cambridge, 1989); M. T. Clanchy, *From Memory to Written Record. England 1066–1307*, 2nd edn (Oxford, 1993); D. R. Woolf, 'The "common voice": history, folklore and oral tradition in early modern England', *Past and Present*, 120 (1988), 26–54; and P. Thompson, *The Voice of the Past*, 2nd edn (Oxford, 1988).
3. R. Samuel, *Theatres of Memory* (London, 1994), 3–50, 315–80.
4. H. Vollrath, 'Das Mittelalter in der Typik oraler Gesellschaften', *Historische Zeitschrift*, 233 (1981), 571–98.
5. J. Vansina, *Oral Tradition* (Harmondsworth, 1961); and *Oral Tradition as History* (London, 1985).
6. E. Tonkin, *Narrating our Pasts. The Social Construction of Oral History* (Cambridge, 1992), 93–4; J. Fentress and C. Wickham, *Social Memory* (Oxford, 1992), 96–7.
7. D. H. Green, *Medieval Listening and Reading. The Primary Reception of German Literature 800–1300* (Cambridge, 1994) though written from a different perspective also emphasizes the social component of listening and reading.
8. R. McKitterick, *The Carolingians and the Written Word* (Cambridge, 1989).
9. J. Nelson, 'Literacy in Carolingian government', *The Uses of Literacy in Early Medieval Europe*, ed. R. McKitterick (Cambridge, 1990), 258–96.
10. M. Innes, 'Memory, orality and literacy in an early medieval society', *Past and Present*, 158 (1998), 3–36.
11. B. Stock, *The Implications of Literacy. Written Language And Models of Interpretation in the Eleventh and Twelfth Centuries* (Princeton, 1983), 42–58, 88–150.
12. M. Richter in his *The Oral Tradition in the Early Middle Ages*, Typologie des sources du moyen âge occidental, 71 (Turnhout, 1994), on the other hand, pays exclusive attention to oral tradition.
13. B. Guenée, 'Temps de l'histoire et temps de la mémoire au moyen âge', *Annuaire-Bulletin de la Société de l'histoire de France. Années 1976–77* (Paris, 1978), 25–35; J. Dunbabin, Discovering a past for the French aristocracy', *The Perception of the Past in Twelfth-Century Europe*, ed. P. Magdalino (London, 1992), 1–14.
14. J. Fentress and C. Wickham, *Social Memory* (Oxford, 1992), 100, 112–13.
15. K. Stringer, *Rethinking History* (London, 1991), 5–26; Samuel, *Theatres of Memory*, 3–48.

16. M. Carruthers, *The Book of Memory. A Study of Memory in Medieval Culture* (Cambridge, 1990).

17. Hugh of St Victor, cited in Carruthers, *The Book of Memory*, 265.

18. M. de Jong, *In Samuel's Image. Child Oblation in the Early Medieval West* (Leiden, 1996).

19. B. Rosenwein, *To be the Neighbour of St Peter; The Social Meaning of the Property of Cluny 909–1049* (Ithaca, 1989); and S. D. White, *Custom, Kinship and Gifts to Saints: The Laudatio Parentum in Western France, 1050–1150* (Chapel Hill, 1988).

20. N. Huyghebaert, *Les documents nécrologiques*, Typologie des sources du moyen âge occidental, 4 (Turnhout, 1972); O. G. Oexle, 'Memoria und Memorialüberlieferung im früheren Mittelalter', *Frühmittelalterliche Studien*, 10 (1976), 70–95; K. Schmid, 'Die Sorge der Salier um ihre Memoria', *Memoria. Der Geschichtliche Zeugniswert des liturgischen Gedenken im Mittelalter*, ed. K. Schmid, J. Wollasch (München, 1984,) 666–726.

21. A. G. Remensnyder, 'Legendary treasure at Conques: reliquaries and imaginative memory', *Speculum*, 71 (1996), 884–906; and her book *Remembering Kings Past: Monastic Foundation Legends in Medieval Southern France* (Ithaca, 1995).

22. C. Wickham, 'Lawyers' time: history and memory in tenth- and eleventh-century Italy', in H. Mayr-Harting and R. I. Moore (eds), *Studies in Medieval History Presented to R. H. C. Davis* (London, 1985), 53–71.

23. I. Hofmeyer, *'We spend our years as a tale that is told'*, *Oral Historical Narrative in a South African Chiefdom* (Johannesburg and London, 1994,) 25–38, 167–70.

24. L. Vail and L. White, *Power and the Praise Poem. South African Voices in History* (Charlottesville and London, 1991), 231–77.

25. *Hrotsvithae opera*, ed. H. Homeyer (Paderborn, 1970); P. Dronke, *Women Writers of the Middle Ages* (Cambridge, 1984), 55–83; *The Alexiad of Anna Comnena*, trans. E. R. A. Sewter (Harmondsworth, 1969).

26. J. L. Nelson, 'Perceptions du pouvoir chez les historiennes du Haut Moyen Âge', *Les femmes au Moyen Âge*, ed. M. Rouche (Paris, 1990), 77–85.

27. R. McKitterick, 'Frauen und Schriftlichkeit im Frühmittelalter', *Weiblicher Lebensgestaltung im frühen Mittelalter*, ed. W. Goetz (Cologna, 1991), 65–118, esp. 95–111.

28. For a summary of previous scholarship, see E. M. C. van Houts, 'Women and the writing of history: the case of Abbess Matilda of Essen and Aethelweard', *Early Medieval Europe*, I (1992), 53–68 and G. Althoff, 'Gandersheim und Quedlinburg. Ottonische Frauenklöster als Herschafts- und Überlieferungszentern', *Frühmittelalterliche Studien*, 25 (1991), 123–44.

29. P. Geary, *Phantoms of Remembrance. Memory and Oblivion at the End of the First Millennium* (Princeton, 1994), 48–80.

Part I Gender and the Authority of Oral Witnesses

CHAPTER 2 CHRONICLES AND ANNALS

1. *Isidori Hispalensis episcopi Etymologiarum sive Originum libri xx*, ed. W. M. Lindsay, 1 (Oxford, 1910), lib. I, *c.* xli.
2. Quoted by B. and P. Sawyer, *Medieval Scandinavia*, The Nordic Series, 17 (Minneapolis and London, 1993), 25.
3. *Rodulfus Glaber, Opera* (Glaber), ed. J. France, N. Bulst and P. Reynolds (Oxford, 1989), 202; *William Newburgh, Historia rerum Anglicarum* (William Newburgh), ed. R. Howlett (London, 1884), 239; *Walter Map, De Nugis Curialium. Courtiers' Trifles* (Walter Map), ed. M. R. James, C. N. L. Brooke and R. A. B. Mynors (Oxford, 1983), 121, 142; *Otto von Freising, Chronica sive de duabus civitatibus* (Otto of Freising), ed. A. Hofmeister and W. Lammers (Darmstadt, 1961), 504, 556.
4. Glaber, 114, 276; *Wilhelmi Malmesbiriensis de gestis regum Anglorum* (William of Malmesbury, GRA), ed. W. Stubbs (London, 1887–89), vol. I, 198, vol. II, 345–6; William Newburgh, 80–1; *The Chronicle of Battle Abbey* (Battle Abbey Chronicle), ed. E. Searle (Oxford, 1980), 104–6; *Peregrin de Fontaine-les-Blanche, Historia monasterii beatae de Fontanis* (Peregrin), ed. A. Salmon, *Recueil des chroniques de Touraine* (Tours, 1954), 259, 273.
5. *The Waltham Chronicle* (Waltham Chronicle), ed. L. Watkiss and M. Chibnall (Oxford, 1994), 44, 46, 60; *The Gesta Normannorum Ducum of William of Jumièges, Orderic Vitalis and Robert of Torigni* (GND), ed. E. M. C. van Houts (Oxford, 1992–95), 2, 60; *Frutolfs und Ekkehards Chroniken und die anonyme Kaiserchronik* (Frutolf, Ekkehard), ed. F. J. Schmale and I. Schmale-Ott (Darmstadt, 1972), 176–8; and for pre-1000 sections of both chronicles *Ekkehardi chronicon universale* (Ekkehard), ed. G. Waitz, *MGH SS*, vol. 6, 33–265.
6. Walter Map, 144–6; *De moribus et actis primorum Normanniae ducum auctore Dudone sancti Quintini decano* (Dudo), ed. J. Lair (Caen, 1865), 120, 125, 289.
7. *Annales Altahensis maiores*, ed. W. Giesebrecht and E. ab Oefele, *MGH SS*, vol. 20, 817–18 ; *La chronique de Saint-Maixent, 751–1140* (Chronicle of Saint-Maixent), ed. J. Verdon (Paris, 1979), 148 ; *Adémar de Chabannes, Chronique* (Adémar), ed. J. Chavanon (Paris, 1897), 175.
8. *Chronicon Novaliciense*, ed. L. C. Bethmann, *MGH SS*, vol. 7, 73–133, esp. 95. This particular case was recently translated and discussed by P. J. Geary, *Phantoms of Remembrance. Memory and Oblivion at the End of the First Millennium* (Princeton, 1994), 71–2.
9. Translation from Geary, *Phantoms*, 71–2.
10. S. Shahar, *Growing Old in the Middle Ages. 'Winter clothes us in Shadow and Pain'* (London, 1997), 82–6.
11. R. I. Page, *Chronicles of the Vikings. Records, Memorials and Myths* (London, 1995), 26.
12. Ibid., 26–7.

13. *Leonis Marsicani et Petri Diaconi, chronica monasterii Casinensis*, ed. W. Wattenbach, *MGH SS*, vol. 7, 657–8; the translation was made available by Dr Graham Loud.

14. Walter Map, 462–4 (King Henry II), and 80, 136–8; for other examples see William of Malmesbury, GRA, vol. 1, 322; Glaber, 244, 258; Peregrin, 259, 273.

15. *Hugonis Flaviacensis chronicon* (Hugh of Flavigny), ed. G. Pertz, *MGH SS*, vol. 8, 285–502, esp. 369.

16. Hugh of Flavigny, 394.

17. Waltham Chronicle, 18; Walter Map, 122.

18. Shahar, *Growing Old in the Middle Ages*, 72, 82–6.

19. Waltham Chronicle, 18.

20. William of Malmesbury, GRA, vol. 2, 333.

21. *Fragmentum historiae Andegavensis* (Fulk of Anjou), ed. L. Halphen and R. Poupardin, *Chroniques des comtes d'Anjou et des seigneurs d'Amboise* (Paris, 1913), 232; *Lamberti Waterlos, Annales Cameracenses* (Lambert of Wattrelos), *MGH SS*, vol. 16, 511–12; *Lamberti Ardensis, Historia comitum Ghisnensium*, ed. I. Heller, *MGH SS*, vol. 24, 607, 636.

22. Walter Map, 490; William Newburgh, 86.

23. Frutolf of Michelsberg, see Ekkehard, 182. Another example of relics being exchanged as part of the diplomatic mission of Duke Hugh of the Franks to King Aethelstan can be found in William of Malmesbury, GRA, vol. 1, 150, although in this case he says that he relied on a tenth-century poem, now lost (C. R. Dodwell, *Anglo-Saxon Art. A New Perspective* (Ithaca, 1982), 74, 156. Since part of the relics had subsequently been given to Malmesbury, he presumably saw them himself and had heard about them.

24. Battle Abbey Chronicle, 90, 96, 104, 128; and *Guibert de Nogent, Autobiographie*, ed. E. R. Labande (Paris, 1981), 188–90.

25. *Annales Fuldensis*, ed. G. Pertz, *MGH SS*, vol. 1, 370.

26. William of Malmesbury, GRA, vol. 2, 332, 342, 432; *William of Malmesbury, Historia Novella* (William of Malmesbury, HN), ed. K. Potter (London, 1955), 70.

27. Walter Map, 344; William Newburgh, 82.

28. William Newburgh, 80-1.

29. Glaber, 52.

30. William of Malmesbury, GRA, vol. 1, 259.

31. *Robert of Torigni, Chronicle*, ed. R. Howlett (London, 1889), 310.

32. *Gesta Herewardi incliti exulis et militis*, ed. T. D. Hardy and C. T. Martin, *Lestorie des Engles solum la translacion maistre Geffrei Gaimar* (London, 1888), 339–40; and P. G. Schmidt, 'Biblisches und hagiographisches Kolorit in den *Gesta Herwardi*' ed. K. Walsh and D. Wood *The Bible in the Medieval World. Essays in Memory of Beryl Smalley*, Studies in Church History, Subsidia, 4 (Oxford, 1985) 85–95.

33. Battle Abbey Chronicle, 104–6.

34. *Orderic Vitalis, Historia Ecclesiastica*, ed. M. Chibnall, 3 (Oxford, 1972), 218.

35. William of Malmesbury, GRA, vol. 1, 155, 165, 229.

36. Walter Map, 404.

37. Lamberti Ardensis, 607, 636.
38. Ekkehard, 186.
39. Lambert's text can be found in Appendix 5.
40. Fulk of Anjou, 233.
41. William of Malmesbury, GRA, vol. 2, 484; William of Malmesbury, HN, 77.
42. *Robert of Torigni, Chronicle*, 239, 303.
43. Glaber, 66–8.
44. William of Malmesbury, GRA, vol. 1,122, 129, 164, 181.
45. William Newburgh, 21–2; cf. Orderic Vitalis, vol. 3, 106–8. Eadmer, *Historia Novorum*, ed. M. Rule (London, 1884), 25; William of Malmesbury, GRA, vol. 2, 337–8; *Le Roman de Rou de Wace*, ed. A. Holden (Paris, 1971), vol. 2, 231–3; B. Guenée, *Histoire et culture historique dans l'Occident médiéval* (Paris, 1991), 80–1.
46. *Robert of Torigni, Chronicle*, 135.
47. *Regino of Prüm, Chronicon*, ed. G. Pertx, *MGH SS*, vol. 1, 598–600.
48. Adémar, 175, *Oxford Latin Dictionary*, ed. P. G. W. Glare (Oxford, 1982,) 766: *glattio*.
49. P. Damian-Grint, 'Truth, trust and evidence in the Anglo-Norman *Estoire*,' *Anglo-Norman Studies* 18 (1995), 63–78.
50. This is a well known fact. For discussions and more examples, see Guenée, *Histoire,* 91–109.
51. B. Guenée, 'Temps de l'histoire et temps de la mèmoire au Moyen Âge', *Annuaire-Bulletin de la Société de l'histoire de France, années 1976–77* (Paris, 1978), 25–35; H. W. Goetz, 'Zum Geschichtsbewusstsein in der alamannisch-schweizerischen Klosterchronistik des hohen Mittelalters (11–13 Jahrhundert)', *Deutsches Archiv,* 44 (1988), 454–88, esp. 466–7; E. M. C. van Houts, *Local and Regional Chronicles,* Typologie des sources du moyen âge occidental, 74 (Turnhout, 1995), 28.
52. P. Brand, 'Time out of mind: the knowledge and use of the eleventh- and twelfth-century past in thirteenth-century litigation', in *Anglo-Norman Studies*, 16 (1993), 37–54.
53. Frutolf, see Ekkehard, 130; Otto of Freising, 332.
54. D. H. Green, *Medieval Listening and Reading. The Primary Reception of German Literature 800–1300* (Cambridge, 1994), 242–3.
55. P. Dronke, *Women Writers of the Middle Ages* (Cambridge, 1984), 64–7, 76–7.
56. *The Alexiad of Anna Comnena*, trans. E. R. A. Sewter (Harmondsworth, 1969), 125, 460–1.
57. Ibid., 46, 460.
58. Ibid., 133, 143.
59. Ibid., 461. Recently it has been suggested that Anna's work was the result of close co-operation between herself and her (late) husband Nikephoros Bryennios, who would have been responsible for the substantial 'warfare' sections, see J. Howard-Johnston, 'Anna Komnena and the *Alexiad*', *Alexios I Komnenos*, ed. M. Mullett and D. Smythe, Belfast Byzantine Texts and Translations, 4:1 (Belfast, 1996), 260–302, esp. 276–88. I owe this reference to Jean Dunbabin, who kindly drew my attention to this important study.

CHAPTER 3   SAINTS' LIVES AND MIRACLES

1. B. Bischoff, 'Wer ist die Nonne von Heidenheim?', *Studien und Mitteilungen zur Geschichte des Benediktinerordens*, 49 (1931), 387–97; and P. Dronke, *Women Writers of the Middle Ages* (Cambridge, 1984), 33–4.

2. *Lupus de Ferrières, Correspondence*, ed. L. Levillain (Paris, 1927), 52–6, see esp. 52–4. *The letters of Lupus of Ferrières*, trans. G. W. Regenos (The Hague, 1966), 18–19.

3. *The Anglo-Saxon Missionaries in Germany*, trans. C. H. Talbot (London, 1981), 205–6.

4. T. Head, *Hagiography and the Cult of Saints. The Diocese of Orleans, 800–1200* (Cambridge, 1990), 83.

5. *Three Lives of English Saints*, ed. M. Winterbottom (Toronto, 1972), 67; and Head, *Hagiography*, 79.

6. *Sancti Odonis de vita sancti Geraldi Aureliacensis comitis libri quatuor*, ed. Migne, *PL*, 133, 641–704, esp. 641; *St Odo of Cluny, being the Life of St Odo of Cluny by John of Salerno and the Life of St Gerald of Aurillac by St Odo*, trans. D. G. Sitwell (London, 1958), 91. For a discussion of the date of the different versions of the *Life of Saint Gerald*, see A. M. Bultot, 'Le dossier de saint Géraud d'Aurillac' *Francia*, 22/1 (1995) 173–206.

7. E. M. C. van Houts, 'Women and the writing of history: the case of Abbess Matilda of Essen and Aethelweard', *Early Medieval Europe*, 1 (1992), 53–68 where references to older literature can be found.

8. *Vita Adelheidis abbatissae Vilicensis auct. Bertha*, ed. O. Holder-Egger, *MGH SS*, vol. 15:2, 754–63.

9. The best survey of Goscelin's career and literary life can be found in *The Life of King Edward who rests at Westminster*, ed. and trans. F. Barlow, 2nd edn (London, 1992), 133–49.

10. The following section is indebted to G. Whalen, 'Patronage engendered: how Goscelin allayed the concerns of nuns' discriminatory publics', in *Women, the Book and the Godly*, ed. L. Smith and J. H. M. Taylor (Cambridge, 1995), 123–35, esp. 129–30. My conclusions, however, are different.

11. A. Wilmart, 'La légende de Ste Edith en prose et vers par le moine Goscelin', *Analecta Bollandiana*, 56 (1938), 5–101, 265–307, esp. 37–8.

12. Ibid., 36–7.

13. Matthew 28:10; John 20:18; and Acts 1:34, 2:2, 2:18.

14. M. L. Colker, 'Texts of Jocelin of Canterbury which relate to the history of Barking Abbey', *Studia Monastica*, 7 (1965), 383–460; and M. Esposito, 'La vie de Sainte Vulfhilde par Goscelin de Cantorbéry', *Analecta Bollandiana*, 32 (1913), 10–26.

15. *Heremanni archidiaconi miracula sancti Eadmundi*, ed. F. Liebermann, and *Ungedruckte Anglo-Normannische Geschichtsquellen*, ed. F. Liebermann (Strassburg, 1879,) 234; for the suggestion that the author is Bertran, see A. Gransden, 'The composition and authorship of the "De miraculis sancti Eadmundi" attributed to "Hermann the archdeacon"', *Journal of Medieval Latin*, 5 (1995), 1–52.

16. R. Nip, *Arnulfus van Oudenberg, bisschop van Soissons (d. 1087), mens en*

model (Groningen, 1995), 280.

17. E. A. Pigeon, *Histoire de la cathédrale de Coutances* (Coutances, 1876), 367–83 at 367.

18. Ibid., 382–3.

19. D. Gonthier and C. Le Bas, 'Analyse socio-économique de quelques recueils de miracles dans la Normandie du XIe au XIIIe siècle', *Annales de Normandie*, 24 (1974), 3–36.

20. *Inventio et miracula sancti Vulfranni*, ed. J. Laporte, *Mélanges publiés par la Société de l'Histoire de Normandie*, 14 (Rouen, 1938); *Miracula s. Vulfranni episcopi*, in *AA SS*, III (March), 150–61; A. Poncelet, 'Miracula s. Nicolai conscripta a monacho Beccensi', *Catalogus codicum hagiographicorum latinorum Bibliotheca Nationali Parisiensi* (Bruxelles, 1890), 405–32.

21. *Historia mulieris suspensae ad vitam revocatae descripta a Marsilia abbatissa Rotomagensi*, in *AA SS*, I (Feb.), 902–3; M. J. Cacheux, 'Histoire de l'abbaye de Saint-Amand de Rouen des origines à la fin du XVIe siècle', *Bulletin de la Société des Antiquaires de Normandie*, 44 (1936), 5–289.

22. *AA SS*, I (Feb.), 902–3.

23. *Catalogue général des manuscrits des bibliothèques publiques de France. Départements*, 25 (Paris, 1894), 403–5.

24. B. Abou-El-Haj, *The Medieval Cult of Saints. Formations and Transformations* (Cambridge, 1997), 86, 156–9, 250 nt. 6.

25. *The Life of Ailred of Rievaulx by Walter Daniel*, ed. and trans. F. M. Powicke (London, 1950), 67, 69.

26. *Der sog. Libellus de dictis quatuor ancillarum s. Elisabeth confectus*, ed. A. Huyskens (Kempten, München, 1911); and P. G. Schmidt, 'Die zeitgenössische Überlieferung zum Leben und zur Heiligsprechung der heiligen Elisabeth', *Sankt Elisabeth, Fürstin, Dienerin, Heilige. Ausstellung zum 750. Todestag der hl. Elisabeth, Marburg, Langrafenschloss und Elisabethkirche 19. November 1981–6 Januar 1982* (Sigmaringen, 1981), 1–6.

27. ' . . . and by the witness of a certain noble maiden of good conduct and of that man', see *Hildegard of Bingen, Scivias*, trans. C. Hart and J. Bishop (New York, 1990), 60.

28. A. L. Clark, *Elisabeth of Schönau. A Twelfth-Century Visionary* (Philadelphia, 1992), 50–68.

29. I. Short, 'Patrons and polyglots: French literature in twelfth-century England', *Anglo-Norman Studies*, 14 (1991), 236.

30. D. Elliott, *Spiritual Marriage. Sexual Abstinence in Medieval Wedlock* (Princeton, 1993), 266–96 gives numerous examples of family links between women with similar ascetic ideals; most, however, date from after 1200.

Part II   Remembrance of the Past

CHAPTER 4   ANCESTORS, FAMILY REPUTATION AND FEMALE TRADITIONS

1. *Dhuoda, Manuel pour mon fils*, ed. P. Riché (Paris, 1975), 318, 354; and *Handbook for William: a Carolingian Woman's Counsel for her Son by Dhuoda*, trans. C. Neel (Lincoln and London, 1991), 87, 100.
2. *Vita Mahthildis reginae antiquior*, ed. R. Koepke, *MGH SS*, vol. 10, 573–82, esp. 581.
3. *Widukindi res gestae Saxonicae*, ed. A. Bauer and R. Rau (Darmstadt, 1971), 16, 82, 124.
4. *Hrotsvitae opera*, ed. H. Homeyer (Paderborn, 1970).
5. K. Leyser, *Rule and Conflict in an Early Medieval Society. Ottonian Saxony* (Oxford, 1989), 49–62.
6. E. M. C. van Houts, 'Women and the writing of history in the early Middle Ages: the case of Abbess Matilda of Essen and Aethelweard', *Early Medieval Europe*, 1 (1992), 53–68.
7. E. Könsgen, 'Zwei unbekannte Briefe zu den Gesta Regum Anglorum des Wilhelm von Malmesbury', *Deutsches Archiv*, 31 (1975), 204–14.
8. M. D. Legge, *Anglo-Norman Literature and its Background* (Oxford, 1963), 28.
9. *The Gesta Normannorum Ducum of William of Jumièges, Orderic Vitalis and Robert of Torigni*, ed. E. M. C. van Houts, 2 (Oxford, 1992–95), 196–289.
10. N. Lettinck, 'Pour une édition critique de l'Historia Ecclesiastica de Hugues de Fleury', *Revue Bénédictine*, 91 (1981), 392.
11. J. Baldwin, *The Government of Philip Augustus. Foundations of French Royal Power in the Middle Ages* (Berkeley and Los Angeles, 1986), 370–1, 575 nt. 65.
12. *De moribus et actis primorum Normanniae ducum auctore Dudone sancti Quintin*, ed. J. Lair (Caen, 1865), 289; E. Searle, *Predatory Kinship and the Creation of Norman Power 840–1066* (Berkeley and Los Angeles, 1988), 65.
13. *The Life of King Edward who Rests at Westminster*, ed. F. Barlow, 2nd edn (Oxford, 1992), 22, 36–8.
14. *The Letters and Charters of Gilbert Foliot*, ed. A. Morey and C. N. L. Brooke (Cambridge, 1967), 60–66, esp. 66.
15. For Empress Matilda's claim to the English throne, see M. Chibnall, *The Empress Matilda, Queen Consort, Queen Mother and Lady of the English* (Oxford, 1991), 64–88.
16. J. Martindale, ' Succession and politics in the romance-speaking world, c. 1000–1140', *England and her Neighbours 1066–1453: Essays in Honour of Pierre Chaplais*, ed. M. Jones and M. Vale (London, 1989), 19–41; J. Holt, 'Feudal society and the family in early medieval England: the heiress and the alien', *Transactions of the Royal Historical Society*, 5th s., 35 (1985), 1–28; J. Green, 'Aristocratic women in early twelfth-century England', *Anglo-*

Norman Political Culture, ed. W. Hollister (Woodbridge, 1997), 59–82.
17. J. C. Andressohn, *The ancestry and Life of Godfrey of Bouillon* (Bloomington, 1947).
18. L. Huneycutt, 'The idea of the perfect princess; the Life of St Margaret in the reign of Matilda II (1100–1118), *Anglo-Norman Studies*, 12 (1989), 81–98.
19. *The Gesta Normannorum Ducum*, ed. E. M. C. van Houts, vol. 1, lxxxvii–lxxxviii.
20. R. Nip, 'Godelieve of Gistel and Ida of Boulogne', *Sanctity and Motherhood. Essays on Holy Mothers in the Middle Ages*, ed. A. B. Mulder-Bakker (New York, 1995), 191–223; G. Duby, *Love and Marriage in the Middle Ages*, trans. J. Dunnett (Oxford, 1994), 36–55.
21. W. L. Warren, *Henry II* (Berkeley, 1973), 449.
22. G. M. Spiegel, *Romancing the Past. The Rise of Vernacular Prose Historiography in Thirteenth-Century France* (Berkeley and Los Angeles, 1993), 71, 75; for the historical circumstances, see Baldwin, *The Government of Philip Augustus*, 200–2.
23. J. Dunbabin, 'Discovering a past for the French aristocracy', *The Perception of the Past in Twelfth-Century Europe*, ed. P. Magdalino (London, 1992), 1–14, esp. 12–13; *Guillaume de Tyr, Chronique*, ed. R. B. C. Huygens, H. E. Mayer and G. Rösch (Turnholt, 1986), 425–7.
24. J. L. Kupper, 'Mathilde de Boulogne duchesse de Brabant', *Femmes, mariages, lignages, XIIᵉ–XIVᵉ siècles. Mélanges offerts à Georges Duby* (Bruxelles, 1992), 233–55.
25. *Le Conte de Floire et de Blancheflor*, ed. J. L. Leclanche (Paris, 1980), 20.
26. Ibid., 20; my discussion is heavily indebted to R. L. Krueger, *Women Readers and the Ideology of Gender in Old French Verse Romance* (Cambridge, 1993), 7–11.
27. *De obsessione Dunelmi et de probitate Uchtredi comitis*, in: *Symeonis Dunelmensis opera*, ed. H. Hinde (Durham, 1868, 154–57; trans. (inc. errors) J. Stevenson, *The Church Historians of England*, 3:2 (London, 1855), 765–68. I am very grateful to Dr Susan Kelly for discussing this text with me.
28. C. Fell, *Women in Anglo-Saxon England* (1984), 139–40; C. R. Hart, *The Early Charters of Northern England and the North Midlands* (London, 1975), 143–50; R. Fleming, *Kings and Lords in Conquest England* (Cambridge, 1991), 49–50.
29. *English Historical Documents, vol. 1 c. 500–1042*, ed. D. Whitelock (New York, 1955), 556.
30. L. W. Vernon Harcourt, *His Grace the Steward and Trial of Peers. A Novel Inquiry into a Special Branch of constitutional Government* (London, 1907), 125–6, for Latin text, see 125 nt. 2.
31. *Frutolfs und Ekkehards Chroniken und die anonyme Kaiserchronik*, ed. F. Schmale, and I. Schmale-Ott (Darmstadt, 1972), 78–9.
32. *The Ecclesiastical History of Orderic Vitalis*, ed. M. Chibnall (Oxford, 1969–80), 6, 16.
33. *The Gesta Normannorum Ducum*, ed. van Houts, vol. 2, 242–5.
34. *Rotuli de dominabus et pueris et puellis de xii comitatibus*, ed. J. H. Round (London, 1913). Translated excerpts can be found in E. Amt, *Women's Lives*

in Medieval Europe. A Source Book (London, 1993), 154–7; as a source of family history it is discussed by J. S. Moore, 'The Anglo-Norman family: size and structure,' *Anglo-Norman Studies*, 14 (1991), 153–96.

35. *De rebus gestis Rogerii Calabriae et Siciliae comitis et Roberti Guiscardi ducis fratris*, ed. E. Pontieri, *Rerum Italicarum Scriptores*, 5:1 (Bologna, 1924), 76.

36. Holt, 'Feudal society and the family in early medieval England: The heiress and the alien', 1–28.

37. *Havelok*, ed. G. V. Smithers (Oxford, 1987), xvi–xxxii for an account of the various versions of this romance. The earliest written version is reported by Gaimar in c. 1135–40.

38. *Waltharius and Ruodblieb*, ed. and trans. D. M. Kratz (New York and London, 1984), 187.

39. The arrangement was part of a direct swap since Constance's brother Duke Conan IV had married Malcolm's sister Margaret. The letter is printed in *Recueil des Historiens de France*, 16, 23; and discussed in *Regesta regum Scottorum, 1: The Acts of Malcolm IV King of Scots 1153–1165*, ed. G. W. S. Barrow (Edinburgh, 1960), 13.

40. *The Gesta Normannorum Ducum*, ed. van Houts, vol. 2, 260–74.

41. A., Porée, *Histoire de l'abbaye du Bec*, 1 of 2 vols (Evreux, 1901), 183–4.

42. *Miracula sanctae Mariae*, Migne, *PL*, vol. 150, 738–42.

43. *Frutolfs und Ekkehards Chroniken*, ed. Schmale and Schmale-Ott, 20–1, 186–8.

44. K. J. Leyser, *Medieval Germany and its Neighbours 900–250* (London, 1982), 171–2.

45. *Hermanni monachi de miraculis s. Mariae Laudunensis de gestis venerabilis Bartholomaei episcopi et s. Nortberti libri tres*, Migne, PL, vol. 156, 961–1018, esp. 965–7.

46. F. Vercauteren, 'Une parentèle dans la France du Nord au XIᵉ et XIIᵉ siècles', *Le Moyen Âge*, 69 (1963), 223–45; G. Duby, *La société chévâleresque. Hommes et structures*, 1 (Paris, 1988), 145–57.

47. *Lamberti Waterlos*, 511–12.

48. *Les Annales de Flodoard*, ed. Ph. Lauer (Paris, 1905). liii–lviii, 158–9: under the year 966.

49. C. B. Bouchard, 'Consanguinity and noble marriages in the tenth and eleventh centuries', *Speculum*, 56 (1981), 268–87.

50. For letter 261 of Bishop Ivo of Chartres, see Migne, *PL*, vol. 162, 265-6; my discussion of it can be found in 'Robert of Torigni as genealogist', *Studies in Medieval History Presented to R. Allen Brown*, ed. C. Harper-Bill, C. Holdsworth and J. L. Nelson (Woodbridge, 1989), 215–33, esp. 225–6.

51. *S. Anselmi Cantuariensis archiepiscopi opera omnia*, ed. F. Schmitt (Edinburgh, 1951), 5, 369-70. *The Letters of Saint Anselm of Canterbury*, trans. W. Frölich, 3 (Kalamazoo, 1990–94), no. 424.

52. *Liber epistularum Guidonis de Basochis*, ed. H. Adolfsson, Acta Universitatis Stockholmiensis, Studia Latina Stockholmiensia, 18 (Stockholm, 1969), esp. 95 no. xxiii, 128–9 no. xxx, 141-2 no. xxxiii. For an altogether different interpretation, see M. Bur, 'L'image de la parenté chez les comtes de

Champagne', *Annales*, 38 (1983), 1016–39, esp. 1031–34.

53. *Gesta Herewardi incliti exulis et militis*, ed. T. D. Hardy and C. T. Martin, *Lestorie de Engles solum la translacion maistre Geffrei Gaimar*, 1 (London 1888) 339-404; trans. in M. Swanton, *Three Lives of the Last Englishmen* (New York and London, 1984), 45–88

54. A. Williams, *The English and the Norman Conquest* (Woodbridge, 1995), 49–50.

55. *Gesta Herewardi*, 357–8; trans. in Swanton, 57.

56. J. H. Round, *Feudal England. Historical Studies on the Eleventh and Twelfth Centuries*, rev. edn (London, 1964), 132–6.

CHAPTER 5   OBJECTS AS PEGS FOR MEMORY

1. E. Tonkin, *Narrating our Pasts. The Social Construction of Oral History* (Cambridge, 1992), 93–5, 109.

2. M. Carruthers, *The Book of Memory. A Study of Memory in Medieval Culture* (Cambridge, 1990), 221–9.

3. *Guillaume de Poitiers, Histoire de Guillaume le Conquérant*, ed. R. Foreville (Paris, 1952), 205.

4. *The Waltham Chronicle*, ed. L. Watkiss and M. Chibnall (Oxford, 1994), 50–6, xliii–xlvi

5. *Rodulfus Glaber, Opera*, ed. J. France, N. Bulst and P. Reynolds (Oxford, 1989), 162.

6. *Guillaume de Pouille, la Geste de Robert Guiscard*, ed. M. Mathieu (Palermo, 1961), 254–9, 336–7.

7. *Reading Abbey Cartularies*, ed. B. R. Kemp, 1 (London, 1986–87), 301–2, 353, 403–5.

8. J. L. Nelson, 'Women at the court of Charlemagne: A case of monstrous regiment?', *Medieval Queenship*, ed. J. C. Parsons (1993), 43–62.

9. For a colour photograph of the illuminated page, Wolfenbüttel, Herzog August Bibliothek, MS Guelph 105 Noviss. 2, folio 171v., see C. R. Dodwell, *Pictorial Arts of the West 800–1200* (Yale, 1993), 285.

10. This section is based on J. Jesch, *Women in the Viking Age* (Woodbridge, 1991), 48–74; R. I. Page, *Chronicles of the Vikings. Records, Memorials and Myths* (London, 1995), 168–72; B. and P. Sawyer, *Medieval Scandinavia. From Conversion to Reformation c. 800–1500* (Minneapolis and London, 1993), 188–213.

11. Jesch, *Women*, 61.

12. B. and P. Sawyer, *Medieval Scandinavia*, 193 Fig. 9.1.

13. Page, *Chronicles*, 169–70; Jesch, *Women*, 58.

14. Page, *Chronicles*, 170.

15. Jesch, *Women*, 54–6.

16. *Otto von Freising, Chronica sive de duabus civitatibus*, ed. A. Hofmeister and W. Lammers (Darmstadt, 1961), 486.

17. *The Ecclesiastical History of Orderic Vitalis*, ed. M. Chibnall, 2 (Oxford, 1969), 168.

18. *Willelmi Malmesbiriensis, De gestis Regum Anglorum*, ed. W. Stubbs, 1 (London, 1887), 218.

19. *The Chronicle of Battle Abbey*, ed. E. Searle (Oxford, 1980), 15–6, 36–8, 60–2.
20. *Actes des comtes de Flandre 1071–1128*, ed. F. Vercauteren (Bruxelles, 1936), 16–19.
21. B. S. Bachrach, *Fulk Nerra, the neo-Roman consul 987-1040. A Political Biography of the Angevin Count* (Berkeley and Los Angeles, 1993), 131–5. For the consecration and subsequent collapse of the church, see *Rodulfus Glaber*, 58–64.
22. D. Wilson, *The Bayeux Tapestry* (London, 1985), Pl. 17; D. Bernstein, *The Mystery of the Bayeux Tapestry* (London, 1986).
23. S. A. Brown and M. Herren, 'The Adelae comitissae of Baudri of Bourgueil and the Bayeux Tapestry', *Anglo-Norman Studies*, 16 (1993), 55–74.
24. D. Whitelock, *Anglo-Saxon Wills* (Cambridge, 1930), 15.
25. Ibid., 65.
26. *Liber Eliensis*, ed. E. O. Blake (London, 1962), 136.
27. C. R. Dodwell, *Anglo-Saxon Art. A New Perspective* (Ithaca and New York, 1982), 134–6, 188–9.
28. *Eadmeri: Historia Novorum in Anglia*, ed. M. Rule (London, 1884),107–10; trans. G. Bosanquet, *Eadmer's History of Recent Events in England* (London, 1964), 111–13. See also, V. Ortenberg, *The English Church and the Continent 900-1100* (Oxford, 1992), 104.
29. Whitelock, *Anglo-Saxon Wills*, 15, 110
30. C. Duhamel-Amado, 'Femmes entre elles. Filles et épouses languedociennes (XIe et XIIe siècles)', *Femmes, mariages, lignages, XIIe–XIVe siècles. Mélanges offerts à Georges Duby* (Bruxelles, 1992), 126–55, esp. 153–4. For a similar conclusion with regard to fifteenth-century bequests at Douai, see M. C. Howell, 'Fixing movables: gifts by testament in late medieval Douai,' *Past and Present* 150 (1996), 3-45 at 25–9.
31. P. Skinner, 'Women, wills and wealth in southern Italy', *Early Medieval Europe*, 2 (1993), 133–52; esp. 136–7, 138–9, 142–3.
32. Dodwell, *The Pictorial Arts*, 27–9.
33. R. H. C. Davis, *The Normans and their Myth* (London, 1976), 74-5; Pl. 36.
34. D. Abulafia, *Frederick II* (London, 1992), 10–12; plate on 10 shows Emperor Charles V in the same coronation mantle.
35. Dodwell, *Pictorial Arts*, 25.
36. *The Life of King Edward Who Rests at Westminster*, ed. F. Barlow, 2nd edn. (Oxford, 1992), 24.
37. *English Romanesque Art 1066–1200*, ed. G. Zarnecki (London, 1984), 291–2.
38. *Suger, Vie de Louis VI le Gros* , ed. H. Waquet (Paris, 1929), 276; trans. R. C. Cusamo and J. Moorhead, *Suger, The Deeds of Louis the Fat* (Washington 1992), 154.
39. *Abbot Suger on the Abbey Church of St Denis and its Art Treasures*, ed. E. Panofsky, 2nd edn (Princeton, 1979), 78–9. G. Beech, 'The Eleanor vase: witness to Christian-Muslim collaboration in early 12th-century Spain', *Ars Orientalis*, 22 (1992), 69–79. I am very grateful to Professor Beech for sending me his article.
40. *Early Yorkshire Charters*, ed. W. Farrer and C. T. Clay (York, 1939), 3, 60–70, at 69.

41. Whitelock, *Anglo-Saxon Wills*, 11.
42. Ibid., 21.
43. Ibid., 65.
44. Skinner, 'Women, wills', 138, 144.
45. Whitelock, *Anglo-Saxon Wills*, 15.
46. *Beowulf*, trans. D. Wright (Harmondsworth, 1970), 98, lines 3015–16. For an attempt to identify the surviving weapons, see O. Bouzy, 'Les armes symboles d'un pouvoir politique: l'épée du sacre, la sainte lance, l'oriflamme au VIIIᵉ–XIIᵉ siècles', *Francia*, 22–1 (1995), 45–57.
47. Whitelock, *Anglo-Saxon Wills*, 59.
48. Dodwell, *Anglo-Saxon Art*, 74.
49. M. Clanchy, *From Memory to Written Record, England 1066–1307*, 2nd edn. (Oxford, 1993), 35–6.
50. *The Gesta Normannorum Ducum*, ed. van Houts, vol. 1, lxi–lxv, vol. 2, 184–91.
51. A. Porée, *Histoire de l'abbaye du Bec*, 1 (Evreux, 1901), 650–1; Chibnall, *Empress*, 189–90.
52. *Suger*, ed. Panofsky, 77.
53. P. Stafford, *Queen Emma and Queen Edith. Queenship and Woman's Power in Eleventh-Century England* (Oxford, 1997), 143.
54. *Leonis Marsicani et Petri diaconi chronica monasterii Casinensis*, ed. W. Wattenbach, *MGH SS*, vol. 7, 743–4.
55. *Orderic Vitalis*, ed. Chibnall, vol. 2, 42.
56. Marjorie Chibnall points out that the Psalter of the story was probably the 'psalterium magnum' mentioned in the twelfth-century catalogue of Saint-Evroult. A tenth-century Anglo-Saxon Psalter formerly belonging to Saint-Evroult is now in the public library of Rouen (BM 24) but this is not likely to be the Psalter mentioned here by Orderic.
57. *Les actes de Guillaume le conquérant et de la reine Mathilde pour les abbayes caennaises*, ed. L. Musset (Caen, 1967), 112–13.
58. E. M. C. van Houts, 'The Norman conquest through European eyes', *English Historical Review*, 110 (1995), 832–53; P. McGurk and J. Rosenthal, 'The Anglo-Saxon gospelbooks of Judith, countess of Flanders: their text, make-up and function', *Anglo-Saxon England*, 24 (1995), 251–308.
59. New York, Pierpont Morgan Library, MS 709, fol. 105v; see also Dodwell, *Anglo-Saxon Art*, 60.
60. See note 51 above; and *The Gesta Normannorum Ducum*, ed. van Houts, vol. 2, 244–5.

Part III   One Event Remembered

Chapter 6   The Memory of the Norman Conquest of England in 1066

1. *The Chronicle of Battle Abbey*, ed. E. Searle (Oxford, 1980), 90, 102–6, 128.
2. *Guillaume de Poitiers, Histoire de Guillaume le Conquérant*, ed. R. Foreville (Paris, 1952),180–2.

3. *The Chronicle of Battle Abbey*, 90. This states that most of the relics hanging on the Battle shrine had come from King William's predecessors, the Anglo-Saxon kings.
4. Ibid., 106.
5. *Guibert de Nogent, Autobiographie*, ed. E.-R. Labande (Paris, 1981), 188–91.
6. *The Chronicle of Battle Abbey*, 130–2 and R. W. Southern, *Saint Anselm. A Portrait in a Landscape* (Cambridge, 1990), 372–6.
7. E. M. C. van Houts, 'The Brevis Relatio de Guillelmo nobilissimo comite Normannorum written by a monk of Battle Abbey, edited with a historical commentary', *Camden Miscellany*, 34; Camden 5th s., vol. 10 (Cambridge, 1997), 1–48.
8. For examples from modern history, see J. Fentress and C. Wickham, *Social Memory* (Oxford, 1992), 127–43
9. *The Waltham Chronicle*, ed. L. Watkiss and M. Chibnall (Oxford, 1994), 45–6, 56–7. The two versions regarding Harold's burial need not be mutually exclusive.
10. Ibid., 56–7.
11. *The Life of King Edward who Rests at Westminster*, ed. F. Barlow, 2nd edn (Oxford, 1992),150–63.
12. E. M. C. van Houts, 'Wace as historian', *Family Trees and the Roots of Politics. The Prosopography of Britain and France from the 10th to the 12th Century*, ed. K. S. B. Keats-Rohan (Woodbridge, 1997), 103–33.
13. *Le Roman de Rou de Wace*, ed. A. Holden, 2 (Paris, 1970–73), 205–6 lines 8585–8602.
14. The expedition is mentioned by William of Poitiers (*Guillaume de Poitiers*, 106–15), and *The Bayeux Tapestry*, ed. D. Wilson (London, 1985), Pl. 18–24.
15. *Guillaume de Poitiers*, 192, 260; D. Crouch, *The Beaumont Twins. The Roots and Branches of Power in the Twelfth Century* (Cambridge, 1986), 3; *The Gesta Normannorum Ducum of William of Jumièges, Orderic Vitalis and Robert of Torigni*, ed, E. M. C. van Houts, 2 (Oxford, 1995), 98; *The Ecclesiastical History of Orderic Vitalis*, ed. M. Chibnall (Oxford, 1980), 6, 146–8, 180; N. Hooper, 'Edgar the aetheling: Anglo-Saxon prince, rebel and crusader', *Anglo-Saxon England*, 14 (1985) 197–214.
16. Crouch, *The Beaumont Twins*, 78–9, 95–6.
17. F. Barlow, *William Rufus* (London, 1983), 441–5.
18. R. W. Southern, 'Aspects of the European tradition of historical writing, 4. The sense of the past', *Transactions of the Royal Historical Society*, 5th s., 23 (1973) 243–63; J. Campbell, 'Some twelfth-century views of the Anglo-Saxon past', *Essays in Anglo-Saxon History* (London, 1986), 209–28; A. Gransden, *Historical Writing in England* c. 550 to c. 1307 (London, 1974),105–6, 136, 167–8.
19. J. Coleman, *Ancient and Medieval Memories. Studies in the Reconstruction of the Past* (Cambridge, 1992), 155–91.
20. *The Life of King Edward*, 88; see also 110 for a section that was probably written in 1067 (p. xxxii). Countess Gytha fled the country after the fall of Exeter in 1068 (*ASC* 'D' 1067).

21. *English Historical Documents*, vol. II, 1042–189, ed. D. C. Douglas and G. W. Greenaway (London, 1968), 107–9 (Introduction), and 110–203 (text of all versions).

22. Two sections of this poem have survived in Old Norse as part of the saga on Harold Hardrada (*King Harald's Saga. Harald Hardradi of Norway from Snorri Sturluson's Heimskringla*, trans. M. Magnusson and H. Pálsson (Harmondsworth, 1966),157–8).

23. E. M. C. van Houts, 'The Norman Conquest through European eyes',*English Historical Review*, 110 (1995), 832–53.

24. For recent evaluations of Hereward's role in the Fenland, see the uncritical study by J. Hayward, 'Hereward the outlaw', *Journal of Medieval History*, 14 (1988), 293–304; and the much more stimulating discussions in C. Hart, 'Hereward the Wake and his companions', *The Danelaw* (London, 1992), 625–48; and A. Williams, *The English and the Norman Conquest* (Woodbridge, 1995,) 49–50.

25. Particularly instructive is the insertion in two places of almost identical lists of Hereward's companions. The author presumably had two lists which he gave integrally rather than amalgamating them. Some of the individuals have been identified by Hart and Williams. It seems to me that all are historical persons of whom only the most important as landholder can now be traced and identified.

26. *Henry, Archdeacon of Huntingdon, Historia Anglorum*, ed. D. Greenaway (Oxford, 1996); N. Partner, *Serious Entertainments: the Writing of History in Twelfth-Century England* (Chicago and London, 1977), 11–48; D. Greenaway, 'Henry of Huntingdon and the manuscripts of his Historia Anglorum', *Anglo-Norman Studies*, 9 (1987), 103–26 and 'Authority, convention and observation in Henry of Huntingdon's Historia Anglorum', *Anglo-Norman Studies*, 18 (1995), 105–22; Williams, *The English and the Norman Conquest*, 177–80.

27. *Gaimar, Lestoire des Engleis*, ed. A. Bell (Oxford, 1960).

28. I. Short, 'Patrons and polyglots: French literature in twelfth-century England', *Anglo-Norman Studies*, 14 (1991), 229–50, esp. 243–4.

29. *The Gesta Normannorum Ducum*, ed. van Houts, vol. 2, 164–73, 182–5.

30. *Guillaume de Poitiers*, ed. Foreville.

31. *The Ecclesiastical History*, ed. Chibnall, vol. 2, xviii–xxi, 208–58.

32. Ibid., 258.

33. F. Lot, *Études critiques sur l'abbaye de Saint-Wandrille* (Paris, 1913), 207.

34. *Anglo-Saxon Chronicle Version E* for the year 1087 (*English Historical Documents*, vol. 2, 165); F. Barlow, *William Rufus* (London, 1983), 65.

35. *Guillaume de Poitiers*, ed. Foreville, vii.

36. Ibid., 244; *The Ecclesiastical History*, ed. Chibnall, vol. 2, 198.

37. *The Carmen de Hastingae proelio of Guy of Amiens*, ed. C. Morton and H. Muntz (Oxford, 1972), 42–9 lines 653–752.

38. G. Orlandi, 'Some afterthoughts on the "Carmen de Hastingae Proelio", *Media Latinitas. A Collection of Essays to Mark the Occasion of the Retirement of L. J. Engels*, ed. R. Nip, H. van Dijk and E. M. C. van Houts (Turnhout, 1996), 117–28.

39. *The Gesta Normannorum Ducum*, ed. van Houts, vol. 2, 158-72; and vol. 1,

lxxiii–lxxv, where the suggestion is made that some of the interpolations are based on William of Poitiers's biography.

40. *The Ecclesiastical History*, ed. Chibnall, vol. 2, xvii, 232.

41. Ibid., 2, 272–8, esp. 272: It is interesting to note that neither Guitmund nor, for that matter, Orderic minded Guitmund's acceptance in *c*. 1088 of the bishopric of Aversa in Norman occupied Italy!

42. *De statu hujus ecclesiae ab anno 836 ad 1093*, ed. *Gallia Christiana*, 9, Instrumenta, 217–24 at 220. For the authorship, see L. Delisle, 'Notice sur un traité inédit du douzième siècle intitulé: miracula ecclesiae Constantiniensis', *Bibliothèque de l' École des Chartes*, 2nd s., 4 (1847–48), 339–52, see esp. 368; M. Chibnall, 'La carrière de Geoffroi de Montbray', *Les évêques normands du XIᵉ siècle*, ed. P. Bouet and F. Neveux (Caen, 1995), 279–93, esp. 282.

43. *De statu hujus ecclesiae*, 220.

44. *The Brevis Relatio*, ed. van Houts, 31.

45. Ibid., 31.

46. *Willelmi Malmesbiriensis, De gestis regum Anglorum*, ed. Stubbs, vol. 2, 475.

47. *Chronica monasterii de Hida juxta Wintoniam ab anno 1035 ad annum 1121*, ed. E. Edwards, *Liber monasterii de Hyde* (London, 1866), 284–21.

48. See Chapter 2 above, 28.

49. P. Brand, 'Time out of mind: the knowledge and the use of the eleventh- and twelfth-century past in thirteenth-century litigation', *Anglo-Norman Studies*, 16 (1993), 37–54.

50. E. M. C. van Houts, 'The trauma of 1066', *History Today*, 46:10 (1996), 9–15.

51. E. Searle, 'Women and the legitimization of succession at the Norman conquest', *Proceedings of the Battle Conference 1980*, ed. R. Allen Brown (Woodbridge, 1981), 159–70, 226–7.

52. P. Stafford, 'Women and the Norman conquest', *Transactions of the Royal Historical Society*, 6th s., 4 (1994), 221–49.

53. Brand, 'Out of time out of mind', 46, 47, 48–9.

54. van Houts, 'The Norman Conquest through European eyes', 838–9.

55. *The Letters of Lanfranc, Archbishop of Canterbury*, ed. H. Clover and M. Gibson (Oxford, 1979), 166–7.

56. Searle, 'Women', 166–9.

57. E. M. C. van Houts, 'The Ship List of William the Conqueror', *Anglo-Norman Studies*, 10 (1987), 159–83 at 173.

58. 'The Liber Confortatorius of Goscelin of Saint Bertin', ed. C. H. Talbot, *Analecta Monastica*, 3rd s., (Rome, 1955), 1–118 at 22–3, 41.

59. The evidence is discussed by J. Wogan-Browne, '"Clerc u lai, muine u dame": women and Anglo-Norman hagiography in the twelfth and thirteenth centuries', *Women and Literature in Britain 1150–1500*, ed. C. Meale (Cambridge, 1993), 61–85.

60. *Vita et passio Waldevi comitis*, ed. J. A. Giles *Original Lives of Anglo-Saxons and Others Who Lived before the Conquest* (London, 1854), 18–19.

Chapter 7 Conclusions

1. Petri Damiani, *De parentelae gradibus*, ed. Migne, *PL*, 144, 191–208; and discussion in C. Bouchard, 'Consanguinity and noble marriages in the tenth and eleventh centuries', *Speculum*, 56 (1981), 268–87; J. Goody, *The Development of the Family and Marriage in Europe* (Cambridge, 1983), 134–46; C. Brooke, *The Medieval Idea of Marriage* (Cambridge, 1989), 70–4, 134–7.

2. G. Duby, *La société chévâleresque. Hommes et structures*, vol. 1 (Paris, 1988), see: Ch. 8 'Structures de parenté et noblesse dans la France du Nord au XIe et XIIe siècles', 143–66; and Ch. 9 'Remarques sur la littérature généalogique en France au XIe et XIIe siècles', 167–80.

3. P. Geary, *Phantoms of Remembrance. Memory and Oblivion at the End of the First Millennium* (Berkeley, 1994), 43–80.

4. S. Kay, *The 'Chansons de geste' in the Age of Romance: Political Fictions* (Oxford, 1995), 33, 103–15.

5. The lack of source material for the central Middle Ages has often been discussed, though snippets strongly suggest common patterns north and south of the Alps, see K. Leyser, *Rule and Conflict in an Early Medieval Society. Ottonian Saxony* (Oxford, 1979), 49–62, esp. 51–2; D. Herlihy, *Medieval Households* (Harvard, 1985), 103–11; and Duby, *La Société chévâleresque*, Ch. 7 'Les jeunes dans la société aristocratique dans la France du Nord-Ouest au XIIe siècle', 129–42. I am most grateful to Richard Smith for discussing this material with me.

6. D. Herlihy, *Medieval Households* (Harvard, 1985), 103–11; D. Herlihy, 'The generation in medieval history', *Viator*, 5 (1974), 347–64; R. M. Smith, 'Geographical diversity in the resort to marriage in late medieval Europe: work, reputation and unmarried females in the household formation systems of northern and southern Europe', *Woman is a Worthy Wight. Women in English Society c. 1200–1500*, ed. P. J. P. Goldberg (Stroud, 1992), 16–59, esp. 27–46.

7. J. Goody, *The Development of the Family*, Figs 4 and 6.

FURTHER READING

Medieval Historiography

General introductions can be found in R. W. Southern's series of four presidential lectures for the Royal Historical Society, 'Aspects of the European tradition of historical writing', *Transactions of the Royal Historical Society*, 5th s., 20–3 (1970–73), 173–96, 159–79, 159–86, and 243–63. For a comprehensive survey of western Europe, see H. Hoffmann, *Artikulationsformen historischen Wissens in der lateinischen Historiographie des hohen und späten Mittelalters, La littérature historiographique des origines à 1500*, ed. H. U. Gumbrecht, U. Linkheer and P. M. Spangenberg, *Grundriss der romanischen Literaturen des Mittelalters*, 11:1 (Heidelberg 1987), 1. 2, 367–687.

'National and regional' overviews and introductions

England
A. Gransden, *Historical Writing in England c. 550–c. 1307* (London, 1974); and her articles, 'The chronicles of medieval England and Scotland', *Journal of Medieval History*, 16–17 (1990–91), 129–50, 217–43. N. Partner, *Serious Entertainment: The Writing of History in Twelfth-Century England* (Chicago, 1977).

France
The indispensable collection is by A. Molinier, *Les sources de l'histoire de France des origines aux guerres d'Italie (1496)*, 6 vols (Paris, 1901–6); and R. H. Bautier, 'L'historiographie en France au Xe et XIe siècles (France du Nord et de l'Est)', *La Storiografia altomedievale*, Settimane di studio del centro italiano di studi sull'alto medioevo, 17 (Spoleto, 1970), 793–850.

Germany
W. Wattenbach, W. Levison, H. Löwe and R. Holzmann, *Deutschlands Geschichtsquellen im Mittelalter*, 8 vols (Darmstadt 1952–71), T. Reuter, 'Past, present and no future in the twelfth-century "regnum teutonicum"', *The Perception of the Past in Twelfth-Century Europe*, ed. P. Magdalino (London, 1992), 15–36.

Italy
C. Wickham, 'The sense of the past in Italian communal narratives', *The Perception of the Past*, ed. Magdalino, 173–90; and T. S. Brown, 'The political use of the past in Norman Sicily', *The Perception of the Past*, ed. Magdalino, 191–210.
Spain
B. Sanchez Alonsa, *Historia de la historiografia espanola*, 2nd edn (Madrid, 1947); R. McCluskey, 'Malleable accounts: views of the past in twelfth-century Iberia', *The Perception of the Past*, ed. Magdalino, 211–26.
Scandinavia
B. and P. Sawyer, 'Adam and Eve of Scandinavian history', *The Perception of the Past*, ed. Magdalino, 37–52.

For a more thematic approach, see B. Guenée, *Histoire et culture historique dans l'Occident médiéval*, 2nd edn (Paris, 1991). Discussions of individual genres can be found in the series Typologie des sources du moyen âge occidental (Turnhout, 1972): L. Genicot on genealogies, 1 (1972); M. McCormick on annals, 14 (1975), K. H. Krüger on world chronicles, 16 (1976); M. Sot on serial biographies of bishops and abbots, the so-called 'gesta', 37 (1981); and E. M. C. van Houts on local and regional chronicles, 74 (1995).

Medieval Hagiography

The classic studies for the writing of hagiography are H. Delehaye, *The Legends of Saints*, (Chicago, 1961); B. de Gaiffier, *Étude critique d'hagiographie et d'iconologie* (Bruxelles, 1967); and M. Goodich, *Vita perfecta. The Ideal of Sainthood in the Thirteenth Century* (Stuttgart, 1982). C. W. Jones, *Saints' Lives and Chronicles in early England* (Ithaca, 1947); and M. Heinzelmann, *Translationsberichte und andere Quellen des Reliquienkultes*, Typologie des sources du moyen âge occidental, 33 (Turnhout, 1979) concentrate on surveys of written texts. Extremely useful for the interaction between oral and written versions of saints' lives in France are: T. Head, *Hagiography and the Cult of Saints, the Diocese of Orléans, 800–1200* (Cambridge, 1990); and J. Smith, 'Oral and written: saints, miracles and relics in Brittany, 850–1250', *Speculum*, 65 (1990), 309–43. The genre of saints' miracles, and the preponderance of women amongst those involved, is discussed by P. Sigal, 'Histoire et hagiographie:

les miracula au XIe et XIIe siècles', L'historiographie en Occident du Ve au XVe siècles', *Annales de Bretagne*, 87 (1980), 237–57, and his *L'homme et le miracle dans la France médiévale (XIe–XIIe siècles)*, (Paris, 1985); D. Gonthier and C. Le Bas, 'Analyse socio-économique de quelques recueils de miracles dans la Normandie du XIe au XIIIe siècles', *Annales de Normandie*, 24 (1974), 3–36; and D. W. Rollason, 'The miracles of St Benedict: a window on early medieval France', *Studies in Medieval History Presented to R. H. C. Davis*, ed. H. Mayr-Harting and R. I. Moore (London, 1985), 73–90. B. Abou-el-Haj, *The Medieval Cult of Saints. Formations and Transformations* (Cambridge, 1997) focuses on the pictorial representations of saints' stories. For the German tradition of sainthood promoted in the royal family by its women, the crucial work is P. Corbet, *Les saints ottoniens. Sainteté dynastique, sainteté royale et sainteté féminine autour de l'an Mil*, Beihefte der Francia, 15 (Sigmaringen, 1986).

Oral and Written Traditions

The major study of oral and written traditions in the Middle Ages is M. T. Clanchy, *From Memory to Written Record. England 1066–1307*, 2nd edn (Oxford, 1993); as well as his earlier article, 'Remembering the past and the good old law', *History*, 55 (1970), 165–76. A much more general sketch for Germany is H. Vollrath, 'Das Mittelalter in der Typik oraler Gesellschaften', *Historische Zeitschrift*, 233 (1981), 571–98. More recent studies emphasize the parallel existence of oral and written traditions J. Fentress and C. Wickham, *Social Memory* (Oxford, 1992), 96–7; and M. Innes, 'Memory, orality and literacy in an early medieval society', *Past and Present*, 158 (1998) 3–36. D. H. Green, *Medieval Listening and Reading. The Primary Reception of German Literature 800–1300* (Cambridge, 1994).

Exclusive attention to oral traditions in the Middle Ages is given by M. Richter, *The Formation of the Medieval West: Studies in the Oral Culture of the Barbarians* (Dublin, 1994) and his *The Oral Tradition in the Middle Ages*, Typologie des sources du moyen âge occidental, 71 (Turnhout, 1994), see also his 'Kommunikationsprobleme im lateinischen Mittelalter', *Historische Zeitschrift*, 222 (1976), 43–80.

Literacy, both pragmatic and literary, is the central theme of R. McKitterick, *The Carolingians and the Written Word* (Cambridge, 1989); J. Nelson, 'Literacy in Carolingian government', *The Uses of Literacy in Early Medieval Europe*, ed. R. McKitterick (Cambridge, 1990), 258–96;

and B. Stock, *The Implications of Literacy. Written Language And Models of Interpretation in the Eleventh and Twelfth Centuries* (Princeton, 1983).

Studies for other periods offer interesting insights and parallels for the Middle Ages: R. Thomas, *Oral Tradition and Written Record in Classical Athens* (Cambridge, 1989); D. R. Woolf, 'The "common voice": history, folklore and oral tradition in early modern England', *Past and Present*, 120 (1988), 26–54; P. Thompson, *The Voice of the Past*, 2nd edn (Oxford, 1988); and R. Samuel, *Theatres of Memory* (London, 1994), 3–50, and 315–80. For anthropological research in the same areas, see J. Vansina, *Oral Tradition* (Harmondsworth, 1961), and *Oral Tradition as History* (London, 1985); J. Goody, *The Logic of Writing and the Organisation of Society* (Cambridge, 1986), and *The Interface between Written and the Oral* (Cambridge, 1987); W. J. Ong, *Orality and Literacy. The Technologizing of the Word* (New York, 1982); and E. Tonkin, *Narrating our Pasts. The Social Construction of Oral History* (Cambridge, 1992).

Memory and Family Tradition

For memory in the Middle Ages, see P. J. Geary, *Phantoms of Remembrance. Memory and Oblivion at the End of the First Millennium* (Princeton, 1994); M. Carruthers, *The Book of Memory. A Study of Memory in Medieval Culture* (Cambridge, 1990); and J. Coleman, *Ancient and Medieval Memories. Studies in the Reconstruction of the Past* (Cambridge, 1992). For the range of memory in historical works, both B. Guenée, 'Temps de l'histoire et temps de la mémoire au moyen âge', *Annuaire-Bulletin de la Société de l'histoire de France. Années 1976–77* (Paris, 1978), 25–35; and H. W. Goetz, 'Zum Geschichtsbewusstsein in der alamannisch-schweizerischen Klosterchronistik des hohen Mittelalters (11–13 Jahrhundert)', *Deutsches Archiv*, 44 (1988), 454–88 are essential reading.

Family commemoration of the dead is introduced by O. G. Oexle, 'Memoria und Memorialüberlieferung im früheren Mittelalter', *Frühmittelalterliche Studien*, 10 (1976), 70–95; K. Schmid, 'Die Sorge der Salier um ihre Memoria', *Memoria.Der Geschichtliche Zeugniswert des liturgischen Gedenken im Mittelalter*, ed. K. Schmid and J. Wollasch (München, 1984), 666–726; and N. Huyghebaert, *Les documents nécrologiques*, Typologie des sources du moyen âge occidental, 4 (Turnhout, 1972).

For memory and families in more general terms, see K. Hauck, 'The literature of house and kindred associated with medieval noble families illustrated from eleventh- and twelfth-century satires on the nobility', *The Medieval Nobility*, ed. T. Reuter (Amsterdam, 1979), 61-85; J. Dunbabin, 'Discovering a past for the French aristocracy', *The Perception of the Past in Twelfth-Century Europe*, ed. P. Magdalino (London, 1992), 1–14; E. M. C. van Houts, *Local and Regional Chronicles*, Typologie des sources du moyen âge occidental, 74 (Turnhout, 1995), Ch. 3, F. Vercauteren, 'Une parentèle dans la France du Nord au XIe et XIIe siècles', *Le Moyen Âge*, 69 (1963), 223–45; M. Bur, 'L'image de la parenté chez les comtes de Champagne', *Annales*, 38 (1983), 1016–39; G. Duby, *La société chévâleresque. Hommes et structures*, 1 (Paris, 1988), Ch. 8 'Structures de parenté et noblesse dans la France du Nord au XIe et XIIe siècles', 143–66, and Ch. 9 'Remarques sur la littérature généalogique en France au XIe et XIIe siècles', 167–80. G. M. Spiegel, *Romancing the Past. The Rise of Vernacular Prose Historiography in the Thirteenth-Century France* (Berkeley, 1993).

Legendary memory and distortions are discussed by A. G. Remensnyder in *Remembering Kings Past: Monastic Foundation Legends in Medieval Southern France* (Ithaca, 1995), and in her 'Legendary treasure at Conques: reliquaries and imaginative memory', *Speculum*, 71 (1996), 884–906.

For legal memory and the past, see M. T. Clanchy, 'Remembering the past and the good old law', *History*, 55 (1970), 165–76; C. Wickham, 'Lawyers' time: history and memory in tenth- and eleventh-century Italy', in *Studies in Medieval History Presented to R. H. C. Davis*, ed. H. Mayr-Harting and R. I. Moore (London, 1985), 53–71; J. P. Delumeau, 'La mémoire des gens d'Arezzo et de Sienne à travers des dépositions de témoins', *Temps, mémoire, tradition au Moyen Âge. Actes du XIIIe congrès de la société des historiens médiévistes de l'enseignement supérieur public Aix-en-Provence, 4–5 Juin 1982* (Aix-en-Provence, 1983), 45–67; R. Fleming, 'Oral testimony and the Domesday inquest', *Anglo-Norman Studies*, 17 (1994), 101–22; P. Brand, 'Time out of mind: the knowledge and use of the eleventh- and twelfth-century past in thirteenth-century litigation', *Anglo-Norman Studies*, 16 (1993), 37–54; and S. Shahar, *Growing Old in the Middle Ages. 'Winter clothes us in Shadow and Pain'* (London, 1997), 82–6.

Gender and Memory

General introductions on women and family memory can be found in P. Geary, *Phantoms of Remembrance. Memory and Oblivion at the End of the First Millennium* (Princeton, 1994), 48–80; E. M. C. van Houts, 'Women and the writing of history: the case of Abbess Matilda of Essen and Aethelweard', *Early Medieval Europe*, I (1992), 53–68; J. L. Nelson, 'Perceptions du pouvoir chez les historiennes du Haut Moyen Âge', *Les femmes au Moyen Âge*, ed. M. Rouche (Paris, 1990), 77–85; R. McKitterick, 'Frauen und Schriftlichkeit im Frühmittelalter', *Weiblicher Lebensgestaltung im frühen Mittelalter*, ed. W. Goetz (Cologne, 1991), 65–118, esp. 95–111; G. Althoff, 'Gandersheim und Quedlinburg. Ottonische Frauenklöster als Herschafts-und Uberlieferungszentern', *Frühmittelalterliche Studien*, 25 (1991), 123–44; and K. Leyser, *Rule and Conflict in an Early Medieval Society. Ottonian Saxony* (Oxford, 1989), 49–62. For France in the twelfth century, see S. Gaunt, *Gender and Genre in Medieval French Literature* (Cambridge, 1995), with separate chapters on *chansons de geste*, romances and hagiographical writing; G. Duby, *Women of the Twelfth Century, No. 2: Remembering the Dead*, trans. J. Birrell (Cambridge, 1998).

For wills, see M. Sheehan, *The Will in Medieval England from the Anglo-Saxon Conversion to the End of the Thirteenth Century* (Toronto, 1963); and D. Whitelock, *Anglo-Saxon Wills*, Cambridge Studies in English Legal History (Cambridge, 1930). For women and wills in particular, see C. Duhamel-Amado, 'Femmes entre elles. Filles et épouses languedociennes (XIe et XIIe siècles)', *Femmes, mariages, lignages, XIIe–XIVe siècles. Mélanges offerts à Georges Duby* (Bruxelles, 1992), 126–55; P. Skinner, 'Women, wills and wealth in southern Italy, *Early Medieval Europe*, 2 (1993), 133–52. And for the late Middle Ages, see P. Cullum, '"And her Name was Charite": charitable giving by and for women in late-medieval Yorkshire', *Woman is a Worthy Wight. Women in English Society c. 1200–1500*, ed. P. J. P. Goldberg (Stroud, 1992), 182–211; M. C. Howell, 'Fixing movables: gifts by testament in late medieval Douai', *Past and Present* 150 (1996), 3–45.

For female testimonies, see D. Elliott, *Spiritual Marriage. Sexual Abstinence in Medieval Wedlock* (Princeton, 1993), 266–96.

For gender and the past in other societies, see I. Hofmeyer, '*We spend our years as a tale that is told': Oral Historical Narrative in a South African Chiefdom* (Johannesburg and London, 1994), 25–38, 167–70;

and L. Vail and L. White, *Power and the Praise Poem. South African Voices in History* (Charlottesville and London, 1991), 231–77.

The Memory of the Norman Conquest in 1066

Different aspects of the memorial tradition of 1066 are discussed in E. M. C. van Houts, 'The trauma of 1066', *History Today*, 46: 10 (1996), 9–15, and her 'Wace as historian', *Family Trees and the Roots of Politics. The Prosopography of Britain and France from the 10th to the 12th Century*, ed. K. S. B. Keats-Rohan (Woodbridge, 1997), 103–33.

For the place of 1066 in historical writing, see R. W. Southern, 'Aspects of the European tradition of historical writing, 4. The sense of the past', *Transactions of the Royal Historical Society*, 5th s., 23 (1973), 243–63; J. Campbell, 'Some twelfth-century views of the Anglo-Saxon past', *Essays in Anglo-Saxon History* (London, 1986), 209–28.

For the legal and administrative memory of 1066, see P. Brand, 'Time out of mind: the knowledge and the use of the eleventh- and twelfth-century past in thirteenth-century litigation', *Anglo-Norman Studies*, 16 (1993), 37–54; J. Hudson, 'Administration, family and perceptions of the past in late-twelfth-century England: Richard fitz Nigel and the Dialogue of the Exchequer', *The Perception of the Past in Twelfth-Century Europe*, ed. P. Magdalino (London, 1992), 75–98. C. Wickham draws attention to interesting contrasts between eleventh-century Italy and twelfth-century England in '"Lawyers" time: history and memory in tenth- and eleventh-century Italy', in *Studies in Medieval History presented to R. H. C. Davis*, ed. H. Mayr-Harting and R. I. Moore (London, 1985), 53–71.

Women's role in the legitimization of landholding and memorial tradition is discussed in E. Searle, 'Women and the legitimization of succession at the Norman conquest', *Proceedings of the Battle Conference 1980*, ed. R. Allen Brown (Woodbridge, 1981), 159–70, 226–7; and P. Stafford, 'Women and the Norman Conquest', *Transactions of the Royal Historical Society*, 6th s., 4 (1994), 221–49. For women and the patronage of the post-Conquest hagiographical tradition, see J. Wogan-Browne, "Clerc u lai, muine u dame": women and Anglo-Norman hagiography in the twelfth and thirteenth centuries', *Women and Literature in Britain 1150–1500*, ed. C. Meale (Cambridge, 1993), 61–85.

INDEX

187

Ida, countess of Boulogne, wife of
Rainald Dammartin, 75, 139
Ida of Lower Lotharingia, countess of
Hainault, wife of Baldwin II, 89
Immid, brother of Queen Matilda I of
Germany, 85
Inga, wife of Ragnfast and of Eirik, 99
Ingelmarius, knight, 82
Ingvar, son of Tola, brother of Harald,
97
Innocent III, pope, 146
Ireland, 130
Irmengard, servant of Saint Elisabeth
of Hungary, 60
Isabel of Hainault, queen of France,
wife of Philip II Augustus, 71
Isembert, chaplain of Robert the
Magnificent duke of Normandy, 23
Isentrudis, maid of Saint Elisabeth of
Hungary, 60
Isidore of Seville, bishop, 20, 38, 150
Isleif, bishop, 25–6
Ivo, bishop of Chartres, 88
Ivo of Taillebois, 137

J
Jerome, saint, 44
Jerusalem, 43, 75
jewellery, 2, 15, 30, 93, 106–9, 114,
118, 145
John of Coutances, canon, 54, 134–5
John, king of England, 111
John of Worcester, 128, 130
jongleurs, 20, 31–3, 37, 88
Jordan Fantosme, 36
Jordanes, 37
Judith, countess, wife of Earl Waltheof,
130, 141
Judith of Flanders, wife of Earl Tostig
and of Welf IV of Bavaria, 116–18,
124, 139, 140
Judith, mother of Charles the Bald,
66–7
Julius Caesar, 136
Justin, historian, 35
Justinian, emperor of Byzantium, 150

K
Kilvert, husband of Ecgthryth, 78
King's Lynn, 111
Kol, son of Hall, 26
Kunigunde, Holy Roman Empress, wife
of Henry II, 105

L
La Lande Patry, 127
Lambert, abbot of Lobbes, 88
Lambert, abbot of Saint-Bertin, 88
Lambert of Ardres, 29, 32
Lambert of Wattrelos, canon, 29, 33,
87, 90
Lanfranc, archbishop of Canterbury,
138, 140
Languedoc, 104
Le Bec, monastery, 55, 84, 112, 116–18
Lebowa, 11
Leo of Ostia, 27, 113
Leo IX, pope, 100
Leoba, saint, 44–6
Leofflaed, wife of Thurkil the White,
79–80
Leofric the Black, 90, 130
Leofric the Deacon, 31, 90, 130
Leofric, earl, 130
Leofwine, brother of King Harold of
England, 94
Leofwine, thegn of Warwickshire, 137
Letaldus of Micy, 46–7, 48–9
Letitia, daughter of Atenolf, 104, 109
Limoges, 24, 35
Lisbon, 31
Lisiard, bishop of Soissons, 53, 62
Lisieux, 56
literacy, 1, 3, 4–5, 37–8, 67, 143–4
Liudolf, duke of Saxen, 69
Liudolf, duke of Swabia, 69
Liutgard, daughter of Emperor Otto I
and Edith, 69
Loretta, countess of Leicester, wife of
Robert, 80
Lothar II, king of Germany, 96
Louis IV, king of France, 88
Louis VI, king of France, 22, 27, 107,
125
Louis VII, king of France, 33, 83, 106,
107
Louis IV, landgrave of Thuringia, 60
Louis the Pious, king of the Franks, 96,
111
Louvain, 76
Lucy of Bolingbrooke, 137
Lupus of Ferrières, abbot, 43–4
Lyons-la-Forêt, 95

M
Mago, priest, 45–6
Maio, son of Autari, 105

Makapansgat, 11–12
Malcolm III, king of Scotland, 74
Malcolm IV, king of Scotland, 83
Maldon, battle of, 102
Malfosse, 100
Marburg, 60
Margaret, saint, 71, 74, 139, 140
Marelda, wife of Peter, sister of Maio, 105
Marie, abbess of Barking, sister of Thomas Becket, 62
Marie, nun at Chatteris, 141
Marsilia, abbess of Saint-Amand at Rouen, 56–7
Martin of Monopli, 104, 109
Martin of Tours, saint, 46
Martin of Vertou, saint, 46–7
Mary, abbess of Romsey and countess of Boulogne, wife of Matthew of Flanders, 75
Mary of Brabant, wife of Otto IV, 76
Mary of Scotland, countess of Boulogne, wife of Eustace III, 74, 140
Mary Magdalene, 51, 52
Mary, saint, the Virgin, 51, 52, 53–4, 87
Matilda, abbess of Essen, 69–70, 108
Matilda, abbess of Quedlinburg, 67–8, 69
Matilda, daughter of King Louis IV of France, 88
Matilda, duchess of Brabant, wife of Henry, 75–6
Matilda, duchess of Saxony, wife of Henry the Lion, 96–7
Matilda, empress and countess of Anjou, wife of Henry V and of Geoffrey Le Bel, 33, 71, 73, 82, 96, 112, 116–18
Matilda, nun at Barking Abbey, 141
Matilda I, queen of England, wife of William I the Conqueror, 73, 112, 115, 117–18
Matilda II, queen of England, wife of Henry I, 71, 73, 74, 137–8, 139, 140
Matilda IV, queen of England, wife of Stephen, 74–5
Matilda I, queen of Germany, wife of Henry I, 49–50, 67–8, 85
Matthew of Flanders, count of Boulogne, 75
Matthew Paris, 106, 108

Maud of Senlis, daughter of Countess Judith, 141
Maurice, 58
Maurice, bishop of London, 52
Mele, son of Martin of Monopli, 104, 109
memorials, 2
  runic stones, 97–100
  of war, 100
Meningoz, father of Saint Adelheid, 50, 86
Milo Crispin, 85, 88
Miranda, daughter of Peter, 105, 109
Monte Cassino, abbey, 27, 113
Morcar, 109
Morcar, earl, 132–3
Muriel, daughter of Colswein of Lincoln, 137
Muslims, 10, 24, 35, 107

N
Nana, nun at Bishofsheim, 45
necrologies, 9, 68
New Forest, 29
Nicholas II of Rumigni and Florennes, 89
Nordhausen, nunnery, 49–50
Norway, 25–6, 98, 99
Notre Dame at Soissons, nunnery, 13
Notre-Dame-des-Prés, priory, 95
Novalesa, 24–5, 37, 38
  Chronicle of, 72

O
Oda, wife of Duke Liudolf of Saxen, 69
Odd, son of Kol, 26
Odo, abbot of Cluny, 48–9
Odo, abbot of Saint-Germer at Fly, 31, 125
Odo, bishop of Bayeux, 101
Odo II, count of Blois, 94
Odolric, bishop of Orléans, 23
Offa, king of Mercia, 109–10, 119
Olaf, saint, 26
Olaf Tryggvason, king of Norway, 26
Orderic Vitalis, 32, 34, 82, 100, 114, 132, 133–4, 135, 138, 142, 149
Orm, father of Sigrid, 98
Osbert of Clare, 127
Oswald, saint, 116
Otranto, battle of, 39
Otto, bishop of Freising, 22, 23, 37, 90, 100